D1615246

KA 0128207 7

HISTORICAL MANUSCRIPTS COMMISSION

JP 20

Wells Cathedral Chapter Act Book 1666–83

Edited with an introduction by

DERRICK SHERWIN BAILEY, PH.D., D.LITT.

Precentor of Wells

LONDON
HER MAJESTY'S STATIONERY OFFICE
1973

First published 1973

This volume, which has been prepared by the Somerset Record Society, forms no. 20 in the Joint Publication series of the Historical Manuscripts Commission.

SBN 11 440041 5*

Contents

PREFACE i

INTRODUCTION

I The Chapter before the Restoration iii

II The Residentiaries, 1666–1683 ix

III The Chapter, its Meetings and Records xix

IV The Residence and Remuneration of Canons xxiii

V The Ashbury Lease xxx

VI The Vicars Choral and their Stipends xxxii

VII The Library xxxv

APPENDICES

I Letter from Roger Walker to the Chapter xxxix

II Orders and Injunctions exhibited att the . . . Lord Bishopp of Bath and Wells att his Primary Visitation of the Deane and Chapter . . . xli

III A full answer to the desires of the Deane left with Dr Peirs to be communicated to the Chapter xliii

IV Draft of a letter from Dr Holt to the Dean xlv

CALENDAR 1

INDEX 105

Preface

In his introduction to the second volume of the calendar of Wells manuscripts,[1] Mr W. P. Baildon noted that there were certain regrettable gaps in the series of Wells chapter act books, one of which occurred between 1666 and 1683. Unknown to Mr Baildon, however, the act book covering this period was in fact extant, though its whereabouts at the time remain an unsolved mystery. Like several other act books it bears on the front cover a blue label inscribed in an unidentifiable 19th century hand—clear evidence that it once had a place in the series. But it must have been missing from the library at the time when the Revd J. A. Bennett compiled the edition of Wells documents published in 1885,[2] for after presenting items from the act book of 1635–45 he continued with "extracts from the *next* volume of chapter acts"[3]—that of 1683–1705. On the other hand, since a label on the spine is in the handwriting of Mr R. S. Bate, who did valuable work in the library between 1935 and 1940, the book must have reappeared by that time. It is impossible now to discover whether it had been removed from the library or simply mislaid there—though it seems very improbable that it could have been overlooked by both Mr Bennett and Mr Baildon. Its recovery, however, makes it possible to fill a gap in the printed records of Wells cathedral bridged hitherto only by a few extracts from the accounts of the communar and the master of the fabric, and from the ledger or register book for 1624–81.[4]

In the calendar of 1914 the act books of the 17th and 18th centuries were treated selectively, with the result that valuable or interesting material was frequently omitted. In the present edition, however, the act book for 1666–83 has been calendared in full, in order to give an accurate account of its contents and of the way in which the capitular records were kept; even the entries (and they are numerous) which minute no business supply important information about the time, place, and frequency of chapter meetings, and the residentiaries who attended them. Details such as these add a little to our meagre knowledge of the life and work of the chapter in the years following the Restoration.

All the formal entries in the act book—the dates, times, and places of meeting; the names and titles of those present; the records of enthronements, installations, and appointments to capitular offices—and most of the minutes of business transacted are set down in Latin, and the substance of all such entries has been fully presented in the calendar. Some entries are in English, and these occur with increasing frequency during and after 1680, when Richard Healy had assumed the duties of deputy chapter clerk; they have been transcribed literally (save for the extension of abbreviations) and set within quotation marks.

Editorial insertions are enclosed within square brackets, and spaces within square brackets indicate gaps in the manuscript itself. For the sake of brevity, surnames only have been given in the attendance lists of residentiaries, vicars choral, and others; and all surnames, wherever they occur, have been transcribed exactly as written, no attempt having been made to harmo-

[1] *Calendar of the Manuscripts of the Dean and Chapter of Wells* (hereafter cited as *Cal.*), edited on behalf of the Historical Manuscripts Commission by W. P. Baildon (London, 1914), ii, vii.

[2] *Report on the Manuscripts of Wells Cathedral*, prepared for the Historical Manuscripts Commission by J. A. Bennett (London, 1885).

[3] Ibid., 263 (my italics); Mr Bennett seems also to have overlooked the small act book for 1664–66—unless this, too, was missing. It is curious that he should state that from 1599 the chapter act books, "allowing for the necessary interruption of the Commonwealth period, run on in unbroken succession to the present time": ibid. vii.

[4] See *Cal.* ii. 440–6.

nize the variations which not infrequently occur. But all other spellings, including those of place-names, have been modernized except when they occur in transcriptions or quotations.

My thanks are due to Dr R.W. Dunning, to Mr L. S. Colchester, and the staff of the Somerset Record Office at Taunton for help in the preparation of this volume.

Wells Cathedral
July 1972

SHERWIN BAILEY

Introduction

I The Chapter before the Restoration

The early history of the chapter, and its reconstitution about 1140–43 by bishop Robert of Lewes on the model of the 'Institution Charter' provided by St Osmund for Salisbury cathedral, have already been described more than once,[1] and most recently and accurately by Dom Aelred Watkin,[2] while the English secular cathedrals of the middle ages (of which Wells was one) have been exhaustively studied by Dr Kathleen Edwards.[3] It will be sufficient, therefore, simply to recall the principal features of the mediaeval establishment at Wells before giving an account of the changes and developments during the 16th and 17th centuries which are reflected in the somewhat different constitution of the chapter in the post-Restoration period with which we are particularly concerned here.

In the 13th century the Wells chapter of 54 canons shared with that of Lincoln the distinction of being the largest in England, and at the Reformation the number was not reduced below the present complement of 49. Each canon was appointed by the bishop and was assigned a prebend from which he drew a regular income, irrespective of any emoluments to which he might be entitled as a residentiary. Not all the canons resided, though originally this seems to have been the intention. A few preferred to remain on their prebendal estates and to serve the churches there. Some were tied to duties at the royal or papal chancelleries, or kept residence in other cathedrals, or were engaged in academic pursuits, while others held their canonries in plurality with higher offices in the Church. Moreover, at Wells as elsewhere, attempts were made to restrict the admission of new residentiaries by requiring expensive hospitality or charging large entrance fees; and although the Papacy tried to check this abuse, election to residence on payment of a caution of 100 marks or 100 *l*, had become the established practice before the end of the 15th century, and possession of a canonical house was often stipulated.

This state of affairs was advantageous to the small number of canons who kept residence—usually no more than a quarter, or at most a third, of the whole chapter—since each enjoyed a proportionately larger share of the common fund in addition to his personal prebendal income. They were also free to add to their body congenial or serviceable colleagues, though capitular harmony and continuity of policy could not always be secured by this means. Thus the government of the cathedral came to be concentrated in the hands of a select and privileged oligarchy, with the result that the powers and status of the non-residentiary canons eventually underwent a marked diminution. Very often, however, the latter had other interests to pursue and acquiesced in the situation; they were generally kept informed of capitular business and were consulted on matters of great importance, and at Wells there seems to have been little friction between them and the residentiaries.

The principal residentiaries were five dignitaries known as the *quinque personae*, who received double quotidians or daily commons. Four of them (dean, precentor, chancellor, and treasurer) had special administrative responsibilities, and at first were bound to perpetual residence (which

[1] See e.g. C. M. Church, *Chapters in the Early History of the Church of Wells* (London, 1894); T. S. Holmes, 'Ecclesiastical History' and 'The Religious Houses of Somerset', in *Victoria County History of Somerset*, ii. 8ff and 162ff.

[2] 'The Precentors, Chancellors, and Treasurers in Wells Cathedral', in *Collectanea III*, ed T. F. Palmer (Som.Rec.Soc.57), 51ff.

[3] *The English Secular Cathedrals in the Middle Ages* (2nd edition, Manchester, 1967); see also 'The Cathedral of Salisbury' in *Victoria County History of Wiltshire*, iii. 156ff.

did not exclude absence for some "compelling and evident reason")—though at the end of the 15th century, and probably long before then, this statutory requirement had ceased to be strictly observed. Upon them the constitutional structure of the cathedral was based; they were the pillars or corner-stones supporting the spiritual and institutional fabric, and they united under their direction and control the subordinate ministers and officers of the church, functions well symbolized by their being assigned the four terminal canonical stalls in quire.[1] They enjoyed a large measure of freedom in the administration of their departments, but were answerable to the chapter, and could be censured if they exceeded or neglected their duties.[2]

The dean was president of the chapter; within the cathedral he exercised spiritual, pastoral, and disciplinary oversight of all its members, ministers, and servants, though in relation to the other dignitaries and canons he stood simply as *primus inter pares*. Traditionally he was elected by the canons from among themselves, while the other dignitaries were appointed by the bishop from the chapter. The precentor ruled the quire in all musical and liturgical matters, and directed the singing. The chancellor controlled the schools, lectured in theology and canon law, cared for and corrected the books, kept the muniments, attended to correspondence and drafted charters, and held the chapter's seal in his custody. The treasurer was responsible for all valuables and ornaments, and for the trees on the Cathedral Green, and had to provide whatever was necessary for the services.

The fifth dignitary, the archdeacon of Wells, was not bound to reside and had no special capitular duties, being occupied with the care of the parishes and the cure of souls therein. In addition to the *quinque personae* there were also four other canons who ranked as lesser dignitaries: the archdeacons of Bath and Taunton, the subdean, and the succentor. On the last two, subject to certain relaxations, the early statutes also imposed an obligation of continual residence, in order that they might be available to deputize in quire for the dean[3] and the precentor whenever the need arose. The treasurer was assisted by a subtreasurer who was an officer of lower status, usually a vicar choral.

Important areas of cathedral administration lay outside the jurisdiction of the dignitaries as such, but for these any dignitary, canon, vicar choral, or even chantry priest might be made responsible at the annual election of officers on St Jerome's day, 30th September, when the cathedral's business year began. The master of the fabric was clerk of the works and administrator of the fabric fund, which he expended on the wages of masons and other workmen, and on the purchase of building materials. Two overseers of the houses made an annual inspection of the canonical dwellings in the Liberty and assessed the cost of any necessary repairs, which the occupants were then required to carry out at their own charges before the next Michaelmas. The chapter's common fund was managed by the communar, who was particularly responsible for paying quotidians to the bishop and the residentiaries; his accounts were examined each year by two auditors under the supervision of the baron of the exchequer. Another financial officer, the escheator, received rents from certain lands and houses in Wells and the revenues from vacant prebends, and met various expenses connected with the observance of obits and anniversaries.

[1] This is true even at Wells, where the stalls of the archdeacons of Wells and Bath were (and still are) located to the east of (i.e., outside) those assigned respectively to the chancellor and the treasurer, for the two last-named dignitaries still stood in correct relation to their other two colleagues, the dean and the precentor, and to the rest of the canons. Confusion has resulted from transposition of the stalls of the treasurer and the archdeacon of Taunton, presumably when the quire was remodelled in 1848–52—a solecism which calls for early rectification.

[2] See, e.g., the case of treasurer Hugh Sugar in *Collectanea* III (Som.Rec.Soc.57), 71–3.

[3] In the dean's absence the subdean took his place in quire and discharged some of his other duties in and outside the cathedral, but it is uncertain whether he ever acted as president of the chapter before the Reformation. There is admittedly evidence of a mandate for installation being addressed *decano vel eo non presente subdecano* (Wells Diocesan Registry, *Reg. Stafford*, f.70), but the precentor took precedence next to the dean and would normally preside in the latter's absence.

Two other officers were not elected annually. One was the provost of Combe, who administered the large prebend of Combe St Nicholas and distributed its income among the fifteen prebendaries whom it supported. He himself was *ex officio* prebendary of Combe XII, but was not entitled to place and voice in chapter unless he had also been collated to a second prebend; this was the sole exception to the rule that no canon might hold more than one prebend at a time. Secondly, there was the steward, whose task was to sell each year before Michaelmas for the benefit of the common fund all the grain which had been brought into the chapter's stores in settlement of rents and tithes.

When we compare the mediaeval establishment at Wells with that of the post-Restoration era revealed by the act book of 1666–83, it is evident that changes of many kinds had occurred during the intervening centuries. Those of greatest consequence for the cathedral took place at the time of the Reformation. Being a secular foundation, Wells was less affected than the monasteries by the course of events under Henry VIII, though its revenues were depleted by propitiatory grants and for nearly three years it suffered an absentee lay dean in the person of Thomas Cromwell, from whose attainder in 1540 the deanery was expressly exempted. But early in the reign of Edward VI Cromwell's successor, William FitzWilliam, was persuaded to surrender to the Crown the deanery and all its possessions. The dean's house and his manors were then granted to Protector Somerset, while the deanery itself was recreated by private act of Parliament as a Crown donative and recompensed with the estates of the archdeaconry of Wells (handed over to Henry VIII by Polydore Vergil in 1546), the prebend of North Curry (instead of the prebend of Wedmore I formerly annexed to the deanery), and the endowments belonging to the provostship and the succentorship. The next dean, John Goodman, was assigned by royal mandate the canonical house of chancellor Thomas Dakyn,[1] and when Somerset acquired the episcopal manors and the palace at Wells in 1548 he conferred the dean's residence upon bishop William Barlow.

Goodman found the revenues of the new deanery insufficient, and proceeded to augment them by obtaining the lucrative prebend of Wiveliscombe, thus infringing the rule against the holding of prebends in plurality—for he was already prebendary of Curry. Consequently he was deemed to have vacated the deanery, which was granted to William Turner, a physician, botanist, and vigorous polemicist on behalf of the Protestant cause. Goodman, however, continued to maintain his claim to be the rightful dean of Wells, and on Mary's accession this claim was upheld; Turner was deprived and he was reinstated, still holding the prebend of Wiveliscombe—presumably as some compensation for the alienated decanal estates. At the same time the palace was restored to the bishop, and the dean regained possession of his own house. But when Elizabeth I came to the throne Turner reappeared from the Continent, where he had taken refuge from the troubles of the last reign, and successfully asserted his own right to the deanery before the Ecclesiastical Commission in 1560; Goodman protested, but was in turn deprived and died two years later.

The vicissitudes of these two decades seem to have caused some uncertainty about the constitution of the dean and chapter of Wells; allegations appear to have been made, either that it was no longer a lawful ecclesiastical corporation, or that it had been dissolved automatically by FitzWilliam's surrender of the deanery and the erection of a new one by the act of 1547. It was vital, therefore, to establish the legal continuity and identity of the Elizabethan with the mediaeval dean and chapter, and politic to secure as good a title as possible to all that had been recovered of the estates and endowments alienated under Edward VI. It is not clear when or why this became

[1] This house was on the site of what is now 17, The Liberty; *V. C. H. Somerset*, ii. 37 says that Goodman does not appear to have lived there, but he certainly paid an obituary rent of 43*s*. 4*d*. to the escheator for the year 1553–4. Goodman was also granted by bishop Barlow a house on the site of 6, Cathedral Green, described in 1558 as "that . . . decayed and ruynouse house . . . wherein M. John Goodman now deane latelye dwellyde" W(ells) C(athedral) L(ibrary), Ledger E, f. 106).

a matter of urgency, but when John Herbert, her majesty's master of requests, was appointed dean in January 1590 he lost no time in taking it up. Two months after his installation he wrote from the Court to assure the chapter that, acting on the instructions of Dr Bisse and Dr Powell (canons residentiary and archdeacons respectively of Taunton and Bath), he had moved the queen "to give her royall assente to incorporate our churche by one certaine name, and soe to endowe the same with the present revenues and to enjoye all suche immunities as presentlie wee doe".[1] On 24th April it was decreed in chapter that all dignitaries, prebendaries, and canons were to be cited to the annual Whitsun visitation to treat with the residentiaries about difficult and urgent matters of business concerning the common good of the cathedral and the individual benefit of every prebendary.[2] Thus began the negotiations which were completed by the issue on 25th November 1591 of royal letters patent confirming the endowments of the cathedral and redefining the constitution of the chapter.

This charter[3] stated that in response to a petition Elizabeth had determined to "create, erect, found, and establish the . . . cathedral church anew". As in the past, there were to be the five great dignities of dean, precentor, archdeacon of Wells, chancellor, and treasurer; the lesser dignities of archdeacon of Taunton, archdeacon of Bath, and subdean; and forty-nine prebends —and each of these offices or benefices was confirmed to its existing holder. Next, "certain other offices or dignities" were founded with the title of "canon residentiary", to which were appointed the eleven canons then keeping residence; and it was stipulated that as their number was reduced in course of time, so it should never exceed eight or fall below six, of whom the dean might be one, should he so desire. Canons residentiary were each to reside for three months in the year, or for four months if they were also dignitaries; they were to be "of themselves a body corporate and politic in deed and name" and were to be known as "the dean and chapter", and in them was vested exclusively the "rule, management, and government, and the disposal of the affairs" of the cathedral. The other (non-residentiary) canons were to be joined perpetually to this dean and chapter, having their prebends and their own stalls in quire but no place or voice in chapter save at the election of a bishop. The deanery was confirmed as a Crown appointment, but the other dignities and prebends remained, as formerly, in the gift of the bishop; and vacancies in the body of canons residentiary were to be filled by the co-option of approved dignitaries or other prebendaries, who must already be in possession of a canonical house. The remaining provisions dealt mainly with capitular property, endowments, and revenues.

There are certain obvious and important constitutional differences between the charter and the ancient statutes of Wells. It was a principle of the secular cathedrals that every canon, without distinction, was a member of the chapter and had the right to keep residence; and this principle was not negated by the fact that in practice the number of residentiaries came to be limited by personal choice, circumstances, and restrictive devices. Now, however, this right itself was taken away—first, by creating the novel "office or dignity" of canon residentiary, and secondly, by incorporating the canons residentiary as the "dean and chapter" of Wells. The non-residentiary canons were not really affected by this deprivation, and in practice their situation remained unchanged. They continued to enjoy the revenues from their prebends and to exercise the patronage of their prebendal churches, and in addition to joining with the residentiaries in episcopal elections they retained their traditional associations with the cathedral. It was their duty periodically to preach there, or to find someone to supply their turn; some of them were responsible for the payment of stall wages to vicars choral; and they could attend and even officiate at installations of new prebendaries. Each year they were cited to appear at the Whitsun

[1] *Cal.* ii. 316. [2] W.C.L. Act Book H, f.60.

[3] See H. E. Reynolds, *Wells Cathedral, its Foundation, Constitutional History, and Statutes* (1881), 241ff.

visitation held by the dean and chapter, though the business on these occasions seems usually to have been formal. They might also be summoned for special consultations, as in 1608, when arrangements for preaching were discussed. In short, the non-residentiaries lost nothing but a theoretical right which had long ceased to have any practical significance.

The charter also left the four principal dignitaries in an anomalous position. The precentor, the chancellor, and the treasurer were neither relieved of their ancient statutory duties, nor confirmed in them, nor given *ex officio* any right to the residentiary status without which it was difficult to perform them properly. It happened that in 1591 all three were residentiary, and were accordingly included among the eleven canons nominated as the first members of the refounded dean and chapter; but not all of their successors managed to secure election. Some apparently did not seek it, and others, though co-opted, declined to reside. The dean's situation was different but equally curious. The charter expressed the queen's desire that he should always be one of the residentiary canons if that were his wish [*si voluerit*], and all dean Herbert's successors took advantage of their right until it was lost in the reforms which followed the recommendations of the Cathedrals Commission of 1835. But now, consistent with the terms of the charter, the governing body of the cathedral might at any time lack one or more of the persons designated by mediaeval theory as the pillars and corner-stones of the capitular structure; and in fact this occurred not infrequently during the next three hundred and fifty years. Constitutional anomalies like these, however, meant little, for by the end of the 16th century many of the traditional responsibilities of the dignitaries, if not obsolete, were beginning to lapse through neglect or had already passed to the chapter, while others were being assumed by minor officials.

The aim of the charter was simple, practical, and limited, and it achieved the objects of its promoters; it secured the dean and chapter in possession of rights, properties, and endowments which had been called in question, and it set the seal of legality upon the existing capitular structure and administrative arrangements of the cathedral. Although its provisions thus reflected the actual conditions at Wells in the closing decades of the 16th century, the charter did not wholly supersede the constitution established four hundred years earlier by Robert of Lewes and developed in the meantime. Ancient statutes and approved customs which had not become obsolete and had not been abrogated by contrary usage remained in force and were invoked from time to time—though with diminishing frequency. Both the mediaeval constitution and the Elizabethan charter contributed to the traditions of the cathedral, and this explains why, during the last three centuries, Wells often presented the ambiguous character of an ancient secular church upon which certain features of the New Foundations had been grafted; not until 1967 was this ambiguity removed, so far as modern circumstances and legal requirements would allow, by a revision of its constitution and statutes on lines broadly consistent with the principles of the *Statuta Antiqua*.

Before leaving the charter one point calls for comment. According to Professor E. A. Freeman, "it is evident that the residentiaries took this opportunity to procure something like a legal confirmation of the usurpations by which the non-residentiary canons were gradually cheated out of their rights and powers".[1] But the imputation is not well grounded, and such evidence as we have points in quite another direction. It is true that the non-residentiary canons lost their original rights as members of the chapter, but it is naive to dismiss as a cheat and a usurpation the historical process by which this came about; there is even no indication of resentment against the restrictive practices by which the number of residentiaries was controlled. And as for the residentiaries of 1590, there is no evidence that they contrived to obtain a legal ratification of the fraud alleged to have been perpetrated by their predecessors. On the contrary, there is good reason to suppose that the non-residentiaries were consulted about the terms of the charter and

[1] E. A. Freeman, *History of the Cathedral Church of Wells* (London, 1870), 151–2.

approved them; otherwise it is difficult to believe that they would have assented on 10th June 1590 to the decree passed at the Whitsun visitation that "the charge and burden [of the charter] ... shalbee ratablie borne as well by the dignities and prebendaries not residentiaries as the residentiaries ... according to the rate and proportion of the particular livings of the saide dignities and prebendaries not residentiaries as they bee valued in the Queen's booke".[1] Professor Freeman was commendably jealous for Wells and its ancient institutions, but in this instance his zeal seems to have betrayed him into special pleading which took no account of historical realities.

During the 17th century, and particularly after the Restoration, the vicars choral were far less prominent in the administration of the cathedral than they had been in the middle ages. Then, and until the Reformation, they usually supplied the important offices of master of the fabric, communar, and escheator; in other words, they handled much of the day-to-day financial business of the chapter, while the dignitaries were responsible for the worship and government of the church. The vicars, too, were often closely associated with the canons in the management of the cathedral's external affairs, and the two groups generally were then less widely separated than they afterwards became. After the Reformation, however, only the escheatorship remained with the vicars, who annually nominated two of their number from whom the chapter selected one to act in that capacity for the ensuing year; obits and anniversaries being no longer observed, he had only to distribute the surplus of his account in fixed proportions among the residentiaries and vicars. All other offices were normally filled by residentiaries, though between 1572 and 1589 two notaries, John Dane and Bartholomew Haggat, successively acted as communar, while between 1690 and 1712 another layman, Dr Richard Healy, was to hold this office simultaneously with the mastership of the fabric. In fact, for many decades after the Restoration it was common for one person to be elected to the same office year after year, or to hold two offices at once, though the practice was not always viewed with favour.[2] The steward was now always appointed biennially, and his responsibilities were wider in scope and more diversified than formerly; he negotiated leases, held manorial courts, inspected properties, and generally supervised the chapter's estates and those who administered them.

It is significant that while the responsibilities of the various officers increased and were largely taken over by the residentiary canons, so those of the dignitaries, as we have seen, diminished and even disappeared. No longer were the latter like pillars upholding the capitular fabric; that function, if it still existed, belonged rather to the communar, the master of the fabric, and the steward. In the post-Restoration cathedral the dean's situation had perhaps altered least, though he was no longer called upon to exercise the spiritual and disciplinary powers of his mediaeval predecessors; and the substitution of appointment by the Crown for election by his fellow canons was not in all respects a gain. The precentor's concerns were more and more shared by the organist and master of the choristers, whose professional status was slowly growing. There is no evidence of their respective roles at Wells in the latter part of the 17th century, but the organist would obviously have considerable scope when the precentor was an absentee like Sebastian Smith (1635–74), and would rarely serve under a musician with the competence of Smith's successor, Robert Creyghton II (1674–1734). The chancellor's legal and secretarial duties, already to some extent delegated in mediaeval times, now devolved almost entirely upon professionals such as the chapter clerk and his deputy, and the various notaries

[1] W.C.L., Act Book H, f.61.

[2] Dr Healy was succeeded as communar and master of the fabric by chancellor Marshall Brydges in 1713, but the latter was not re-elected to the mastership of the fabric in 1719, and in 1720 his monopoly of the office of communar was successfully challenged by dean Brailsford and archdeacon Archer on the ground that it deprived other canons of administrative experience—though it may be suspected that another motive was to break the dominance of the Creyghton faction in the chapter, Brydges being a son-in-law of the precentor, Robert Creyghton II. See below, p.xvii.

public, registrars, and other agents who helped to conduct the business of the chapter; and his obligation to lecture had long been considered sufficiently discharged by the delivery of an occasional homily. The treasurer's task of providing for the services was greatly simplified by the modest requirements of the Book of Common Prayer and the liturgical practice of the time, and he had fewer vestments, valuables, and pieces of plate in his charge than before the Reformation. In spite of all these changes, however, the dignitaries retained theoretical jurisdiction over their respective departments, one indication of this being their duty to nominate minor officials for appointment by the chapter.

Nothing, perhaps, illustrates the difference between the circumstances of the dignitaries before and after the Reformation better than the loss by precentor, chancellor, and treasurer of their customary precedence in the cathedral. The charter always lists the *quinque personae* in their traditional order (dean, precentor, archdeacon of Wells, chancellor, treasurer), but it does not confirm this as an order of precedence, nor does it define the standing of the dignitaries, whether resident or not, in relation to the non-dignified members of the dean and chapter. When Sebastian Smith attempted in 1639 to revive ancient usage by asserting his precedence as precentor, claiming with some justification that this was implicit in the charter, Robert Creyghton I (then treasurer) protested that precedence was now reckoned by seniority of co-option as a residentiary;[1] and the matter was not raised again.

II The Residentiaries, 1666–83

In 1666 only two residentiary canons remained from the pre-Commonwealth chapter.

Robert Creyghton I,[2] a Scotsman descended on his mother's side from the royal house of Stuart, became treasurer and canon residentiary on 17th December 1633, having been appointed prebendary of Taunton six days earlier; he already held the prebend of Castor in Lincoln cathedral and the regius professorship of Greek at Cambridge (which he resigned in 1639), and to his preferments at Wells he added the deanery (or rectory) of St Buryan, Cornwall, in 1637, the archdeaconry of Stowe and the rectory of Huggate, Yorkshire, in 1641, and the vicarage of Greenwich in 1642. On the outbreak of the Civil War he appears to have remained at Wells and was present on 28th January 1644–5 at the last recorded meeting of the chapter before the residentiaries were compelled to leave the city.[3] He then repaired to Oxford, where he was made D.D. and was appointed chaplain to the king. On the fall of Oxford in 1645 he escaped to Cornwall disguised as a labourer, and from there crossed to the Continent where he joined the royalist court in exile; John Evelyn the diarist heard him preach there in 1649.[4] In 1552 he was at The Hague, acting as tutor to Sir Ralph Verney's son.

At the Restoration Dr Creyghton became dean of Wells and took an active part in repairing the damage done to the cathedral during the Commonwealth; he himself gave to the church a

[1] *Cal.* ii: 421—18th April.

[2] See *Dict.Nat.Biog.;* A. Wood, *Athenae Oxonienses* (Oxford, 1691), I, i. 861 and ii. 692; J. and J. A. Venn, *Alumni Cantabrigienses* (Cambridge, 1922), *s.v.*; J. Le Neve, *Fasti Ecclesiae Anglicanae*, ed T. D. Hardy, (Oxford, 1854), i. 147, 154, 174, 194; ibid. ii. 128; J. Evelyn, *Diary*; S. Pepys, *Diary*; A. G. Matthews, *Walker Revised* (Oxford, 1948), 96–7.

[3] An entry by Creyghton in the Steward's Book for 1640–42 referring to completion of a transaction in August 1642 "whilst I was prisoner in Bristoll" suggests that he had already been in trouble on account of his royalist sympathies before his departure from Wells; see S[omerset] R[ecord] O[ffice], DD/CC 110004, 31.

[4] Creyghton's wife remained in Wells, at least for a time. The Parliamentary Survey of the manor of Canon Grange made in June and July 1649 states that his house (later partly reconstructed to form the present no 3. The Liberty) was then still occupied by Mrs Creyghton "who pretends an interest in the same by lease, collacion or otherwise dureing her . . . husband's life (who is now beyonde Sea) . . . but doth manifest unto us noe evidence in confirmacion of any such right . . ."; S.R.O., DD/CC 111733–5, 2.

fine brass lectern (still in use in the nave) with a Bible thereon, and a new window costing 400*l.* for the west end of the nave. In 1663 he took the oaths for naturalization, in 1664 he obtained the benefice of Uplowman in Devon, and in 1665 he was presented to the chapter living of Cheddar. On 25th June 1670 he was consecrated bishop of Bath and Wells on the decease of Dr William Peirs; little more than two years later, on 21st November 1672, he died at the age of 79 and was buried in the cathedral in the chapel of St John the Evangelist, having prepared for himself there at great expense a marble tomb and effigy.

Dr Creyghton had the reputation of an eloquent and spirited preacher, though he was not without a certain eccentricity, either of delivery or of exposition. Samuel Pepys records several occasions on which he listened to sermons by "the great Scotchman". On 7th March 1661–2 at Whitehall chapel, upon Micah i.10 ("Roll yourselves in dust") "he made a most learned sermon . . . but in his application, the most comical man that ever I heard in my life"; and on 3rd April in the following year from the same pulpit he preached "a most admirable, good, learned, and most severe sermon, yet comicall" on St Luke xi.27–28, railing "bitterly ever and anon against John Calvin and his brood, the Presbyterians, and against the present terme, now in use, of 'tender consciences' ". He did not hesitate to condemn in front of the king the morals of the court and the state of the nation, as on 29th July 1667, when Pepys heard that he had delivered on the previous day a "strange, bold sermon . . . against the sins of the Court and particularly adultery . . . and of our negligence in having our castles without ammunition and powder when the Dutch came upon us; and how we have no courage now-a-days, but let our ships be taken out of our harbours". John Evelyn, too, tells of an "extravagant sermon at St Margaret's before the House of Commons" on 29th May 1663. Creyghton's strictures, says Anthony Wood, were "well taken by some tho' sneared at by others". His boldness and 'comical' manner in the pulpit seem, unfortunately, to have turned at times to an aggressive testiness in his relations with the Wells chapter and certain of its members. There is general testimony to his scholarship as an "admirable Grecian", and his translation into Latin of Sguropulus's history of the Council of Florence[1] is proof of his ability.

Dr Creyghton married Frances, daughter of William Walrond of Ile Brewers, by whom he had three sons, Robert II,[2] Thomas who died in 1674, and George who died in 1685, and a daughter Katherine who married Francis, son of John, 1st baron Poulet of Hinton St George; Frances Creyghton died on 3rd November 1683.

Sebastian Smith,[3] son of Edward Smith of Bristol and a graduate of Oxford, succeeded Edward Abbott as precentor on 12th March 1634–5 and was elected to residence on 4th April 1638; in the next year, as we have seen, he came into conflict with Robert Creyghton over the question of precedence in chapter.[4] At this time he also held a canonry at Peterborough, which he resigned in 1640, having secured the Somerset benefices of Compton Dando in 1638 and North Curry in 1639; he had already obtained the prebend of Combe VIII in 1635, which he exchanged for that of Worminster in 1642. He was deprived of his livings under the Commonwealth, but was granted an annuity of 60*l.* for life by the House of Commons; there is no other record of his fortunes at that time. At the Restoration he resumed his precentorship, but never resided and rarely visited Wells, so far as can be ascertained; he became canon of Christ Church, Oxford, in 1661, and in the same year rector of Hambledon, Buckinghamshire, and he died in

[1] *Vera Historia Unionis non Verae inter Graecos et Latinos* . . ., Hagae Comitis, ex typ. Adriani Ulacq, 1660, translated from the Greek of Sylvester Sguropulus.

[2] See below, pp.xv–xvii.

[3] See Wood, op.cit. I, i. 901; J. Foster, *Alumni Oxonienses, 1506–1714* (Oxford, 1892), 1381; Le Neve-Hardy, op.cit.,i. 171, 182, 207; ibid. ii. 520 (the 2nd stall at Oxford) and 546 (the 3rd stall at Peterborough); Matthews, op.cit., 319.

[4] See above, p.ix.

possession of all these preferments in 1674 at the age of 67. His persistent non-residence at Wells, as the act book and other records show, was a cause of some annoyance and acrimony in the chapter, and more will be said about this later in a discussion of the residence and remuneration of canons.[1] It is possible that for much of his time at Oxford he was in ill health.

Five members of the chapter came into residence at the Restoration. William Peirs[2] was the elder son of bishop William Peirs of Bath and Wells by his first wife Anne. After graduating at Oxford he was instituted as rector of Buckland St Mary in 1637, and in 1638 was granted the prebend of Cudworth, which he exchanged for that of Whitchurch in the following year; in 1638 also he became vicar of Kingsbury Episcopi, and was made archdeacon of Bath, resigning this dignity in 1643 on being appointed archdeacon of Taunton. In 1639, out of respect for his father, who presumably had spoken for him, the chapter promised that on the occurrence of the next vacancy Mr Peirs should be co-opted; but when one arose in 1643 his request on 2nd October for admission was rebuffed by dean Raleigh—probably because another candidate, Dr William Watts, had been commended in royal letters dated 18th September. When Watts, however, had not appeared in person to apply for election and to deposit his caution by 4th January, the archdeacon's claim was reconsidered; but it was concluded that the pre-election made in 1639 was contrary to the customs and the interest of the cathedral, and it was revoked accordingly. Mr Roger Wood was then co-opted to the vacant place.

In January 1641 Mr Peirs was cited by the House of Commons on a charge of using malicious words against the last Parliament. Later, under the Commonwealth, he was deprived of his archdeaconry and benefices, and suffered severe privations. He was forced to seek a living by labouring on a small holding, and by selling cheese in Ilminster market and apples at Taunton. Sometimes he was reduced to such necessity that a pitcher of whey, for which he had to trudge at least a mile, was all that kept him from starvation; and he was often seen with other deprived clergymen sitting and eating bread and salt, and drinking water because none of them had a penny to buy beer. It was said also that "he used to go about the country with a little poultry horse, and sell tobacco". He was imprisoned for standing sponsor at baptism to the son of John Tarleton, vicar of Ilminster, because the child was named Charles, and this may have been the occasion when he was compelled to beg for charity by hanging a glove out of the window of the jail, an incident said to have occurred at Ilchester.

On returning to Wells in 1660 he resumed his archdeaconry and at last was made a residentiary canon; in 1661 he proceeded D.D. at Oxford, and was preferred to the benefice of East Brent, and a year later he resigned the vicarage of Kingsbury Episcopi to become rector of Christian Malford, Wiltshire. Probably about this time, too, he married Mary Coward, who belonged to a prominent local family, though Walker states that his marriage took place under the Commonwealth. Walker's account, however, is confused: he says that Peirs was "forced out of meer necessity for subsistence ... to marry an ordinary woman with a very small estate ..." on which he was compelled to work, but later he tells that "he was at last received into the country man's house, whose daughter he married". There were Cowards at Ditcheat and elsewhere who were yeomen, and these tales may have resulted from confusion between Mary Coward's family and relatives of the same name who may have befriended him in his troubles.

Before the Civil War Dr Peirs seems to have lived in the canonical house at the south-eastern corner of the Market Place, a house in the gift of the bishop. Soon after the Restoration, however, in circumstances to be described later,[3] he moved first to Dr Smith's house and then to

[1] See below, pp.xxiv–xxvi.

[2] See Wood, op.cit., I, ii. 823; Foster, op.cit., 1138; Le Neve-Hardy, op.cit., i. 165, 168, 191, 203; J. Walker, *The Sufferings of the Clergy* (London, 1714), ii. 73; P. M. Hembry, *The Bishops of Bath and Wells, 1540–1640* (London, 1967), 228–9, 251–3; Matthews, op.cit., 317.

[3] See below, pp.xxvii–xxix.

what was once known as 'the archdeacon's house' (until lately the Theological College library) —the house "on the north side of the cathedral" where several meetings of the chapter took place during 1681 and 1682, the last being at 8 o'clock in the evening of 3rd April 1682. The next day he died, at the age of 70.

Richard Busby[1] succeeded Dr Peirs in the prebend of Cudworth in 1639, one year after his appointment as headmaster of Westminster school, the position with which his name will always be associated. During the time of the Commonwealth he lost his prebend, but retained his headmastership and his studentship of Christ Church, Oxford. At the Restoration he recovered the prebend and received in addition a prebend of Westminster, and on 11th August 1660 became canon residentiary and treasurer of Wells. He, too, was almost entirely non-resident, though he retained possession of his canonical house on the site of the present number 11, The Liberty; he did, however, spend a week in Wells in July 1670, immediately after the appointment of Ralph Bathurst as dean, and took this opportunity to explain to the chapter that ill health and pressing duties elsewhere prevented him from keeping residence.[2] Unlike Dr Smith, he took a keen interest in Wells, and atoned for his absence by presenting the cathedral with 36*l.* for the purchase of a silver alms dish, and the library with 56 folio volumes; indeed, he seems to have intended to give more. But his most munificent benefaction was sums totalling 322*l.* 11*s.* for the repair and improvement of the library, enabling the chapter to have it panelled and furnished with presses and desks.[3] Dr Busby died on 5th April 1695 at the age of 89, leaving behind the reputation of a stern but venerated and most successful schoolmaster, and a pious, benevolent and liberal churchman.

Thomas Holt,[4] an Oxford graduate and fellow of Magdalen college who was also incorporated M.A. at Cambridge, became vicar of Weston Zoyland in 1639, and rector of Lamyat in 1641. Early in 1642 he came under suspicion for expressing virulent malignancy against Parliament, and later in that year was ejected from both his benefices. He was turned out on to the highway with his wife and several children to seek what subsistence they could find; but they were fortunate in obtaining shelter in Gloucestershire at the house of Mr (afterwards Sir) Isaac Newton. Mr Holt was succeeded at Lamyat by "one Snead, an army trumpeter, who paid no fifths"; but "towards the latter end of the usurpation [he] returned . . . and shifted in and out there by stealth until the Restoration". Once during these troubles he was forced to flee into Cornwall dressed as a miller, and for some time after that wandered from place to place. He recovered both his livings in 1660, but exchanged Weston Zoyland for Batcombe in 1666, and in 1686, near the end of his life, he resigned from Lamyat and took Wraxall.

His connexion with the cathedral began in 1641, when he received the prebend of Combe II, which he gave up in 1665 for the prebend of Litton. In 1660 he was made chancellor of Wells and was admitted to residence, and in 1661 was recommended by the king (with his colleague John Selleck) to the vice-chancellor of Oxford for the degree of D.D. without submitting the usual exercises, having been prevented from proceeding in the normal way by his loyalty during the late unhappy time. His own university, however, seems to have been ungracious, for in 1665, with better success, the king addressed a similar request on his behalf to the vice-chancellor of Cambridge.[5] Dr Holt dwelt in the house now number 3, The Liberty, and was assiduous to the end in his residence and capitular duties; in the afternoon of 1st July 1685, after Monmouth's soldiers had ransacked the cathedral in the morning, it was he who went alone to the chapter

[1] See *Dict.Nat.Biog.*; Le Neve-Hardy, op.cit., i. 174, 191; ibid. iii. 360; Evelyn, *Diary*; G. F. R. Barker, *Memoir of Richard Busby* (London, 1895).

[2] See below, p.xxvi.   [3] See further below, p.xxxvi.

[4] See Foster, op.cit., 737; J. and J. A. Venn, op.cit., *s.v.*; Le Neve-Hardy, op.cit., i. 178, 197, 204; Walker, op.cit., ii. 74; Matthews, op.cit., 314.

[5] *Letters and Papers (Domestic)*, *1661–2*, 183; ibid *1664–5*, 193.

house where, with the deputy chapter clerk Nicholas Neblett, he opened and immediately adjourned to a more propitious time the fourth quarterly chapter of the year.[1] He died four years later at the age of 93.

John Selleck,[2] a graduate of Oxford, obtained the rectory of Elworthy, Somerset, in 1643, but was ejected before 5th April 1645 on account of his loyalty to the king. He then seems to have taken refuge with John, son of Thomas, 1st Lord Coventry and Keeper of the Great Seal, by his second wife Elizabeth Pitchford, and to have acted as his chaplain. From Coventry's house in the Close at Salisbury he was despatched to Trent, a village on the Dorset border 2 miles from Yeovil where Charles II was staying with Colonel Francis Wyndham, bearing a letter from Coventry and the precentor of Salisbury, Dr Humphrey Henchman, advising the king for his greater safety to move to the house of Mrs Mary Hyde at Hele, near Salisbury. The letter was rolled up into a ball the size of a musket bullet, which Selleck had orders to swallow in case of danger; he succeeded in reaching the king, and returned with a similar paper bullet containing his majesty's acceptance of the counsel tendered by his friends.[3] Nothing more is known of his fortunes at this time.

When Dr James Dugdale, subdean of Wells, died in 1661 not long after election to residence, the dean and chapter asked Charles II to nominate a successor. Mr Selleck had received the prebend of St Decumans in 1660, but had twice failed to gain a place in the chapter despite recommendations from the king. He now petitioned again for election and his request, supported by Mr Coventry and presented by Colonel Wyndham, at last had the desired result. On 16th March 1660–1 the chapter received another letter from Charles, recommending Selleck for co-option in consideration of his sufferings for loyalty to the royalist cause, and his great service in helping to preserve his majesty's person when in danger; and they complied without delay.[4] Selleck was also preferred to the archdeaconry of Bath and installed on 6th June following.

In 1662 Mr Selleck, in company with Dr John Bargrave, a canon of Canterbury, undertook a mission to Algiers on behalf of the Church of England; probably his earlier success as an emissary suggested that he would be specially suitable for this employment. The bishops and clergy had set aside 10,000*l.* for the redemption of English subjects captured and enslaved by the Turk, but since coin of the realm might not be transported without special licence, goldsmiths had been requested to furnish this sum in foreign currency. The king, however, instructed the Lord Treasurer on 15th September to issue the necessary licence, and the next day the two agents were granted passports and permission to leave the kingdom with the ransom money.[5]

On 18th December 1661, with Thomas Holt (as already mentioned), Selleck was recommended by the king for the degree of D.D. at Cambridge, but in the end it was a Lambeth doctorate which he received in 1665. He recovered his benefice of Elworthy at the Restoration, and in 1664 obtained also the rectory of Clifton Campville, Staffordshire, both of which livings he retained until his death on 30th June 1690 at the age of 80.

Dr Selleck's life at Wells, where he was assigned the canonical house on the site now 21, The Liberty, seems to have been uneventful, apart from several brushes with his colleagues over matters concerned with residence and the payment of various emoluments and other moneys due to them.[6] He seems to have been somewhat contentious, or perhaps pedantic, in disposition, and on several occasions found himself in a minority of one in chapter; it is perhaps not without

[1] *Cal.* ii. 458.

[2] See Foster, op.cit., 1332; Le Neve-Hardy, op.cit., i. 165, 196; Matthews, op.cit., 318–9.

[3] T. Blount, *Boscobel, or The Complete History of His Sacred Majesties most miraculous preservation after the Battle of Worcester* . . . , printed in Allan Fea, *After Worcester Fight* (London, 1904), 136–7, 151.

[4] *Letters and Papers (Domestic), 1660–1*, 534. [5] Ibid. *1661–2*, 490.

[6] For an account of these disputes, see below, pp.xxiv ff.

significance that the 56 books which he donated to the library reveal his strong interest in canon and civil law.

Grindall Sheafe,[1] the last of the residentiaries elected at the Restoration, was a Cambridge graduate and fellow of King's College from 1629 to 1650. He held the livings of Horstead and Coltishall in Norfolk and Westerham in Kent, and was ejected during the Commonwealth, but nothing is known about his life at that time; in 1645 he appears as chaplain to Sir P. Osborne at Castle Cornet, Guernsey. On 12th August 1660 he was installed as archdeacon of Wells, and lost no time in addressing a petition to the king for a letter of recommendation to the dean and chapter, claiming that by virtue of his office he should have precedence in any election to a residentiary canonry—a plea which seems to have met with immediate success. At the same time he sought his majesty's assistance in securing the degree of doctor of divinity, which was granted *lit. reg.* in 1661.[2]

Wood gives Sheafe an unattractive character. He asserts that from his various preferments, including the "golden prebendary" (*sic*) of Huish and Brent,[3] "raking and scraping a good deal of wealth together (for he troubled himself not with learning or the encouragement thereof), it had redounded much to his honour and name to have left it to his church, which he did not, but to lay people and servants, who cared not for him, only for pelf-sake". He died in 1680.

In addition to Dr Creyghton and Dr Smith, a third residentiary survived from the time before the Civil War: Dr Thomas Walker, who had been elected in 1635 to replace the precentor, Edward Abbott. Dr Walker died late in 1665, and his passing gave rise to a sharp contention within the chapter. A letter had come from the king recommending the honourable William Fane for election to the vacant place, and dean Creyghton was prepared to propose his co-option at the general chapter meeting on Tuesday, 2nd January 1665–6. But the other canons (doctors Peirs, Holt, Selleck, and Sheafe) objected on two grounds: such elections could only be made by the full chapter (Dr Smith and Dr Busby were, as usual, absent and had not appointed proxies), and there was a more suitable candidate; the indications are that he was Dr Francis Mundy, the subdean. The business was therefore by common consent deferred until Thursday, 4th January.

When the chapter met after Mattins on that day the dean tried to get a decision about the election, so that the king's letter might be answered; but the others (so he asserted) began to hedge and proceeded to deal with other matters. Accordingly Creyghton entered a written protestation against their disobedience and shuffling: on Tuesday they had wasted two hours in futile argument about the practice of the cathedral and the meaning of certain words, and now they were equally obstructive. They had treated the king's letter with ridicule and had created dissention in the chapter by uniting against him to oppose the co-option of Dr Fane, whom they knew to be well-born, of good standing, and of the highest character, and who never ought to have been involved in such controversy—and all because they wanted to force upon the chapter some one from whom they had greater expectations; no more business, private or public, ought to be transacted until they had done satisfaction to the king's letter.

The other canons demurred at this, and declared that the election should be left to his majesty's determination; in other words, if the will of the majority in the chapter was not to prevail, they preferred to waive their right altogether, leaving the matter to be settled by royal nomination as in the case of Dr Selleck's appointment. However, consultations and negotiations must have followed, of which we have no record, for by 8th January the dissidents had had second thoughts; meeting without the dean, they decreed unanimously to accede to the king's request—

[1] See J. and J. A. Venn, op.cit., *s.v.* (where Sheafe is stated erroneously to have been archdeacon of Wilts); Wood, op.cit., I, i. 798; Le Neve-Hardy, op.cit., i. 161; Matthews, op.cit., 272.

[2] *Letters and Papers (Domestic), 1660–1*, 188, 250.

[3] This prebend was annexed to the archdeaconry of Wells, and was one of the most valuable of those founded in the cathedral church.

but they also declared their approval of Dr Mundy as a person fit (*habilem et idoneam*, the term used in the charter) to be a residentiary canon. Another vacancy, however, did not occur until 1674, by which time (as we shall see) other arrangements had been made. Dr Mundy died in 1678.

William Fane[1] was the sixth son of Francis, Earl of Westmorland, and a graduate of Cambridge from Queens' college. He was ordained priest in 1642 by the bishop of Peterborough and in 1650 was presented under the Great Seal to the rectory of West Huntspill, Somerset; he had been sequestered by 1654, but recovered this benefice in 1662. In 1661 he became prebendary of Taunton, and in 1672 exchanged this stall for the rectory and prebend of Dinder, two miles from Wells, but it is not known whether he often resided there; his canonical house, no longer in existence, was formerly Dr Walker's and lay to the east of the present Dean's Lodging, 25, The Liberty. Apart from attending chapter meetings with fair regularity and serving his turn in the various elective offices, we hear little of Dr Fane during his fourteen years as a residentiary; the fact that he was asked in 1670 to arrange and catalogue the books in the cathedral library suggests that he may have been something of a scholar. He died in 1679.

On 25th May 1670 Robert Creyghton I was elected bishop of Bath and Wells, and on 28th June Ralph Bathurst,[2] president of Trinity college, Oxford, was installed in his stead as dean of Wells. Bathurst was ordained priest in 1644, but during the Civil War he studied medicine and in 1654 graduated M.D. at Oxford, where he practised for some time; he also assisted the ejected bishop of Oxford, Robert Skinner, at private ordinations. He was a good latinist and a scholar of repute with a facility for composing verses, and the breadth of his interests is shown by the part he took at Oxford in the formation of a small group of scientists and others which developed into the Royal Society, of which he himself became a fellow in 1663.

In character Dr Bathurst was genial and hospitable, and generous personally and with money; in Wells he is said to have placed his medical skill at the service of the poor, giving advice and medicines free of charge. But Wells did not see much of him. Immediately following his appointment as dean he came to preside over the July general chapter, and under his inspiration various measures of reform were undertaken. Thereafter, however, his attendance was infrequent; he usually kept residence (nominally with Dr Busby) during the long vacation months of July, August, and September; but in the 12½ years of his tenure of the deanery covered by the act book of 1666–1683 he was present in chapter only on 138 days. Most of his time and energy was given to his duties at Oxford, and to the repair and enlargement of Trinity college; indeed, in 1691 he even refused the bishopric of Bristol with licence to hold both the deanery and his presidency *in commendam*, fearing that episcopal responsibilities would interfere with the university work to which he was so devoted. He died in 1704 at the age of 86, "stark-blind, deaf, and memory lost", wrote his old friend John Evelyn, "after having been a person of admirable parts and learning."

Mindful of the contention that had arisen over the election of Dr Fane, dean Creyghton must have resolved that nothing of the kind should interfere with the promotion of his son Robert. This would explain the terms of a letter from the king, dated from Whitehall on 14th November 1667, in which the chapter was enjoined to elect Robert Creyghton to the next vacant place, and to register its undertaking to comply with this order by an act which all the residentiaries present were required to subscribe.[3] This was dutifully done on 2nd January 1667–8, and even Dr Peirs seems conveniently to have forgotten the arguments against pre-election which were used to oppose his own co-option in 1644. When Dr Smith died, Creyghton was installed as precentor and elected canon residentiary on 2nd May 1674, and on 19th May he was collated to

[1] See J. and J. A. Venn, op.cit., *s.v.*; Matthews, op.cit., 312.

[2] See *Dict.Nat.Biog.*; Foster, op.cit., 87; Evelyn, *Diary*; T. Wharton, *Life and Literary Remains of Ralph Bathurst* (London, 1761); E. H. Plumtre, *Life of Thomas Ken* (London, 1888), 2 vols.

[3] See W.C.L., Parfitt papers, no. 3.

the precentor's official residence, now known as 'Tower House'; previously he dwelt in the house until recently occupied by the principal of the Theological College—one of the houses in the gift of the bishop, which were usually granted to non-residentiaries to establish a qualification for residence.

Robert Creyghton II[1] as a boy had gone with his father into exile, and while abroad is said to have commenced his musical studies. He returned to England before the Restoration, being admitted a pensioner at Trinity college, Cambridge, on 23rd May 1655 and matriculating a year later as a scholar from Westminster school. He graduated B.A. in 1659, M.A. in 1662, and D.D. in 1678; in 1659, too, he was admitted fellow of Trinity college, and from 1666 to 1672 he held the regius professorship of Greek. His first ecclesiastical preferment was to the prebend of Timberscombe, which he resigned in 1667 for that of Yatton; in 1670 he was instituted to the benefice of Ashbrittle, and also succeeded his father as rector of Uplowman, Devon, and he retained these livings and his prebend until his death in 1734 at the advanced age of 96.

Dr Creyghton married Frideswide, daughter of his colleague Dr Peirs, archdeacon of Taunton. She had an unpleasant experience during the occupation of Wells by the insurgents under Monmouth in the summer of 1685. On the same 1st July when Dr Holt, sitting alone, had adjourned the general chapter on account of the crisis, Samuel Storey the duke's commissary general extorted 20*l.* from her. He later confessed that had this sum not been handed over, the canons' houses as well as the cathedral would have suffered the utmost violence at the hands of the rebels. At a chapter meeting on 7th October 1685 it was decreed that the 20*l.* should be repaid by the communar to Mrs Creyghton.[2]

John Evelyn the diarist records several occasions on which Dr Creyghton preached before the Court. On 14th September 1673 he took as his text Isaiah lvii.8; on 2nd September 1676 he "preached the second sermon ... on Psalm xc.12 of wisely numbering our days and well employing our time"; and on 6th September 1685 he again delivered the second sermon on 1 Thess.iv.11, "persuading to unity and peace and to be mindful of our own business". Another sermon, preached at Windsor on 10th September 1682 in his capacity of chaplain in ordinary to the king, was published under the title, *The Vanity of the Dissenters' Plea for their Separation from the Church of England*. Three Latin poems from his pen appeared in 1698 in *Examen Poeticum Duplex*.

Dr Creyghton seems to have been a competent and enthusiastic amateur musician. Nothing is known of his proficiency as a performer or his work as precentor, but his compositions include nine services (morning, ante-communion, and evening) and eleven anthems. The longer service in E flat and the full service in B flat have been published, and also the anthems 'Behold now, praise the Lord', 'Praise the Lord, O my soul', and 'I will arise', but all are now out of print; his other works remain in manuscript, and only the alto, tenor, and bass parts survive in choir books at Wells. Unfortunately Creyghton's music, though no worse than that of some of his contemporaries, can only be described as undistinguished. He was adventurous in his choice of keys (E flat and F minor were unusual at the time) and his modulations, and one of his harmonic mannerisms has established itself in musical theory as the 'Creyghtonian seventh',[3] but his works as a whole are pedestrian in character and sadly lacking in melodic invention; they are clearly the products of a keen amateur of some technical ability but limited creative talent. The anthem 'I will arise' is still performed at Wells and elsewhere, and is superior to most of his other compositions, which have long forfeited their place in cathedral lists.

[1] See *Dict.Nat.Biog.*; Wood, op.cit., I, i. 862; J. and J. A. Venn, op.cit., *s.v.*; Evelyn, *Diary*; Le Neve-Hardy, op.cit., i. 171, 181, 199.

[2] *Cal.* ii. 460.

[3] This is formed by the addition of a diatonic seventh to the chord of the subdominant in its root position, when it immediately precedes a final perfect cadence.

When Dr Selleck died in 1690, Dr Creyghton became virtually the senior residentiary, for Dr Bathurst and Dr Busby, as we have seen, were rarely or never in Wells. Thus he was able to establish in the chapter an ascendancy of which he took full advantage by procuring the election of two sons-in-law as residentiaries. Marshall Brydges, chancellor and husband of Frances Creyghton, was co-opted in 1700, and subdean Henry Layng, who had married Katherine Creyghton, succeeded Edwyn Sandys in 1706. The precentor could count on further support from William Hunt, who was elected in 1712; he was not bound to the Creyghtons by family ties, but was necessitous and financially indebted to them. Only in one respect did Dr Creyghton fail. He was anxious to introduce his son, Robert Creyghton III, into the chapter, to which end he secured a canonical house for him by an ingenious but discreditable manoeuvre;[1] but he was thwarted by the diplomacy of bishop Hooper, who viewed the dominance of the Creyghtons with concern. By making Dr Henry Layng archdeacon of Wells and Henry Pope, who had married the precentor's second daughter Margaret, chancellor of the diocese, the bishop at once placed the Creyghton family under obligation to himself, and drew support to his side; thus he managed to exert enough influence to check any further strengthening of the Creyghton ascendancy in the chapter. Robert Creyghton III, who was master of the cathedral grammar school, had to be content with the prebend of Dinder, which he held from 1718 to 1728, when he acquired instead the prebend of Timberscombe; he was also vicar of Combe St Nicholas from 1703 to 1725, and was appointed rector of Odcombe in 1725, rector of Burnham in 1727, and vicar of Yatton in 1729, three livings which he retained until his death in 1732. He predeceased his father by more than a year, and with the latter's passing the power of the Creyghtons came abruptly to an end. The schoolmaster's son, Robert Creyghton IV, succeeded him as prebendary of Timberscombe, but seems to have played no part in affairs at Wells.

On the death of Dr Fane, Edwyn Sandys[2] was elected to residence in his place on 2nd July 1679, having presented royal letters of recommendation to the chapter on 6th October 1675. He came of a Somerset family well-known at the time, and it seems probable that his great-grandfather Francis Sandys was related to Edwin Sandys, archbishop of York. He matriculated at Magdalen Hall, Oxford, on 25th October 1659 and held a fellowship there from 1665 to 1672. In 1671 he obtained the rectory of Yeovilton and in 1672 the prebend of Wedmore IV, which he relinquished for the prebend of Wanstrow in 1674; in 1675 he acquired the benefice of Puddimore Milton (now Podimore), adjoining the parish of Yeovilton, and retained both livings until his death in 1705. His last preferment was to the archdeaconry of Wells, in which dignity he was installed on 14th November 1683.

When Dr Creyghton moved into the precentor's house from the house at the east end of the cathedral, Mr Sandys was collated to the latter by bishop Mews on 15th June 1674, and remained there until he followed Dr Fane in the canonical house 'in East Wells'. On 10th January 1683–4 the bishop gave him leave to pull down the canonical house in the Market Place and to build another there on new foundations, fit for a canon residentiary. This was in order to obviate the inconveniences due to the close proximity of the market hall, on account of which Dr Piers had refused to occupy the house;[3] but we do not know why Sandys was prepared to go to such trouble and expense. The chapter helped him with a loan of 50*l.* and a grant of one of the trees on the cathedral green for timber, and the communar paid 10*s.* to the workmen when the foundation was laid. It is not recorded when he took up residence in the new house, but he seems to have vacated the canonical house 'in East Wells' some time in 1683, for Dr Levinze paid the obituary rent of the latter for the year 1683–4; he probably lived at his Yeovilton rectory

[1] There is an account of this in *The Life of Richard Kidder, D.D.*, ed. A. E. Robinson, (Som.Rec.Soc.,37), 208; and see also W.C.L., Act Book 1683–1704, f.151 (*Cal.* ii. 465) and ibid., Act Book 1705–25, f.95.

[2] See Le Neve-Hardy, i. 185, 195; *Life of Richard Kidder*, 193–5. [3] See below, pp.xxvii–xxviii.

until the dwelling in the Market Place was finished. Later, and certainly from the beginning of bishop Kidder's episcopate, he retired to Yeovilton and let the house in Wells.

Soon after his election Mr Sandys was involved in a chapter dispute about his emoluments, and in 1681 a more serious controversy arose over the question of his subscription to the Act of Uniformity on co-option to residence; both matters are dealt with later.[1] It appears from the second case that his relations with bishop Mews were cordial, and with Mews's successor Thomas Ken he was on terms of intimate friendship. Though he did not throw in his lot with the non-jurors they had his sympathy, and when Ken was deprived he did all he could to avoid recognition of Richard Kidder's jurisdiction; he would not co-operate in visitations or ordinations, he omitted references to William and Mary from the bidding and other prayers, he never called on Kidder when the latter was in Wells, and once rose from the dinner table and left the room when the bishop's health was being drunk.

Mr Sandys only survived the 'latitudinarian traditor' by two years, dying at Yeovilton on 8th October 1705 at the age of 62 after receiving the holy sacrament from his friend Thomas Ken. In his will he directed that a number of books belonging to him should be carried to Wells and deposited in the cathedral library; they included one of the copies of Nathaniel Chyles's manuscript history of Wells cathedral. The inscription on his tomb in Yeovilton church tells of his "pious and exemplary" life; he seems to have been a man of courage and firm principle, but also somewhat eccentric, if it is true that "he was noted for his hatred to children" and "never would baptize an infant, nor see one of his own several children till they were eight or nine years of age".[2]

Dr Sheafe died on 28th April 1680, and the next day Henry Dutton[3] was elected canon residentiary in his place, having been commended to the chapter in royal letters dated 4th July 1678 and 8th January 1679.[4] He was a graduate of Oxford and fellow of Corpus Christi college, from which he was expelled in 1648 by the parliamentary visitors. In 1650 he occurs as minister of Yanworth, Gloucestershire, and may have been rector of Kirkby Laythorpe, Lincolnshire, and vicar of Clifton Maybank, Dorset, in the time of the Commonwealth. At the Restoration he obtained the benefice of Curry Mallet, which he resigned for that of Mells in 1667; he was also vicar of Evercreech from 1661 to 1690. In 1661 he was installed as prebendary of East Harptree, which he held until 1668, when he received the prebend of Whitelackington. He is described by Walker as "a very good scholar, an admirable preacher, and one of the most accomplished persons for agreeableness of humour and conversation that ever lived. He married the eldest daughter of Dr Dugdale, one of the suffering prebendaries of Wells". Mr Dutton died in 1693 at the age of 72; he seems to have held as his canonical residence the house lately occupied by the Principal of the Theological College, in succession to Mr Sandys.

The last residentiary to be elected during the period 1666–1683 was William Levinze,[5] prebendary of Holcombe from 1679 and subdean from 1682; he was admitted on 20th April 1682 in succession to Dr Peirs, having been recommended by a royal letter which Dr Bathurst sent to the chapter with his own cordial support on 15th December 1679.[6] He was a fellow of St John's college, Oxford, and is recorded as refusing to submit in 1648. He became professor of Greek at Oxford and president of St John's college, and had a considerable reputation for learning and collected a large library, though Wood reports gossip that he was "not thought well of . . . since he beats the students and fights". Like Dr Bathurst, he devoted himself mainly to his work in the

[1] See below, pp.xxix–xxx. [2] Le Neve-Hardy, op.cit., i. 162 n. 52.

[3] See Foster, op.cit., 436; Walker, op.cit., ii. 112; Le Neve-Hardy, op.cit., i. 183, 188, 206; Matthews, op.cit., 312.

[4] W.C.L., Documents, series III, box 4, 190, 192.

[5] *Dict.Nat.Biog.*; Wood, op.cit., I, ii. 840; Foster, op.cit., 905; Matthews, op.cit., 33.

[6] W.C.L., Documents, series III, box 4, 191.

university and was not often in Wells, though he followed Mr Sandys in possession of the canonical house 'in East Wells'. He died unmarried in 1698.

III The Chapter, its Meetings and Records

The Elizabethan charter vested the government of Wells cathedral in the body of eight residentiary canons formally designated 'the dean and chapter', but often termed simply 'the chapter'. A meeting of this body was also called a 'chapter', and its chairman or (more correctly) president was *ex officio* the dean, or in his absence the senior by co-option of the members present. The number of residentiaries necessary to form a quorum was not stated in the charter, but seems to have been defined by custom; an act book entry for 1st July 1672 suggests that a *capitulum plenum* was constituted by the attendance (personally or by proxy) of not less than five, though for an installation three sufficed, two of whom might be non-residentiary canons. While it is sometimes stated that a decision was unanimous, no record is given in the act books of the voting on those occasions when the chapter divided on an issue—though in an entry for 5th January 1669–70, reference to the making of a decree by three named members out of a chapter of five may indicate a majority decision. It does not appear that the president, whether the dean or another canon, had any casting vote.

During the cathedral's business year quarterly or general chapters were regularly convened on 1st October, 2nd January (because 1st January was a 'red letter' day and meetings were normally not held on such days), 1st April and 1st July. Each of these chapters was continued by adjournment from one time of meeting to another until all the business before it had been transacted. Thus any chapter might vary in length from a few days to almost three months, though during such long periods meetings would not be held every day. In the sixteen and a half years covered by our act book, ten chapters extended over more than 30 days,[1] while thirty-five lasted two weeks or less.

Among the routine matters dealt with at the quarterly chapters were the roll-call of vicars choral on the first day, and confirmations of leases granted and elections of canons residentiary made after the conclusion of the preceding chapter; on the strength of a chapter act of 1608[2] Dr Selleck maintained that such elections were invalid and could only be made at a quarterly chapter, but he was overruled.[3] Not many meetings took place outside the times of the general chapters; excluding the annual election of officers on St Jerome's day, 30th September (which really belonged to the October chapter), there were only 58 during our period, and of these 34 were installations of prebendaries which did not require subsequent confirmation.

Only once[4] does the act book specify the exact hour at which the chapter met. The common formula was to record that it met between such and such hours in the forenoon or afternoon of the day in question—for example, between 8 am and 10 am, 9 am and 12 noon, 2 pm and 4 pm, 3 pm and 6 pm, and so forth. It is not clear whether this means that the members assembled at the first of such hours and continued in session until the second, or whether they met and adjourned at their convenience between the times stated, but the latter seems the more likely; it is improbable that life and business in Wells were then conducted with a stricter eye on the clock than was the case elsewhere, and we know from Pepys that the sense of time was generally less precise at this period than modern life demands.[5]

[1] October 1672 (37 days), October 1673 (66), July 1675 (34), July 1676 (40), July 1677 (66), October 1679 (71), April 1680 (33), October 1680 (71), October 1681 (91), and October 1682 (75).

[2] *Cal.*, ii. 355. [3] See 2nd July 1680. [4] 3rd April 1682, 8 pm in Dr Peirs's house.

[5] In the middle ages the chapter was summoned by the ringing of a bell, but there is no evidence that this practice survived into the 17th century.

Meetings were normally held in the chapter house, but during the winter months the chapter was often adjourned to the exchequer or audit room; this was the long room at the northern end of the range of buildings above the west cloister, next to the present choristers' practice room,[1] where the canons could do business in comfort round a fire. If a residentiary was sick the chapter would meet at his house, and meetings were sometimes held in canonical houses during cold weather, late in the evening, or simply for convenience. Once, for the sealing of an important lease, the chapter gathered at the residence of a layman in the Liberty.[2]

Among the formal transactions of the chapter were the admission and perpetuation of vicars choral, the installation of non-residentiary canons and dignitaries, and the admission of canons residentiary. When a vicar choral was to be admitted for his probationary year the vicars, having deliberated in hall, came into the chapter house where the dean or other president, proposing the candidate to them for election, enquired whether they approved him for his voice and skill. If all or most of them answered in the affirmative, he was admitted on probation by the chapter as a vicar choral of the cathedral and of the New Close, and swore allegiance to the sovereign and obedience to the dean and chapter; he was then assigned the vicarial stall of the prebendary by whom part of his emolument, known as stall wages, would be paid, and a senior vicar choral was nominated as his *auscultor* or supervisor. Twelve months later the vicars again deliberated and assembled in the same way, and if the probationer was approved by them and commended by his *auscultor* for voice, skill, and diligence he was perpetuated by the chapter.

The installation of a non-residentiary canon began in the chapter house, where the canon-designate appeared in person or by proxy and presented letters mandatory from the bishop for his installation "to the prebend or canonry of——". The mandate was inspected and read by the chapter clerk or his deputy; then the dean or other president, in the name of the chapter, decreed to proceed accordingly and appointed from those present two canons, either residentiary or non-residentiary, as installers. These conducted the new canon to the quire, and there installed him and inducted him into possession of his prebend;[3] then, returning to the chapter house, they gave him place and voice in chapter and he took the customary oaths. The same procedure occurred at the installation of a dignitary. It seems to have been customary for the newly-installed canon to provide a collation afterwards, for on 20th October 1680 it was decreed by the chapter that instead he should be desired to pay 20*s.* to the library fund.[4]

A canon seeking to enter upon residence appeared before the chapter, appealed to any royal letters in his favour registered in the archives, deposited a caution of 100*l.* if he were a dignitary or 100 marks if he were a simple prebendary,[5] and asked for admission as a residentiary. If he were

[1] It is described on 12th October 1372 as over a gate on the west side of the cloister, *Cal.*, i. 273.

[2] See 4th March 1669–70. [3] It does not appear that this was done, as it is now, in the context of a service.

[4] By the time of bishop Hooper (1704–27) there seems to have been a reversion to the old practice, which was doubtless a survival of mediaeval custom. His daughter Abigail records that when any of the poor prebends became vacant "the Bp used to be ashamed to ask any one to take them, for besides the necessary expence of comeing into one of them, it was so much increased by an unreasonable custom . . . of the Prebends (*sic*) giveing a cold collation at a publick house on the evening of the day he was installed a Prebend (to which were invited all the clergy and gent: in the town) so that he was not made whole for his expenses in seven years time . . . This made the Bishop resolve to break through this custom and upon the vacancy one of these poor prebends, he sent to a clergyman who was well provided for and of known hospitality and gave him the Prebend, and then told him his design to break that evil custom through him, and expressly forbid any entertainment, himself sending a message to the two Prebends, who install'd the new one, to come to the Palace to drink their new brothers health that evening. The Bishop took this method for two or three times, strictly chargeing every one to comply with it, wch intirely broke that custom"; *Some memorandums concerning Bishop Hooper*, (Walton [Hooper] MSS, formerly known as Prowse MS), pp.27–8, reproduced by kind permission of Sir Richard Hamilton Bart.

[5] It is not clear when or how this distinction arose. A bull of pope Boniface IX in 1400 ordered that instead of giving an expensive entertainment on the occasion of his installation, every new residentiary should pay 150 marks (=100*l.*) to the dean and chapter for the fabric and other capitular expenses; no difference was made between dignitaries and simple canons, and nothing is said about the distribution of this sum among the residentiaries and vicars (see *Cal.* i. 392). Presumably the custom of requiring dignitaries to pay a larger caution arose from their enjoyment of larger endowments than other canons.

approved as *idoneus et habilis* (in the words of the charter), his caution was accepted, and he was elected and admitted on condition that he should not enter upon residence before a stated date, usually 1st October in the year following that of his co-option. Provision was made that if he should die in the meantime the amount of his caution would be refunded to his executors. The caution money was then apportioned according to custom: one-tenth went to the fabric fund, one-tenth to the vicars choral, and the remainder was divided equally between the members of the chapter (excluding, of course, the newly-elected canon), so that each received one-seventh of four-fifths of the total sum deposited. After admission the new residentiary was entitled to participate in the conduct of chapter business, but might not claim any emoluments of office (quotidians and dividends) before commencing residence at the time specified. This rule may have been designed to ensure financial provision for an *annus post mortem* payment to his predecessor's estate; it was relaxed in favour of Messrs Sandys and Dutton,[1] but seems to have been reapplied in the case of Dr Levinze. There was no ceremony of admission for a residentiary, who would already have his stall in quire and a place in the chapter house as a prebendary or dignitary.

Among the admissions of residentiary canons recorded in the act book of 1666–83 is that of Dr Bathurst, who succeeded Dr Creyghton as dean of Wells. This raises a point which calls for clarification. Originally, at Wells as at the other secular cathedrals, the dean was a canon elected to that dignity by his fellows; and as he remained a prebendary by virtue of possessing a prebend, so he continued to be a canon by virtue of his membership of the chapter in which he was *primus inter pares*.[2] During the 16th century, however, the situation at Wells (as we have seen) underwent a change. First, the deanery became a Crown appointment and thereafter, with the exception of Robert Creyghton in 1660 and Richard Jenkyns in 1845, it was never filled by the preferment of a prebendary of Wells; the ancient practice virtually disappeared. Second, the charter committed the government of the cathedral to the dean and canons residentiary, who were to be known corporately as 'the dean and chapter', but the dean himself was left free to decide whether or not to seek election as a canon residentiary. If he chose not to do so, it seems that he could still preside in chapter but could not claim any emoluments of residence, though he would enjoy the revenue from the endowments belonging to the deanery. The question never arose, however, for every dean asked for co-option and was admitted a residentiary canon on payment of his caution, subject to the usual conditions—save that he entered immediately upon his residence. He received the same emoluments as the other residentiaries and shared the duties of residence with them; indeed, in some records of attendance in our act book he was specifically counted as one canon among others.[3] Both the provisions of the charter and capitular practice leave no room for doubt that the 17th century deans of Wells, in a different but equally real sense, were canons no less than their mediaeval predecessors.[4]

The election of a new residentiary affected the disposition of the patronage administered by

[1] See below, p.xxix. [2] See K. Edwards, op.cit. 319.

[3] See, e.g., the entries for 25th, 26th, and 27th October 1681.

[4] This still leaves open the question, whether the dean is now a canon. He is not a canon residentiary in the sense defined by the charter, for all elections to residence ceased in the 19th century, when the appointment of all residentiaries other than the dean was at Wells vested in the bishop. Confusion has arisen from a habit, begun in the 18th century, of giving to residentiaries who had no dignity from which to take their title the style of 'canon'—thus, 'Mr Treasurer Woodford', but 'Mr Canon Hill' (never 'Canon Hill'). From this, however, 'canon' gradually became a mode of address, and usage was legalized and extended by section 1 of the Ecclesiastical Commission Act of 1840 (now repealed by the Cathedrals Measure, 1963), which enacted that "from henceforth all members of chapter except the dean . . . shall be styled canons" (3 and 4 Vict. c.113). This, of course, was a matter simply of statutory designation, and has now become obsolete. Properly speaking, all members of an old foundation cathedral who are subject to its constitution and statutes are canons, and distinctions of status within the chapter are correctly expressed in terms of the dignities. In this sense the dean is constitutionally still a canon, and the principal canon, and the current (1967) Wells constitution (§1) implies as much.

the dean and chapter. Fifteen benefices[1] were in its gift, but the rights of presentation were exercised by the members individually; seven of the canons each received the patronage of two livings, and one (always Buckland Abbas in Dorset) went to the eighth. Immediately after an admission these benefices were reallocated; originally it seems that this was done by agreement, but in 1560 there occurs the first reference to 'casting balls', a method mentioned once in the act book and certainly implied by other allusions to the apportionment of benefices by lot.[2] No example or description of the balls has survived, but they were probably made of wood and inscribed with the names of the residentiaries or with identifying numbers; it seems unlikely, from an entry dated 24th April 1590, that they bore the names of benefices.[3] Their use (in what way, we do not know) for the distribution of livings did not preclude the exchange of patronage between members of the chapter.[4]

Two bishops were enthroned during the period with which we are concerned, each of them by proxy, and one feature of the ceremonies is curious. After the usual proceedings in the cathedral the episcopal representative was conducted to the chapter house and was there installed in the accustomed place assigned to the bishop (*locus in capitulo episcopo . . . assignari consuetus*). The accustomed place was, of course, the stall in the centre of the east side of the chapter house reserved for the bishop and used by him at visitations; but it was not, strictly speaking, *locus in capitulo*, for the bishop had no place or voice in chapter since he possessed no prebend.[5] It is possible that the ceremony in question (now disused) signified recognition by the chapter of the bishop's right of visitation in the cathedral—a right unsuccessfully contested in mediaeval times,[6] and implicitly accepted in the charter.

The responsibility for keeping a record of the transactions at chapter meetings rested with the chapter clerk, but he seems to have delegated this task almost entirely to the deputy chapter clerk. The latter usually attended in person, though occasionally he sent a substitute, and it appears that the residentiaries not infrequently met without him; when present, he took notes of attendances and decisions which he, or an assistant, afterwards wrote down in the act book or register. A decree of 16th October 1672 ordered that all acts made during the course of a chapter were to be presented for approval in the chapter house at the concluding session before being entered, but it is not clear how carefully this regulation was observed.

During the whole of the period 1666–83 the office of chapter clerk was held by William Westley. At the beginning Alexander Harrison was his deputy, and made most of the entries until 3rd October 1671, after which a number of unsigned entries occur. Robert Quirke assumed Harrison's duties in March 1672, and continued to act until at least January 1679; a gap then follows in the records, but in July of that year Richard Healy's bold, clear hand appears, and on 30th September he took Quirke's place to commence his long and distinguished career in the service of the dean and chapter. Among the substitutes, all notaries public, who attended meetings from time to time were Guy (or Guydo) Clynton, Nicholas Neblett, Thomas Heath, and John Paine who eventually succeeded Mr Westley as chapter clerk.

[1] Allerton, Bishop's Lydeard, Buckland Abbas (Dorset), Burnham, Cheddar, Dulverton, East Lambrook, Long Sutton, Mudford, North Curry, Pucklechurch (Gloucestershire), Shipham, Stogumber, St Cuthbert's Wells, Winscombe.

[2] See particularly 4th July 1679; also 4th July 1670, 1st July 1674, 2nd July 1680, 20th April 1682.

[3] W.C.L., Act Book H, f.60d.

[4] See an entry for 1st October 1679. The practice of casting balls continued until 24th July 1780, when it was decreed that benefices should be allocated according to seniority (W.C.L., Act Book 1777–1792, 75); but the "old and accustomed manner of casting lotts" was restored on 15th August 1798 (W.C.L., Act Book 1792–1817, 121). Balloting or casting lots for benefices was finally abolished on 1st April 1817 (ibid, 564).

[5] The bishops of Salisbury overcame this disadvantage by the permanent annexation to the bishopric, first of the prebend of Horton, and then of the prebend of Potterne.

[6] K. Edwards, op.cit. 131. The bishop could not, however, examine canons and other ministers individually, and the dean alone answered for the chapter.

At this time all records of formal business were made in Latin,[1] but English entries occur with growing frequency towards the end of the act book, especially after Richard Healy had assumed office. When the vernacular was used, it was generally to note decisions relating to dealings with tenants, lessees, or the vicars choral, or concerning the public at large; nevertheless, it is by no means always clear why one language was chosen in preference to the other, and the choice may to some extent have been dictated by the availability of common forms or precedents.

Common forms occur frequently, and have been drastically abbreviated in the calendar. The first entry in the act book, for example, is typical of the verbose preamble with which most records of meetings began, when any transaction of important business had to be written up. In translation it reads: "On Monday, 1st October, in the year of our Lord 1666, between the hours of 9 and 11 in the forenoon of that day, in the chapter house of the cathedral church of Wells, before the worshipful men Robert Creyghtone, doctor of divinity, dean of the cathedral church of Wells lawfully founded in the county of Somerset, Thomas Holt, doctor of divinity, chancellor of the said church, John Selleck, doctor of divinity, archdeacon of Bath, Grindall Sheafe, doctor of divinity, archdeacon of Wells, canons residentiary of the same church, and before the honourable William Fane, doctor of divinity, also canon of the said church, capitularly assembled and making a chapter, in the presence of me, Alexander Harrison, notary public and deputy chapter clerk:" Similar common forms record such matters as installations of non-residentiary canons and admissions of vicars choral.

Very many entries simply note, in a brief formula, the meeting of certain residentiaries at a prearranged time, and their adjournment of the chapter to a day and hour following. On some of these numerous occasions there may have been no business to transact, but this cannot have been a frequent occurrence—particularly when, as so often happened, a morning meeting was prorogued to the afternoon of the same day. At such times the chapter was doubtless often occupied with matters relating to the administration of its extensive estates; there would be the granting of leases to consider, fines to fix, suits at law to undertake, and revenues to collect—and behind decisions briefly recorded in the act book might lie many hours of report and debate. Cathedral affairs, too, would call for careful and sometimes prolonged discussion; we know that from time to time there were problems connected with the fabric, residence, the vicars choral, and so forth, all of which would demand attention during the sometimes brief periods when the general chapter was in being. The absence of the chapter clerk or his deputy from such meetings explains the lack of any minutes, and points to their informal and often private character.

The act book generally records in the briefest terms the granting or confirming of leases and the sealing of letters patent for the appointment of officials. These and similar documents were usually transcribed in full in a ledger book or register, and one labelled 'G' covers the period 1624–81.

IV The Residence and Remuneration of Canons

Two topics which recurrently engaged the chapter's attention during our period were residence and the entitlement of canons to the regular emoluments of residence. These emoluments consisted of quotidians, escheatory dues, and dividends, and were quite distinct from the revenue which every residentiary derived from his prebend, and if he were also a dignitary, from any endowments annexed to his dignity.

[1] Latin continued in use for all formal entries until 2nd April 1733, from which date English alone was employed, in conformity with the act 4 Geo. II., c. 26 (1731) which authorized the discontinuance of Latin for various kinds of legal instruments and similar documents.

Quotidians were the distributions to residentiary canons, originally made daily in kind but eventually commuted to cash payments of equivalent value; as the *quinque personae*, it will be recalled, qualified in earlier times for double commons, so now (if they were residentiary) they received 20*l.* annually by quarterly instalments, while other residentiaries received 10*l.* Escheatory dues and dividends varied in amount from year to year. The former, in any case, were small, ranging from 7*s.* 10*d.* in 1679 to 18*s.* 9*d.* in 1675; the average sum received by each residentiary during the period 1666–83[1] was 14*s.* 5*d.* By far the most substantial part of a residentiary's income in any year came from his dividend, or share of the revenue accruing to the common fund from fines, rents, pensions, and so forth. In 1670, due mainly to the large fine received from John, Lord Poulett, in consideration of the lease of the rectory of Buckland Abbas for three lives, the dividend amounted to 346*l.* 9*s.* 1*d.*, while in 1680 it was as small as 20*l.* 0*s.* 7*d.*; but the average for the period was 100*l.* 6*s.* 8*d.*—so that with quotidians and escheatory dues a dignitary during the years 1666–1683 received for his emoluments of residence an average round sum of 120*l.*, and a simple residentiary 110*l.*

In addition to these regular annual items of income each canon, as we have seen, benefited at the admission of a new residentiary from his share of the latter's caution money. If this sum were deposited in pounds he would have 11*l.* 8*s.* 6*d.*, or if in marks, 7*l.* 12*s.* 4*d.*[2]

Payment of emoluments other than shares of caution money by the communar was not unconditional, but dependent upon observance of the terms of residence laid down in the charter—four months in the case of a dignitary, and three in the case of an ordinary residentiary. Not infrequently, however, other claims conflicted with those of residence, and when duties at Court or university prevented a member of the chapter from coming to Wells his colleagues were usually disposed to be indulgent, and would grant a dispensation, often in the form of an allowance of so many days to enable him to complete his residence and so qualify for his emoluments. Occasionally they were not so accommodating, but because individual instances were dealt with *ad hoc* and not according to definite principles, the practice of the chapter tended to vary with circumstances.

This is well illustrated by the cases of those inveterate absentees, Dr Smith and Dr Busby, though the first reference to quotidians in our act book does not seem to concern them. A minute of 4th January 1667–8 decreed that payment should be made to the canons for as many days as they had omitted to attend the cathedral [*pro tantis diebus quanti per canonicos in adeundo ecclesiam cathedralem omissi sunt*]—a vaguely worded concession which appears to mean that canons living in Wells but absent from the services should not, on that account, suffer any pecuniary loss. The circumstances of this measure are not known, but it may refer to absence due to illness; it does not seem to have any reference to residence.

Eighteen months later Dr Smith's non-residence was brought into a dispute which had divided the chapter into two equal camps. On 1st July 1669, the general chapter day, dean Creyghton and Dr Selleck proposed Dr Sheafe as steward for the two-year period beginning at Michaelmas, while Dr Peirs and Dr Holt proposed Dr Fane; and nothing seems to have been done to resolve this position of stalemate. On the following afternoon Dr Creyghton was absent and Dr Peirs presided. To strengthen the support for Dr Fane he exhibited a proxy from Dr Smith, whereupon Selleck and Sheafe protested that Smith's proxy was invalid and that he ought to receive neither quotidians nor dividend because of his non-residence. Peirs and Holt again proposed Fane as steward and, invoking Smith's proxy, declared him elected by a majority of one. The other two insisted that it was now too late for the election since Sheafe had already been chosen on the previous day, though the grounds for this assertion are not stated, and it would appear to have been incorrect.

[1] There is no record of the escheatory dues paid in 1666, 1667, 1668, and 1678.

[2] On the denominations in which caution money was paid, see above, p.xx and n.5.

After this the chapter was adjourned to the next morning, when all six canons assembled and Dr Peirs, supported by Drs Holt and Fane, presented a written protestation, presumably against the proceedings of the last two days: its contents are not disclosed in the minutes. They then withdrew, and the dean, Dr Selleck, and Dr Sheafe adjourned the meeting from the chapter house to the deanery. This affair seems to have created a serious rift in the chapter, for Drs Peirs, Holt, and Fane stayed away from the October general chapter and Dr Creyghton and his two supporters transacted at the deanery all the business, except that of 30th September and 1st October. Victory, however, clearly lay with the other side, for the steward's books show that Dr Fane did in fact assume office.

By the beginning of 1670 these differences seem to have been patched up for the moment, and on the morning of 5th January 1669–70 a decree was made by Drs Creyghton, Holt, Selleck, Sheafe, and Fane that for the future no residentiary should receive any quotidians or dividend unless he had completed the period of residence required by the charter, and members of the chapter were to certify that they had complied with its provisions in this respect. In the evening of the same day, however, the old rift reappeared within the chapter when, at a meeting in the dean's house, Creyghton, Selleck, and Sheafe outvoted Holt and Fane to carry a resolution that no canon might appoint a proxy unless he had completed his residence for the past year in conformity with the charter, a decree clearly aimed at Dr Smith, and indirectly at Dr Peirs, who had held Smith's proxy on the occasion of the disputed election to the stewardship, and thereafter did not put in an appearance in chapter until April 1670.

Underlying these events one senses something of an animus on the part of Dr Creyghton against Dr Smith and, other evidence suggests, against Dr Peirs also. In Smith's case this may have been of long standing; they had clashed in 1639 over a question of precedence in the chapter,[1] and some matter (possibly this) in dispute between them had been referred to bishop Peirs at his visitation in 1640.[2] As to Dr Peirs, it is noteworthy that immediately Creyghton became bishop he proceeded against him for removing to Smith's house, and suspended him. These personal tensions may in part have been due to Creyghton's temperament, though Peirs may have resented the fact that Creyghton, though an exile, had enjoyed the safety and privileges of Court life and had returned to receive a deanery, while he had suffered extremes of privation for the same royalist cause and had been rewarded with nothing but the residentiary canonry for which he had applied in 1643.

It may be to this time that an ill-written and undated document[3] relates, in which certain questions about residence are stated:

> May an absent canon constitute a lawful proxy to vote for him in chapter? Granted that he may do so, should not the cause of his absence be declared in the form of proxy?
>
> Is duly certified bodily infirmity, such as would render a canon unfit to travel, a just excuse for not keeping residence? And if such infirmity continues throughout a whole year, should not the afflicted canon be allowed his full residence? [This question may have been framed with Dr Smith in mind]
>
> Ought not time spent on the chapter's business, or as its proctor in Convocation, or in the king's service, to count as residence? [This clearly applied to Dr Busby]
>
> If a dignitary is absent from the cathedral for eight months or a simple residentiary for nine, and is then hindered from keeping residence by any of the causes mentioned, ought not his residence to be allowed to him?

There follows what seems to be the beginning of an opinion. The crucial point at issue, it states, is whether emoluments depend solely upon actual residence, or whether reasonable impedi-

[1] *Cal.* ii. 421; see p. ix.

[2] *Cal.* ii. 422. [3] W.C.L., Documents, series III, box 4, 229.

ments to residence can be taken into consideration. Unfortunately the document breaks off without indicating how the various questions might be answered, and the charter itself affords no clue, for it makes no provision for any of the contingencies described.

Problems connected with residence continued to occupy the chapter's attention for much of 1670. In March the rectory of Buckland Abbas was granted to John, Lord Poulett, for three lives at a substantial fine, which the chapter immediately resolved to divide among the canons. Furthermore, without prejudice to the rule that emoluments should depend on residence, it was decreed on 4th April that in this instance Dr Smith and Dr Busby should receive their shares of the fine. Dr Selleck lodged two objections: first, that this concession was contrary to the charter, and second, that the fine had not been divided formally by the chapter in chapter assembled; but these objections were not upheld.

Two months later, on 25th May, Dr Creyghton was elected to the see of Bath and Wells, vacant by the death of old bishop Peirs at the age of 94, and no time was lost in taking advantage of the opportunities which his preferment afforded. The new dean, installed on 28th June and elected canon residentiary four days later, was the genial and liberal scholar and physician Ralph Bathurst, and he presided over a July general chapter notable for the personal attendance of seven residentiaries, while Dr Smith was represented by his proxy Dr Peirs. The importance of the business to be transacted is indicated by the fact that Dr Busby had come down from Westminster specially to look after his interests and to support Dr Peirs and his associates, who now secured a definite ascendancy in the chapter.

On the afternoon of 4th July the chapter's previous policy in regard to residence and emoluments was reversed at a single stroke; it was decreed that a canon residentiary could at all times act in chapter by proxy as validly and effectively as in person, and all previous measures taken to deprive canons of their quotidians or dividends were annulled. Further, an ingenious attempt was made to prevent revocation of these decrees by a dissident minority; it was resolved that an act of the chapter could be rescinded only by the same number of persons as that by which it had been passed—but this proved inconvenient for the conduct of business and had to be revoked two years later.[1]

Next, on 6th July, Dr Busby explained in chapter why he was unable to keep residence at Wells: he served the chapter as its proctor in Convocation, he laboured under frequent and severe bodily infirmities, and he was continually occupied in the king's service as headmaster of the royal school at Westminster. His colleagues readily accepted these reasons, and ordered that both he and Dr Smith should receive copies of decrees requiring the communar, Dr Selleck, to pay all emoluments due to them before 25th March 1671. The same day, as his receipted cash book shows, Dr Selleck settled accounts with Dr Busby for 1669. On the following day Dr Busby undertook to obtain from legal experts and send to the chapter a standard form of proxy, which every residentiary could use if he were absent. Finally, he and the dean caused it to be recorded on 8th July[2] that unless the chapter approved a canon's absence as necessary, the provisions of the charter concerning the withholding or diminution of emoluments were to be enforced.

It only remained to establish a procedure which would ensure the systematic residence of the canons in conformity with the 44th canon of 1604. This was done at the next general chapter by an act made on 17th October. Annually within the octave of Michaelmas each member of the chapter, according to his precedence, was required to designate the quarter of the year in which he wished to reside, so that not less than two persons were always in residence, the dignitaries being free to decide how and when they kept the extra month's residence which the charter imposed upon them. All emoluments would be paid in full to every canon, irrespective of the

[1] See 19th July 1672. [2] See below, p. 104.

quarter in which he made his residence, so that no one should be prejudiced by selecting a later rather than an earlier quarter. During his period of residence each canon, and particularly the dean, was enjoined to attend to the relief of the poor, provide hospitality, and above all ensure the due conduct of the cathedral's worship and the regular attendance thereat of the vicars choral and choristers; he must not be absent for trivial reasons, but only on account of serious and pressing business. Having thus enacted, the chapter allocated the quarters of the ensuing year to the residentiaries on the lines laid down, Dr Smith being assigned the third quarter with Dr Holt and Dr Busby the fourth with the dean, though there is nothing to show that either Smith or Busby discharged his duty in person at these or any future times.

The decisions about residence and emoluments taken at these two general chapters were clearly displeasing to Dr Selleck, though he seems not to have registered any protest against them at the time. However, being communar for 1669–70, he showed his disapproval by refusing to pay to the canons, or at least to the absentees, the sums due to them for that year. The election of Dr Fane as steward also continued to rankle with him, and he deliberately held up the completion of Dr Fane's accounts by declining to accept and settle his statement of charges for the year. By December things had reached such a pass that on the afternoon of the 14th, in Selleck's absence, the chapter decided to appeal to the bishop as visitor about his handling of the steward's accounts,[1] and on the following day another appeal was lodged complaining that he had withheld the emoluments of the residentiaries "to their no small and serious prejudice".[2] The result of these appeals was not recorded, but it seems that the communar was persuaded or directed to release the moneys due to his colleagues, for their receipts in his account book show that most of them were paid in full before the end of 1670: Drs Peirs, Holt, and Fane on 26th December, Dr Creyghton for what was due to him as dean on the 27th, and Dr Smith (who received his emoluments for 1669 as well as for 1670) and Dr Sheafe on the 29th. Dr Smith's signature in the books, if not given at Oxford, shows that he paid an occasional brief visit to Wells, if only to collect his stipend.

In the next year, 1671, another aspect of residence was the cause of contention between bishop Creyghton and Dr Peirs. It arose in this way. On the occasion of his unsuccessful request for co-option to the chapter in 1643, Peirs had submitted as one qualification his possession of a canonical house. This seems to have been the house at the south-eastern corner of the Market Place, known as 'Dr Young's house' because it had been collated upon John Young who became chancellor in 1611 and was admitted to residence in 1613. Young was excused from residence at the request of James I on account of "his attendaunce on us and employment in our service", and in 1616 was made dean of Winchester. His non-residence was accepted by the chapter in an act of 1626, but George Warburton, appointed dean in 1631, seems to have made an issue of the matter and it was debated at length in 1634. There is no evidence that Young ever dwelt at Wells after his preferment to Winchester and it is probable that his house, in the gift of the bishop, lapsed to William Peirs who conferred it upon his son.

During the Commonwealth the house passed into the hands of Dr Cornelius Burges, who bought much of the property belonging to the abolished bishopric and dean and chapter;[3] he sold it, and it was converted into a court for the quarter-sessions. When Peirs regained it at the Restoration he "built and repaired the same, and converted it again into an habitable house.[4] But . . . since the kinges restauracion there is a greate market house built before the dore of this

[1] See below, p.104. [2] W.C.L., Documents, series III, box 4, 174.

[3] D. Underdown, 'A Case concerning Bishops' Lands: Cornelius Burges and the Corporation of Wells', in *Eng. Hist. Review*, LXXVIII, January 1963.

[4] The cost of these works was 700*l*.—more than six times the amount spent on any other canonical house; see 'Disbursements by the chapter after the Restoration in reparation of canonical houses', "from a bundle of papers in the audit room", in W.C.L., archdeacon Archer's *Note Book*, 55.

canonicall house, which hath drawne the market from other partes to the very dores of this house, to the greate annoyance of the said house"[1]. On account of this inconvenience he left the house, rented it (apparently to a layman), and went to live in Dr Smith's official residence, now called 'Tower House', probably as the latter's tenant.

This arrangement seems to have been acceptable to most of the chapter, but it did not please bishop Creyghton, who asserted that his predecessor, Dr Peirs's father, had often enquired into the matter at his triennial visitations, but without remedy. At Creyghton's own visitation of the cathedral in 1671 the question of residence was raised, and the canons affirmed that all present faithfully observed the statutes and ordinances in this matter, though they complained much of the absences of Dr Smith and Dr Busby.[2] As to whether a canon could keep residence alone, his family being away from Wells; whether he could do so outside or without a canonical house; whether he might live in a canonical house other than his own, if such house were vacant; whether he might do so during the lifetime of the canon upon whom the house had been collated; and whether a canonical house could be leased or sold to a layman—the chapter replied that such questions (which obviously related to Dr Peirs) must be determined according to the charter, the statutes, and the laudable customs of the cathedral.[3] The bishop "entreated Dr Peirs amicably that he would amend his fault", but the latter's only response was to leave the precentor's house and go to live with his stepmother, Mary Peirs, in a "secular [*laicalem*] dwelling"—the old 'archdeacon's house' opposite the north porch of the cathedral, where he settled in the eastern part of the building. For these alleged irregularities he was summoned to the Palace on 16th November where the bishop, in the presence of Dr Sheafe and Dr Fane, censured him and suspended him from all ecclesiastical functions for violating the fundamental statutes of the cathedral.[4] Protesting against the validity of these proceedings, Dr Peirs declared his intention to appeal to the Court of Arches, and an undated document of this period[5] may be a statement of his case for legal opinion in connexion with this appeal.

First, the points at issue are set forth:

1. Is a canon residentiary bound to reside in the house collated upon him by the bishop, or does he fulfil the intention of the charter by residing in the house of another canon who is absent on account of infirmity or other impediment, "especially that other house beinge more commodious and honourable for a canon residentiary to live in, than his house collated on him"?
2. If the charter compels a canon to keep residence in the house assigned to him, may he leave that house and live elsewhere in the city after fulfilling his residence?
3. If a canon may live in some other canonical house, may he let his own house at an annual rent, so long as he maintains it in good repair?

Then the case for Dr Peirs is stated: canonical houses are annually inspected and reported upon (implying that there is no risk of a house let at a yearly rent falling into disrepair, to the prejudice of the bishop or the dean and chapter); he had good cause to move elsewhere; and in the past, for reasons approved by them, the dean and chapter had permitted residentiaries to live elsewhere than in their own canonical houses, provided they performed their duties of residence. Therefore, "the question is, whether may not the deane and chapter (by reason of the inconveniencies the canonical house of the said Dr Peirs is reduced unto) grant licence unto the said Dr Peirs to live either in some other canonical house, or in any other convenient house suitable to his quality, hee in the meane time keepinge his own house in good repair, and performing his duties in the church". Nothing is known of the outcome of this business but it may be inferred

[1] W.C.L., Documents, series III, box 4, 230.

[2] Why they did so in the case of Dr Busby is not clear, for it was not many months since they had accepted his reasons for non-residence.

[3] W.C.L., Documents, series III, box 4, 174, duplicate 176.

[4] Ibid. 177, duplicate 178; also 179 (mandate of suspension). [5] Ibid. 230.

that these arguments prevailed, and that with the death of Creyghton and the arrival of Peter Mews as bishop the matter was dropped, for Dr Peirs continued to live in the 'archdeacon's house' until his death in 1682, and his right to do so never seems to have been challenged again. One cannot but sympathize with him, and feel that in taking up this matter his former colleague was moved by something other than a disinterested concern for the observance of the cathedral's statutes and customs.

No further dispute about residence and emoluments occurred until 1679. On 2nd July in that year Edwyn Sandys was elected to residence, and the usual conditions were laid down: he was to commence residence on 1st October 1680, and would receive no stipend before that date. He seems to have objected to this stipulation, however, for on 6th October the chapter decreed in his absence that according to the statutes and customs of the cathedral and the conditions stated at the time of election, no new residentiary could claim to receive as of right any quotidians, dividend, or other payment before the date when he entered upon full residence. Those present (Drs Bathurst, Peirs, Holt, Selleck, and Creyghton) confirmed this act with their signatures. This drew from Mr Sandys a protest which he delivered to the chapter on 15th October, complaining that the act made nine days earlier was to his disadvantage, and that in particular he was entitled to his quotidians—on which point he appealed to bishop Mews, then engaged on his visitation.

Nothing more is heard of this matter until 1st July 1680, when Dr Creyghton, moved by "certain just and legitimate reasons", withdrew his assent to the act of the previous 6th October. On the next day the chapter confirmed the election of Henry Dutton made on 29th April—Dr Selleck dissenting on the ground that as the election did not take place at a general chapter it should be done again. He protested further when the chapter decided that although Mr Sandys had not yet commenced his full residence he should have his share of Mr Dutton's caution money. That afternoon the validity of Mr Dutton's election was reaffirmed, despite Dr Selleck's renewed objection.

Nine months later the same question arose with reference to Mr Dutton. On 7th April 1681 the communar, Dr Peirs, paid quotidians to the canons up to 1st April and Mr Dutton, though he was not to enter upon his residence until 1st October following, asked if he too might have his quotidians. At this Dr Selleck walked out, and the rest of the chapter then voted unanimously that Mr Dutton should have his arrears of quotidians to date. Two days later Drs Peirs and Holt followed Dr Creyghton's lead and revoked their assent to the act of 6th October 1679. The act itself was not annulled, but its force was greatly weakened by this withdrawal of approval on the part of three canons, and by the subsequent decision of the chapter.

One of the issues in a controversy involving Mr Sandys which arose at the end of our period was his legal qualification for election to residence, but the documentation is unfortunately so slight that it is difficult to piece together the course of events. The first hint of trouble comes in a memorandum dated 7th April 1682, written in a hand which cannot be identified: "Mr Tristram Evans was sent to mee by Mr Chancellor Dr John Baylie [to] let mee know that this the sayd Mr Chancellor had byn with Mr Guido Clinton to know whether the sayd Mr Clinton had sett his hand to any certificate on the behalfe of Mr Edwyn Sandys, that the said Mr Sandys had subscrib'd the declaration imposed by Act of Parliament, which the sayd Mr Clinton utterly deny'd that hee had don".[1] There is nothing to indicate the source of this suspicion about the validity of Sandys's election or how long it had been in doubt, but William and Thomas Peirs, sons and executors of Dr Peirs who had died three days earlier, attempted to make capital out of the affair.

It seems probable (though there is no record of this) that Mr Sandys was collated to the canonical house in the Market Place where Dr Peirs had refused to dwell, and that he found it in

[1] Ibid. 194a, p.4.

a poor state of repair—although, as we have seen, Peirs's defence of his right to live elsewhere included an acknowledgement that a canon so doing was still liable for the condition of his house of residence. This would explain why Sandys found it necessary to proceed against the brothers Peirs for the payment of dilapidations on a canonical house, which could only be the one in the Market Place. They seem to have retaliated by alleging that his election was illegal, that his claim for dilapidations was therefore unfounded, and that he was not entitled to receive any of the emoluments of residence. Mr Sandys took action against the Peirses on all three points, and at a hearing before the bishop in February[1] 1682–3 succeeded in compelling their attorney, Mr Lovell, to accept liability for the dilapidations and to admit that his subscription to the Act of Uniformity was in all respects true and lawful.[2]

Notwithstanding this setback, the brothers addressed to the chapter a caveat[3] not to pay any fine, dividend, or quotidian to Mr Sandys, "supposed to be one of their Members", until he proved that he had been duly and lawfully elected, and this was presented at the beginning of the quarterly chapter in April 1683. A copy was immediately sent to the bishop, who wrote to the chapter on 12th April a characteristically trenchant letter in which he declared that the suggestion of illegality made by the Peirses was " . . . Scandalously false: Mr Sandys having duly perform'd all which the Law required to be done before Mee, as may appeare by my Certificate under my hand and Seale. I should adde much more", he concluded, "did not Religion and Charity command my Passion", and subscribed himself "Your affectionate, though at present affronted Brother".[4] On the following day the chapter replied, regretting the trouble that this matter had occasioned; "Wee were not able", they said, "to foresee or prevent the heats and imprudencies of Youth . . . Wee have not been so far concerned in the Difference between our Bro Sandys and Mr Peirces as to question the Legality of His Election: but wee are concerned that there should be any Reflexion upon your Lordship, especially such a one as carries Scandall with it"; and they begged his aid in making an "effectuall Composure" between the parties.[5]

Despite this correspondence, which was duly entered in the chapter act book, William and Thomas Peirs managed to persuade William Westley the chapter clerk to register their caveat surreptitiously on 15th May, but on 1st August the chapter declared that the entry was null and void, and it was deleted accordingly.[6] Nothing more was heard about the validity of Mr Sandys's election or the dilapidations on the canonical house in the Market Place, which he began to demolish in the following year preparatory to building a more suitable residence on new foundations.

V The Ashbury Lease

Several entries in the act book of 1666–1683 relate to the lease of Ashbury rectory. Ashbury, a benefice on the western border of Berkshire, some 7 miles east of Swindon, was at this time in the gift of the bishop of Bath and Wells. On 4th May 1536 the rector, Peter Vannes, granted the rectory for three years to John Sterky and Thomas Aprice at an annual rent of 30*l*., subject to certain conditions and covenants; the advowsons of the benefice and of the chapel of Wick, in the northern part of the parish, were excluded from the lease, as was also a small wood in Ashbury fields called Parson's Wood. A year later this lease was surrendered, and on 27th[7] or 28th[8] June

[1] The date is uncertain; it is given as *die extra: vizt 29mo die mensis Febrii 82*, but 1682 was not a leap year.

[2] W.C.L., Documents, series III, box 4, 194b. [3] Ibid. 197.

[4] *Cal.* ii, 447 and more accurately transcribed in *Life of Richard Kidder*, 193–4.

[5] *Cal.* ii. 447–8; *Life of Richard Kidder*, 194–5. [6] *Cal.* ii. 450.

[7] *A Case touchinge the Parsonage of Ashburye*, in W.C.L., Documents, series III, box 4, 172a

[8] *Cal.* ii. 248; W.C.L., Ledger D, ff.24–5.

1537 Vannes granted the rectory to Robert Rokes for 51 years at the same annual rent; this was confirmed by John Clerk, bishop of Bath and Wells, Thomas Cromwell, dean of Wells, and the chapter, and William, prior of Bath, on 24th October.[1]

On 9th June 1581 William Cheshire, then rector of Ashbury, leased the rectory to the Crown for 99 years from the termination of the existing lease at Ladyday 1591, in consideration and satisfaction of "certain debptes" due from him to the Crown, and of a sum of money paid to him. The rent still remained at 30*l.* a year and the lease was subject to the same conditions as that of 1537; furthermore the rectors, when resident, were to have the use of two rooms in the rectory house, at the lower end of the hall over the buttery and larder, and stabling for three geldings; and no oaks or great timber were to be felled without licence, except for repairs to the building.[2] It was asserted that this lease, too, was confirmed by the bishop and the dean and chapter.

Towards the end of 1668 the then rector Dr Mundy, subdean of Wells, proposed to procure the surrender of the Crown's lease, which had still more than 20 years to run, in order to grant the rectory to one of his sons for three lives. Bishop Peirs consulted the chapter, who furnished him with seven *Reasons . . . to stop the Confirmacion of Ashbury Lease*[3] which convinced him that Dr Mundy's intention was unwise and should be checked; he sent his chancellor to intimate to the dean his gratitude to the chapter for its advice, and it was decreed on 4th January 1668–9 that this should be recorded in the act book. What happened next is not clear, but it appears that when Robert Creyghton became bishop he took a different view of the matter, for it is asserted in *A Case touchinge the Parsonage of Ashburye*,[4] drawn up about this time, that Dr Mundy obtained the Crown's surrender and granted the new lease, and that this was confirmed by the bishop, but not by the dean and chapter.

Doubt was expressed, however, whether the lease was good in law in the absence of confirmation by the dean and chapter. To resolve this point bishop Creyghton sent his registrar, Mr Guy Clinton, to the chapter on 2nd January 1671–2 with certain documents and papers, one of which was *An Answere to the Reasons offered . . . by the Deane and Chapter . . . against the Confirmacion of the Lease of Ashbury parsonage*,[5] probably drawn up by Dr Mundy himself. The chapter promised the bishop a reply by 4th January, but it was not until 11th January that their statement was drafted and sent to the Palace. In it the arguments set forth in the *Reasons* were trenchantly reiterated and expanded, and a copy was inserted in the records.[6] It seems that Dr Mundy had also tried to enlist the support of the bishop of Salisbury, for the papers relating to the case include an undated *Answer of the Deane and Chapter . . . to a paper lately presented to the Bishopp of Sarum touching the lease of the Parsonage of Ashbury tendered by Dr Mundy to bee confirmed*;[7] this dealt more briefly with three points advanced by the subdean in support of his case. No further reference to the business occurs in the chapter's books or papers, and in the absence of any confirmation of the proposed lease it may be inferred that Dr Mundy failed to succeed in his purpose.

The arguments on both sides are lengthy and involved, and not always easy to follow on account of the incomplete documentation, but a clue to the principal question at issue may lie in the first section of the chapter's *Answer . . . to a paper lately presented to the Bishopp of Sarum.* Dr Mundy had claimed that the rectory of Ashbury was, in effect, a "rurall prebend", and could therefore be let in the same way as an ordinary prebend founded in a cathedral or collegiate church. The chapter was quick to point out that Ashbury was a benefice with cure of souls, and no rector of such a benefice had the same right to make a lease of his parsonage as a prebendary

[1] *Cal.* ii. 248; W.C.L., Ledger D, ff.24–5. [2] *Cal.* ii. 303.

[3] W.C.L., Documents, series III, box 4, 172b. [4] Ibid. 172a. [5] Ibid. 172d.

[6] See 11th January 1671–2. [7] W.C.L., Documents, series III, box 4, 172c.

had to devise his prebendal estate. Nor could Dr Mundy take refuge in the fact that Peter Vannes had let Ashbury rectory for 51 years and William Cheshire for 99. Nothing was known about the circumstances of the first lease, but it might be extenuated in view of the unsettled times and the consequent danger to the Church; in such conditions a long lease might have seemed prudent. As to the second lease, it was clearly invalid, having been made in contravention of the provisions of the Act of 13 Elizabeth "against Frauds", chapter 10, section 2 of which prohibited the letting of ecclesiastical property for more than 21 years or three lives. These past transactions did not alter the fact that Dr Mundy's intention was to grant a benefice with cure of souls in such a manner that the income from its tithes and glebe would be diverted from the rector to the lessee, who was also to receive the parsonage house. At the same time the annual rent was to remain at the sum of 30*l.* fixed over 130 years earlier, though the same sum was currently worth more than 200*l.*

Under the arrangements proposed, a benefice reputed to be worth 300*l.* a year would be let at about one-seventh of its true rental value, and would yield a stipend of 35*l.* for the rector and 5*l.* for a vicar—and out of his 35*l.* the rector must pay tenths and subsidies amounting to more than 30*l.*, leaving him scarcely anything for a livelihood. Furthermore, being deprived of the parsonage house, the rector would have to rent accommodation in the parish; true, he was to have two rooms in the house and stabling whenever he was in residence at Ashbury, but what was this worth when almost all his income was already committed? On the death of the present incumbent the presentation would revert to the bishop, and all he could offer would be a benefice worth less than many curacies.

In *An Answer to the Reasons . . .* Dr Mundy attempted to refute these objections. There were precedents for the letting of rectories, and he instanced the case of Wootton in Wiltshire; a modest yield was less likely to attract the attention of rapacious persons with designs upon ecclesiastical revenues; the charging of a low rent was prudent in the present state of affairs, and created a desirable dependency of tenants upon the Church; and the value of the rectory at the clear improved value was only 200*l.*, and not 300*l.* as had been alleged. Though he maintained that the lease he proposed to grant was more advantageous to the rector than that made to the Crown by William Cheshire, his arguments do not sound convincing, and he always evaded the charge that the provision made for the stipend was insufficient. The chapter clearly had good reason for refusing to confirm the lease, and it seems probable that in the end bishop Creyghton had to agree with them.

VI The Vicars Choral and their Stipends

From two entries recording business done on 3rd January 1669–70 we learn that there was then some question in dispute between the dean and chapter and the vicars choral. That morning Mr Nicholas Dowthwaite, clerk of the chapter's courts, was instructed to hand over to the vicars certain documents relating to their affairs, which they wished to examine; this was to be done in the audit room in the presence of Dr Selleck and Dr Fane. In the afternoon the chapter resolved to propose that the vicars should withdraw a petition which they had laid before the archbishop of Canterbury, and that both parties should disclose their cases and refer them jointly to counsel for an opinion, in the hope that the controversy between them might be terminated; the chapter offered, without prejudice, to pay the legal costs incurred. Some delay occurred, however, in giving effect to this suggestion, for it was only on 8th July 1672 that a decision was taken to proceed with the proposed consultation; and the relevant minute reveals for the first time that the point at issue was the entitlement of the vicars to fines derived from leases of escheatory lands.

This was not the first controversy about emoluments between the dean and chapter and the vicars choral, for another had occurred at the end of the 16th century which dragged on for more than ten years, and originated in a dispute over the stipends which were paid to the vicars from the chapter's common fund. Each vicar received annually at Michaelmas a sum ranging from 20*s.* to 30*s.* according to merit. Towards the close of the 15th century the communar's allocation for this purpose was increased to 76*l.*,[1] which enabled him to augment the stipends of priest vicars to 3*l.* a year and other vicars to 40*s.*—the number of vicars then varied between 20 and 24. This arrangement continued until the beginning of Elizabeth's reign, when the queen's visitors ordered that the establishment should not exceed 20 vicars, and that every one should have 3*l.* a year; if the number fell below 20, the unpaid stipend or stipends were to be divided between as many as there were in the college at the time.

After these *stipendia vicariorum* had been paid the unexpended portion of the allocation of 76*l.* was credited to the common fund and its disposition was at the discretion of the chapter. Part of it was used to pay the salary of the grammar school master, 26*s.* 8*d.* a year went to the choristers,[2] and some or all of the remainder might be distributed according to merit among those vicars present at Christmas and other principal feasts. The vicars took exception to this practice,[3] and complained to the Privy Council, which appointed the archbishop of Canterbury to adjudicate between the parties, and it is to this appeal that entries in the chapter act book for 30th September 1594, 24th October 1595, and 2nd and 15th January 1595–6 probably refer.[4]

The archbishop decided that the whole of the unexpended part of the allocation of 76*l.* belonged by right to the vicars, and should be divided among them by the chapter "according to their several merits and necessities, the better to keep them in order, obedience, and attendance upon their duties".[5] An unidentified document transcribed by Mr Beauchamp could also be an extract from the archbishop's order;[6] if so, he reserved for the choristers the annual sum of 26*s.* 8*d.* which they were accustomed to receive, but no mention is made of this in subsequent discussions, and it may simply have been a recommendation which was not implemented. We learn further from *The true state of the case between the Dean and Chapter . . . and the Vicars*[7] that his grace had expressed the hope that the traditional subsistence allowance might be continued; this was a commutation of the 'diet' or commons which each vicar in earlier times had taken at his canon's table, and in the post-Restoration period was worth 10*s.* a quarter.[8]

The chapter declared in *The true state of the case* that both sides had been satisfied by this order, but the vicars still had their grievances and, probably at the end of 1604, presented a further petition to which the Council replied in February 1604–5.[9] Having heard all the arguments, their lordships confirmed the decisions made by the archbishop, but made a variation in favour of the vicars by directing that their much-reduced stipends were to be augmented by diverting from capitular funds for this purpose the income of six stalls, one valued at 53*s.* 4*d.*, three at 40*s.*, and two at 26*s.* 8*d.* By this means a vicar's quotidians could be increased from 7*d.* to 9*d.* a week. The Council then directed that both the rents and the fines from the escheatory lands were to be divided equally among the vicars, whose numbers must not be enlarged beyond the then establishment of 14 unless the chapter made extra provision accordingly. It seems that soon after this order was made, *The true state of the case* was drawn up—apparently with the object of certifying

[1] Or according to some statements, 77*l.* 18*s.* 9*d.*

[2] W.C.L., 'Mr Beauchamp's Book', a common-place book compiled by a 19th-century vicar choral, 65.

[3] See W.C.L., Documents, series III, box 4, 228: *De Stipendiis Vicariorum.*

[4] *Cal.* ii, 330, 332; W.C.L., Act Book H, ff. 103d, 104. [5] W.C.L., Documents, series III, box 4, 223.

[6] W.C.L., 'Mr Beauchamp's Book', 65. [7] W.C.L., Documents, series III, box 4, 223.

[8] Letter of 1st September 1677 from Dr Selleck to Dr Bathurst, W.C.L., Documents, series III, box 4, 189.

[9] W.C.L., 'Mr Beauchamp's Book', 148.

that the chapter had complied with the directions of the Council, so that the only matter still outstanding between the residentiaries and the vicars was the discipline to be applied to the delinquent Robert Marwood.[1]

Despite the assurances in *The true state of the case*, the vicars do not appear to have been fully satisfied and the controversy continued, for on 1st March 1608–9 the chapter decreed "that the vicars-choralls . . . shall, before the first of Aprill next commyng . . . disclayme and withdrawe all actions, suites and complayntes heretofore had and mad by them or any of them in the behalf of the wholl company of them, viz. concernyng *stipendia vicariorum*, stall wages, chetry, and ther dyett at the master's table . . . and shall submitt them selves to the deane and chapter . . ."[2]. The records do not indicate whether the vicars submitted on the date specified, but as there is no further mention of these questions it may be assumed that they did, or that some settlement of the dispute was effected.

The chapter's decree refers to stall wages, but we do not know what difficulty had arisen in connexion with them. Each vicar, on appointment, was assigned a vicarial stall corresponding to one of the prebendal stalls. He was thus entitled to receive an annual sum representing payment for his services as the prebendary's deputy in quire—though he was now a professional musician, and a 'vicar' only in name; and this sum was charged upon the revenue of the prebend. Stall wages varied from 20*s.* to 53*s.* 4*d.*, but most of them were fixed at 26*s.* 8*d.*, though these amounts were not proportionate to the value of the prebends. Prebendaries who had no "proper and peculiar vicar" paid their assessments directly into the cathedral fabric fund. Nothing could be done to augment stall wages, and the only problems to which they gave rise were due to defaulting prebendaries, who were regularly called to account at the Whitsun visitation made by the chapter.

Apart from mortgages (which seem to have disappeared "for want of a due looking after") and the revenues of vacant prebends, the other sources from which the vicars drew their emoluments were chantry profits and payments for attendance at obits and anniversaries. This income was derived from lands and other property assigned to the dean and chapter for the maintenance of such services, and the lands were known as escheatory lands (the "chetry" mentioned in the chapter act of 1st March 1608–9) because the escheator acted as receiver of the rents and other profits which they yielded. Any sum left over after providing for these commemorations was divided equally among the canons and vicars. By the Act of 1547 dissolving the chantries,[3] that portion of the escheator's receipts designated for the upkeep of obituary services was diverted to the Crown, but the lands themselves were for the most part left in the hands of the dean and chapter, who leased them and appropriated the income without giving any account thereof to the vicars.

The vicars had protested against this action by the chapter, and the order in Council of February 1604–5 enjoined that rents and fines from the escheatory lands should no longer be withheld, but divided equally between all the vicars perpetuate. In *The true state of the case*, however, the chapter is somewhat guarded on the point, and the act of 1st March 1608–9 requiring the vicars to disclaim and withdraw all proceedings and complaints about, *inter alia*, "chetry" may indicate that the business had not been settled as the Council directed. It is possible that the vicars received no satisfaction, for escheatory fines were the principal cause of contention between the two sides seventy years later, as appears by the act of 8th July 1672 already mentioned.

Two undated documents seem to refer to this revival of the dispute after the Restoration—

[1] Marwood's particular offence at this time is not specified, but he had been guilty in the past of various wrongs from neglect of duty to fornication, and he and his wife Mary were troublesome inhabitants of the New Close or Close Hall, as the Vicars' Close was then called.

[2] *Cal.* ii. 357. [3] 1 Edward VI c. 14.

An answer to certain objections made against the Vicars claim to the fines to be raised out of the lands called Escheatry Lands,[1] and an account (*Escheator Ecclesiae Cathedralis Wellensis*) of the revenues received and distributed by that officer.[2] The vicars maintained that although the lands in question were granted to the dean and chapter, this was done subject to the income being divided between them and the residentiaries, and that their right to a share was confirmed by the charter given to the vicars choral by Queen Elizabeth in 1592. This provided that the vicars should continue to receive all such revenues as they had enjoyed during the twenty years prior to that date, and they asserted that within this period they had been paid a portion of the proceeds from the escheatory lands; furthermore, they insisted that account must be taken, not only of the sums they had received, but also of those to which they were by law entitled.

The whole matter seems still to have been under discussion five years after the decree of 1672, and the vicars now had the support of Nicholas Dowthwaite, clerk of the chapter's courts, who may have drawn up the document *Escheator Ecclesiae . . . Wellensis*.[3] He sent to Dr Selleck at Nether Stowey a letter stating the case as between the chapter and the vicars, and contending that there were two principal receivers in the cathedral—the communar, whose surplus was divided among the residentiaries only, and the escheator, whose surplus was divided equally between residentiaries and vicars; and that nothing had happened to affect the right of the vicars to their share of the latter surplus. Dr Selleck would not accept this argument, and wrote a private letter to the dean to say so; Mr Dowthwaite claimed that his presentation of the case was quite impartial, and Dr Selleck had "soe much charity for him to believe that he thinks soe to, although it can hardly bee imagind that preiudice can be indifferent", but he had made "severall materiall and evident omissions". The escheator had in the past received from the escheatory lands only rents and never fines, and the chapter's records would show that no part of the escheatory revenue was paid to, or shared with, the vicars during the twenty years prior to 1592.[4]

Here the controversy rested, and as in other cases the records do not reveal its outcome.

VII The Library

The cathedral library is situated over the east cloister, where it was removed about 1425 from the western aisle of the north transept; it has been described by subdean C. M. Church in 'Notes on the . . . Library of the Dean and Chapter . . . of Wells',[5] and by Mr T. W. Williams in *Somerset Mediaeval Libraries*.[6] These accounts, and particularly the former, assemble such meagre information as we possess about the contents of the library prior to the Reformation, but nothing seems to be known of its furniture and practical arrangements. No doubt some books were lost as a result of the Act of 1549[7] which ordered the surrender and destruction of all superstitious prayer and service books, but the most serious damage probably occurred during the period of the Commonwealth, though no particulars have survived.

After the Restoration it seems that the structure of the library was in need of attention, for on 3rd March 1669–70 the chapter ordered that part of a sum of 100*l*. set aside from the fine paid by Lord Poulett for the lease of Buckland Abbas rectory should be put at the disposal of the master

[1] W.C.L., Documents, series III, box 4, 224. [2] Ibid. 226.

[3] Two fragments of notes on the escheator by Mr Dowthwaite are preserved in W.C.L., Documents, series III, box 4, 225 and 227.

[4] Ibid. 189. [5] In *Archaeologia*, vol. lvii (London, 1901).

[6] Published under the auspices of the Somerset Archaeological and Natural History Society, Bristol, 1897.

[7] 3 and 4 Edward VI c.10.

of the fabric for the restoration of the library. Four months later the chapter turned its attention to the contents. On 4th July arrangements were made for the removal of the capitular books or registers and the manuscripts to the audit room over the west cloister, while the 'archives' (the muniment room at the southern end of the library) was being repaired with all speed. Dr Fane was then given the task of supervising the arrangement and cataloguing of the books and manuscripts, and the care of them (both in the 'archives' and in the audit room) was committed to Mr Nicholas Dowthwaite; he and the chapter clerk, Mr William Westley, were to have separate keys to the outer doors and the store cabinets. All borrowers of books or manuscripts had to enter their names in a register provided for this purpose, and were required to return them to their places within seven days unless a longer loan was permitted by the chapter.

These provisions may have been temporary and makeshift, until an opportunity occurred to do more, for Dr Busby promised that in 1673 he would pay to the common fund 100*l.* for the repair of the library, which was inconveniently placed and arranged and almost covered with dust. On the strength of this undertaking the master of the fabric, Dr Sheafe, expended 100*l.* on various renovations, and on 21st January 1672–3 the chapter asked the communar, Dr Fane, to reimburse him and to charge the payment against Dr Busby's gift, which would come later. Dr Busby followed this donation with others of 20*l.*, 2*l.* 11*s.*, and in 1684 200*l.*; and the last contribution enabled a thorough restoration to be undertaken. On 7th January 1685–6 the chapter ordered that the library should be "repaired . . . and beautifyed as the said Dr Busby doth desire, and that Richard Healy shall take care of the same".

Mr Richard Healy, deputy chapter clerk at the time, had been given charge of the 'public library', as it is often termed,[1] on 20th October 1677, when further orders were made for its management. It was to be put in charge of a graduate of Oxford or Cambridge, skilled in letters, whose duty it would be to arrange the books alphabetically (whether on the shelves or in a catalogue, and whether under authors or titles, is not stated), and to record the donations of benefactors. Books were not to be lent, except for some pressing reason, and then only to the clergy or benefactors by permission of the dean or his deputy; loans must be entered in the register and signed for, and volumes borrowed must be returned within a month; strangers might be allowed to use the library by permission on payment of a fee of 2*s.* 6*d.*; and the librarian would receive a salary of at least 40*s.* a year, to be found from fees and other sums destined for the use of the library. A small income was secured by an act of the chapter on 20th October 1680 decreeing that instead of the collation usually provided by prebendaries after installation, they should pay 20*s.* to the library. Earlier, a portion of the fines exacted from defaulting prebendaries had been allocated for this purpose.[2]

In spite of regulations about borrowing books and manuscripts, it seems that members of the chapter (by no means for the first time) were in the habit of taking out capitular records and retaining them at pleasure. Indeed, in a letter written to the chapter on 3rd July 1680, bishop Mews had to remind residentiaries that all books and papers belonging to the cathedral should be kept in the place provided for them, pursuant to which the chapter ordered on the following 13th January that "every private canon" should surrender whatever books and records were in his possession, and James Williams the *cursor ecclesiae* was instructed to go round to the canonical houses and collect them. Dr Selleck was found to have the arrears book for 1590–1631, two chapter act books, and another register which cannot be identified; Dr Holt had the steward's book for 1629–30; and Mr Sandys had the *Liber Ruber*. Other volumes and manuscripts were in private hands, and on 7th December 1682 one John Gutch returned ledger book 'F'; we do not

[1] This did not mean, of course, that the library was 'public' in the modern sense of being open to the general public, for it has always been the private library of the chapter; it simply meant that it was the common library of the residentiaries. Access to it was permitted at their discretion.'

[2] See Appendix II, p.xli.

know how many more documents had been dispersed during the Commonwealth, and have never been recovered.

Dr Busby was munificent with books as well as with money; further to compensate for his non-residence, he gave 56 volumes to the library. Other residentiaries were also generous: dean Creyghton donated 33 books, Dr Peirs 23, Dr Selleck 56 (mostly works of canon law), Dr Creyghton the precentor 31, dean Bathurst 34, Mr Sandys 8, and Dr Holt the 6 volumes of Walton's *Polyglot Bible* of 1657, while William Westley the chapter clerk and his wife Sarah gave 36 between them.

Appendix I

Letter from Roger Walker to the Chapter[1]

Sarum this 6th of Aug. 70.

Gent:

I have bin suffred to goe to Dr Smith about Bridges mony, which you have made mee to alow and Litle reason for when twas paid before by my Brother,[2] why did you never aske my Brother fort in his life time. I could wish you would pay it me againe amoungst you, for Dr Smith sayeth that it belongs to the Deane and Chapter to pay it, and not to the Deane and hee only, if it did only them too yet it was in the power of the Chapter to have allowed it to me, seeinge it was by my bill paid by my brother. The Chapter act is othenticke to have mad them paye it, if noe reason to the Contrary why it should not be paid by the whole Chapter, but I supose to put mee of, and make mee rune from one to another to spend my time, and that litle or nothing that I have, and Mr Sweetings 15*l.* tto eald to pay it to Dr Selleck, was the worst thinge I ever did, it hath brought mee to be a prisoner all my dayes unlese it be rebersd. My necesity was great for mony, otherwise I would not have done it, but Dr Selleck did forse mee to it, otherwise I should have noe mony. For god sake gentlemen, consider a poore restraind man, and reberse that, and pay mee Bridges mony that I may be at Liberty, for a livelyhoode, I must have also a noat howe and for what you have paid, the Deane and others, otherwise, it must be discusd bye greater powers. I shalbe forst to swere before a master of Chancery what I red at Wells, cause I have noe note of these greate somes paid by you this vast troble you have put mee to with Charge, and god knows I have not wher with to subsist by, I was forst to borrow 5*l.* to carry me to to [*sic*] Oxford to spake Dr Smith, and to joylt along with the Carrier to, which I never did before, I had a plentiful estate I thanke god, firmerly, I never wasted it in any base way tis well knowne, but lost it by plunder, and being in armes for the King, but non of that is Considered by any of you. You are all well paid for your loses, thanks be to god, I enveiy you not, but I would have you Consider my Condition, and not starve me for want of my owne. You doe not know but it may be your own executors case one day. While you are together tis brother and brother, but when the executor of any of you come to demand his rite, the case wille all tred as it is now with mee, god help mee. Sirs, I desier your answers, As the case of my present condition, where it not for some good pious men in other Churches I might starve, haveing lese reason than you of that Church to help a poor man, yet I desir but my owne. If I had what I ought to have thence, I need not aske of you or any other. I spake not my own thought, but severall other Curches of your nater thinkes I have a great deale of wronge in my business, and all is cause I cannot show how not for what you allow those greate somes, Consider my condition for god sake, on hundred pounds would have paid all my brother's Debts, tho ther be 400*l.* and upards owing, but this Sweetings mony ealding to, hath undune, and brought me to all this troble. I have noe more to say but that I am servant to you all. Thus much from your poor servant.[3]

Rog^{r} Walker.

[1] W.C.L., Documents, series III, box 3, 170; see the entry for 13th January 1667–8 and note.

[2] Probably Dr Thomas Walker, canon residentiary 1635–65.

[3] Entries on 4th April, 7th July, and 6th October 1670 may possibly have a bearing on the subject of this letter.

Appendix II

Orders and injunctions exhibited att the Right Reverend Father in God Peter Lord Bishopp of Bath and Wells att his Primary Visitation of the Deane and Chapter begun and held in the Chapter House of the Cathedrall Church of Sainct Andrew in Wells on the sixth day of September Anno Domini 1673.[1]

First that all Dignitaryes and Praebendaryes bring in the Counterpartes of the Leases of theire Corps to the Chapter to the end that they may be registred within one moneth after the sealeing of theire Leases paying to the Chapter Clerke his usuall fees. And if any Dignitary or Praebendary shall faile in this particuler hee shall pay forty shillings to the use of the Library.

Secondly that all Dignitaryes and Praebendaryes bring in an exact terrier of all the Lands and houses together with an Accompt of the Rents and Jurisdictions belonging to theire respective Dignities and Praebends before the five and twentieth day of March next, otherwise to forfeit Forty shillings to the use of the Library. And that for the future noe Lease shalbee confirmed which hath not a Terrier as is above expressed annexed in schedule to itt.

Thirdly that all Dignitaryes and Praebendaryes make augmentacion of the Vicaridges belonging unto them which are not already competently augmented, and that noe Lease be confirmed untill it appeare that such augmentacion bee made.

Fourthly that noe Dignitary or Praebendary presume to preach in the Cathedrall without his surplice and hood.

Fifthly that the Dignitaryes and Praebendaries duely supply theire Courses of preaching in the Cathedrall by themselves or some other to bee allowed of by the Deane if present or else by the Senior Canon, giveing notice at least a weeke before who is to supply the Course if they cannott discharge itt them selves; who ever shall faile to provide for his Turne as aforesaid shall pay Forty shillings to be exacted by the Commoner of which hee who supplyes the Course shall receive thirty shillings and tenn shillings shalbee payd to be use of the Library.

That if any refuse to pay any of the above said forfeitures he shall incur the penalty of suspencion as disobedient to the good order and government of the Church untill payment bee made.

That a coppy of these orders and iniunctions shall bee sent to every respective Dignitary and Praebendary within a moneth to the end none may pretend ignorance.

Guydo Clynton
Deputy Registrar.

[1] W.C.L., Documents, series III, box 4, 183.

Appendix III

A full answer to the desires of the Deane left with Dr Peirs to be communicated to the Chapter.

Octob: 1°, 1673.[1]

1. It is impossible at the present to imburse the commoner with mony out of the Rents of the church quarterly, and therefore noe dividend can well be made until the end of the yeare, unless some considerable sum happen to come in and be soe conclu[d]ed by Chapter; if you divide quarterly the commoner can have noe mony in his hand but his owne, but it is the habite[?] of the church to divide *in fine anni.*
2. The Steward and clerke of the Courts have order from the chapter for speedy nomination of lives in the several Mannours.
3. Mr Pottinger hath resigned the free schoole, and Dr Holt as Chancellour of the church presented Mr Charles Thirlby who was Admitted schoolemaster and hath at present 50 schollars under him.[2]
4. The Vicars have had full liberty to enquire into our Records &c.
5. An allowance of 2*l.* 1*s.* shall certainely be performed the Deane *in fine anni.*
6. An effectual course shal be taken to demand and recover the mulkts of such Praebendaryes as neglect their preaching Turne if we can lay pecuniary mulkts. *But it is a Quaere whither we can lay pecuniary mulkts or noe.* Our Act of Chapter declares 20*s.* for every omission but my Ld Bps decree in his primary Visitation was 40*s.* of which 30*s.* to the preacher that supplyes and 10*s.* to the library or fabrick *ad libitum Decani et Capituli.*[3]
7. The chapter Fees for confirming your patent made to Guydo Clinton were remitted as desired.[4]
8. Upon the desire and request of the Deane and Chapter Dr Sheafe hath accepted of the Commoners office for the next yeare to the Content of the whole body.
9. As for the Rayles before the Altar, we conceive that if they be taken lower every dog will leap over them. There are frames lyned with cloth to set upon the steps, very easy and convenient for the Communicants to kneele upon and it will be a very great charge to make any alteration in the steps or stone asscent to the Altar.
10. The Appointing of Anthems and Services is the Duty and office of the precentor, in whose perpetual absence and non-Residence the Deane or the senior Canon present is to give orders to the Queire.
11. Dr Peirs the Steward hath waved his election of any reversion for himselfe as Steward until the Deane be served, and Mr Douthwayt the clerke of the courts in this their last progress having found out another reversion to supply the defects of Tulchils in East Surry, it is granted to our good Deane by his faithful Brethren and servants now Resident upon the place, Wm. Peirs, Tho: Holt, Grindal Sheafe, Wm: Fane.

[1] W.C.L., Documents, series III, box 4, 184—a rough draft, probably in the handwriting of Dr Holt. The date, 1st October 1673, must indicate that the answer related to the October general chapter, for it seems to have been drawn up at the same time as the draft letter printed in Appendix IV, which was written on 9th October.

[2] Cf. the entries for 7th and 8th October 1673.

[3] See Appendix II, xli. The bishop's decree specifies that 10*s.* shall go to the library, and does not mention the fabric.

[4] See the entry for 6th October 1673.

Appendix IV

Draft of a Letter from Dr Holt to the Dean[1]

Reverend and Good Mr Deane,
I acknowledge my selfe very much obliged for both your kind letters which I received, especially for your care of my sonns admission into your colledge. I neglected the opportunity of sending the summ required by Mr Sandys, depending without trouble to returne it by a clothier of Shepton, but he fayling I have sent 8*l.* 9*s.* by Dr Mundy's son a student in your colledge, and I humbly desire he may be forthwith entred a Commoner under Mr Cudworth whome I nominate with your approbation to be his Tutor; his name is Francis Holt. As to your Concernes here I hope this inclosed paper[2] wil give you ful satisfaction. Your Course in Octob: was performed by me and it deserves noe thankes, being a just debt from me, and we are most of us soe truely kind, that you need not much trouble your selfe for future supplys, for they shall never fail. Dr Peirs hath kept a noble Audit, but this our chapter hath bin very mean [though it be yet continued];[3] The country is generally poore especially where our lands lye by the late inundations, and mortality among their cattell. The 4th of December is our second Audit. God send mony then, that we may give you a comfortable account of your Dividends. [We have not seene the face of our Brother Selleck a long time, nor soe much as heard from him, perhaps the next Audit wil give us his Company].[3] We have bin ill used by our Tennant of Mudford, Mrs Beaton her selfe and her son wiche from time to time promising our great arreare of Rent but nothing is performed, wherefore this chapter we gave Mr Douthwayte and others with him Commission under our Chapter seale this day[4] to demand the whole Rent, and if not payd upon demand, to enter upon the things. The clause in the lease is absolute forfeiture for non-payment of Rent if legally Demanded. God forbid she should be utterly cast out, but this course must be taken otherwise if she dye you loose al the rent behind, and noe satisfaction for great delapidations; It shal not be disposd of without your privity and at a ful chapter; there shal be noe helping one another as was suggested to you. Yet I humbly desire this favour, if she will upon reasonable termes part with her estate, I may have leave to buy it and give a just value for two lives after her. Her husband bought it for 500*l.* and had 8 yeares time to pay that fine; as we heare from her, you shal accordinly heare from me.

[1] W.C.L., Documents, series III, box 4, 185. At the head of the page are the words (crossed out) "A full Answer to the Dean".

[2] Probably the "Full Answer to the desires of the Deane" printed in Appendix III.

[3] The words in brackets have been deleted.

[4] 9th October 1673, see the entry for that date.

Calendar

Chapter Act Book 1666–83

pp1–6 blank

1666

p7 **Oct 1** In the chapter house between 9 am and 11 am. Present: Creyghtone, Holt, Selleck, Sheafe, and Fane; Harrison in attendance.

[Roll-call of vicars choral] Present: Benford, Thomas Standish, Alderley, Francis Standish, Moss, Beaumont, Davis, Clarke, Edmonds, Hobbs, and Browne.

The stall of St Decumans was assigned to Mr Augustine Benford.

p8 The chapter was continued and adjourned to the afternoon.

In the chapter house between 2 pm and 6 pm. Present: Creyghtone, Holt, Selleck, Sheafe, and Fane; Harrison in attendance.

The bishop would be asked to select a date before Oct 9 on which to hear certain matters of capitular business which concerned him.

The chapter was continued and adjourned to the next morning.

Oct 2 Between 10 am and 12 noon; Creyghtone, Holt, Selleck, and Sheafe assembled and adjourned the chapter to the afternoon.

In the chapter house between 2 pm and 6 pm. Present: Creyghtone, Holt, Selleck, and Sheafe; Harrison in attendance.

The stall of Compton Bishop was assigned to Mr John Moss, vicar choral, of the New Close.

For the current year, only so much would be paid to the choristers as had been paid at the ends of the three preceding years; and no more ought to be paid to them than was customary of old, and justly due from the chapter.

p9 The next day [Wednesday] being a fast day, the chapter was adjourned to Oct 4.[1]

Oct 4 In the chapter house between 10 am and 12 noon. Present: Holt, Selleck, Sheafe, and Fane; Harrison in attendance.

Resolved that Mr Nicholas Dowthwayte should have copies made of the court rolls relating to Mr Strangwayes and Digory Gordge, and that the copies should be handed to them.

The dean then arrived, took his place in chapter, and gave his assent [to the foregoing resolution].

Citations were to be affixed to the stalls of prebendaries John Duncombe, Samuel Lanfire, and [Lambert] Osbaston, requiring them to attend and pay their stall wages.[2] The following prebendaries were also to be cited for non-payment of stall wages: Dr Byam, Dr Bytall,[3] Mr John Head, Mr Henry Dutton, Mr Stephen Berrier, and Mr Francis Atkins.

p10 In the absence of the master of the fabric, the communar was to demand and receive all sums due to the fabric.

A citation was to be affixed to the stall of Mr Hanson, vicar of Twerton, requiring

[1] Cf a similar entry on 3rd July 1666, also relating to a Wednesday, *Cal.* ii. 439.

[2] On stall wages, see p.xxxiv.

[3] Prebendary of Easton-in-Gordano; his name is given in Wells Diocesan Registry, *Reg. Peirs*, f.85d as William Bristall, and in Le Neve-Hardy, op.cit. i. 191 as William Birstall.

him to attend and pay the annual pension of ten pounds outstanding for the past six years.

The chapter was continued and adjourned to the afternoon.

In the chapter house between 4 pm and 6 pm. Present: Creyghtone, Holt, Selleck, Sheafe, and Fane; Harrison in attendance.

The widow of Mr Samuel Yerwoth was freely and *ex gratia* released from the bond of ten pounds given by him to the dean and chapter.

The chapter was continued and adjourned to the next morning.

Oct 5 Between 10 am and 12 noon. Creyghtone, Holt, Selleck, Sheafe, and Fane assembled and adjourned the chapter to the afternoon.

p11 In the chapter house between 2 pm and 6 pm. Present: Creyghtone, Selleck, and Sheafe (speaking for Holt), who adjourned the chapter to the next morning.

Oct 6 In the chapter house between 10 am and 12 noon. Present: Selleck, Sheafe, and Fane (speaking for Creyghtone and Holt), who continued and adjourned the chapter to the afternoon.

In the chapter house between 4 pm and 6 pm. Present: Selleck, Sheafe, and Fane (speaking for Creyghtone and Holt), who continued and adjourned the chapter to Oct 8.

p12 **Oct 8** In the chapter house between 10 am and 12 noon. Present: Creyghtone, Selleck, Sheafe, and Fane; Harrison in attendance.

Two of the bottom seats or stalls on the north side of the quire, where the principal women usually sat, were assigned to Joan Selleck and Grizella Hurdacre, sisters of Dr Selleck, for their own use.

The chapter was adjourned to the afternoon.

In the chapter house between 4 pm and 6 pm. Present: Creyghtone, Selleck, and Fane, who continued and adjourned the chapter to the next morning.

Oct 9 In the chapter house between 9 am and 11 am. Present: Creyghtone, Selleck (proxy for Sheafe), and Fane; Harrison in attendance.

p13 James Williams, sacrist, appeared and confirmed that he had affixed to the outer doors of the cathedral a notice, with a schedule of names annexed, stating the day, hours, and place for the visitation to be held by the dean and chapter.

Then appeared Mr Robert Creyghtone jnr, prebendary of Timberscombe and one of those named in the above-mentioned schedule of prebendaries.

The chapter was continued and adjourned to the afternoon.

In the chapter house between 4 pm and 6 pm. Present: Creyghtone, Selleck (proxy for Sheafe), and Fane; Harrison in attendance. It was enacted as follows [no further entry].

pp14–16 blank

p17 **Nov 2** Between 4 pm and 6 pm; place not stated. Present: Creyghtone, Peirs, Selleck, Sheafe, and Fane; Harrison in attendance.

Although Dr Peirs had been elected master of the fabric, it was decreed at his request, and on account of certain reasonable causes which he then alleged, that Dr Sheafe should execute that office as his deputy for the year beginning at Michaelmas last. Dr Sheafe agreed to this.

Letters patent were sealed, granting the office of registrar of the archdeaconry of Wells to Mr William Westley,[1] and that of apparitor general of the bishop to Robert and Nicholas Thomas of Wells.[2]

p18 Letters of attorney were sealed, directed to Dr Selleck, steward of the dean and chapter, and to Dr Sheafe, communar, for initiating and prosecuting all actions, pleas, processes, and suits touching the dean and chapter.

Letters of attorney were also sealed, directed to John Gray, Richard Kingsbury, and others for requesting, demanding, and receiving all revenues, arrears of revenue, and fines due and payable to the dean and chapter.

1666-7

p19 **Jan 2** In the chapter house between 9 am and 11 am. Present: Creyghtone, Peirs, Holt, Selleck, Sheafe, and Fane; Harrison in attendance.

The following vicars choral of the New Close appeared: Benford and Thomas Standish (principals), Alderley, Francis Standish, Beaumont, Davis, Clarke, Edmonds, Hobbs, and Browne. Absent: Moss, sick.

p20 Mr George Bisse of the Liberties had pledged himself to pay a fine of 100*l.* for the rectory of St Cuthbert's Wells; he had paid this sum, but could not return his bond to the chapter because it had been lost or mislaid. It was resolved to have an instrument[3] drawn up and sealed for his security, but that this must not be treated as a precedent.

The chapter was then adjourned to the afternoon, to meet in the audit room in the cloisters, this being more convenient.

In the audit room between 2 pm and 5 pm. Present: Creyghtone, Peirs, Holt, Selleck, Sheafe, and Fane; Harrison in attendance. The chapter was continued and adjourned to the next morning.

Jan 3 In the audit room for convenience between 9 am and 11 am. Present: Creyghtone, Peirs, Holt, Selleck, Sheafe, and Fane; Harrison in attendance. The chapter was continued and adjourned to the afternoon.

p21 In the audit room between 2 pm and 5 pm. Present: Creyghtone, Peirs, Holt, Selleck, Sheafe, and Fane, who continued and adjourned the chapter to the next morning.

Jan 4 In the chapter house between 9 am and 11 am. Present: Creyghtone, Peirs, Holt, Selleck, and Sheafe; Harrison in attendance.

William Britten[4] and John Breathers appeared, charged "For causing a paper to be read at the high alter in the Cathedrall"; they admitted the offence, and were dismissed.

The chapter was continued and adjourned to the afternoon in the audit room for convenience.

p22 In the audit room between 2 pm and 5 pm. Present: Creyghtone, Peirs, Holt, Selleck, and Sheafe, who continued and adjourned the chapter to the next morning.

[1] See W.C.L., Ledger G, 569. [2] See ibid. 572. [3] See the entry below for 12th January 1666–7.

[4] Possibly the carpenter of this name living at the time in the corner house (since demolished) on the east side of Mountroy lane, now The Liberty, at its junction with the present St Andrew street; see W.C.L., Bargain Book 1, 4.

Jan 5 In the audit room between 10 am and 12 noon. Present: Holt, Selleck, and Sheafe, who adjourned the chapter to Jan 7.

Jan 7 In the audit room between 8 am and 12 noon. Present: Holt, Selleck, Sheafe, and Fane, who adjourned the chapter to the afternoon.
In the audit room between 2 pm and 5 pm. Present: Holt, Selleck, and Sheafe, who adjourned to chapter to the next morning.

Jan 8 In the audit room between 8 am and 12 noon. Present: Creyghtone, Holt, Selleck, Sheafe, and Fane, who adjourned the chapter to the afternoon.
In the audit room between 2 pm and 5 pm. Present: Creyghtone, Holt, Selleck, and Sheafe, who adjourned the chapter to the next afternoon.

p23 **Jan 9** In the audit room between 2 pm and 5 pm. Present: Creyghtone, Holt, Selleck, Sheafe, and Fane; Harrison in attendance.

Two indentures were sealed, one granting the manor or farm of Lovington to Emanuel Hole for three lives,[1] and the other granting March Close, North Curry, to John Pyne for three lives.[2]

The chapter was continued and adjourned to the next morning.

Jan 10 In the audit room between 9 am and 11 am. Present: Creyghtone, Holt, Selleck, and Sheafe, who continued and adjourned the chapter to the afternoon.
p24 In the audit room between 2 pm and 5 pm. Present: Holt, Selleck, and Sheafe, who continued and adjourned the chapter to the next morning.

Jan 11 In the audit room between 9 am and 12 noon. Present: Creyghtone, Holt, Selleck, and Sheafe, who adjourned the chapter to the afternoon.
In the audit room between 2 pm and 5 pm. Present: Creyghtone, Holt, Selleck, and Sheafe, who adjourned the chapter to Jan 12.

Jan 12 In the audit room between 2 pm and 5 pm. Present: Creyghtone, Selleck, Sheafe, and Fane; Harrison in attendance.

The following document was sealed: "Be it knowne unto all men by these presents that wee the Deane and Chapter of the Cathedrall Church of Wells . . . do in and by these presents fully and absolutely remise release and quit claime unto George Bisse of the Liberties of the said Cathedrall Church . . . Esqr of and from all bonds bills claimes or demaunds whatsoever which now or hereafter may be made of for or *p25* concerning the last fine for the Rectory of the parish Church of St Cuthberts in Wells . . . being the summe of one hundred pounds according to a Contract made betweene us and the said George Bisse. In Testimony whereof wee have hereunto caused our Common or Chapter Seale to be Sett: Dated the twelveth day of January *Anno Domini Stylo Angliae* 1666."

p26 blank

[1] See W.C.L., Ledger G, 578. [2] See ibid. 574.

1667

p27 **April 1** In the chapter house between 9 am and 11 am. Present: Peirs and Sheafe; Harrison in attendance.

The following vicars choral of the New Close appeared: Benford, Thomas Standish, Alderley, Moss, Beaumont, Davis, Clarke, Edmonds, Hobbs, and Browne. Absent: Francis Standish, excused.

The chapter was continued and adjourned to the next day.

p28 **April 2** In the chapter house between 8 am and 10 am. Present: Holt (speaking for Peirs), Sheafe, and Fane, who continued and adjourned the chapter to the afternoon. Between 3 pm and 5 pm; place not stated. Present: Holt, Sheafe, and Fane, who continued and adjourned the chapter to the next morning.

April 3 In the chapter house between 8 am and 12 noon. Present: Peirs, Holt, Selleck, Sheafe, and Fane; Harrison in attendance. The chapter was continued and adjourned to the afternoon.

In the chapter house between 3 pm and 6 pm. Present: Peirs, Holt, Selleck, Sheafe, and Fane; Harrison in attendance.

p29 Mr Robert Creyghtone jnr was installed by Dr Holt and Dr Sheafe in the prebend or canonry of Yatton, vacant by the death of Mr Stephen Berrier.

The chapter was then continued and adjourned to the next morning.

April 4 In the chapter house between 8 am and 12 noon. Present: Peirs, Holt, Selleck, and Sheafe; Harrison in attendance.

p30 Dr Selleck, steward for the time being, was empowered to give copies of licences forthwith to Dr Peirs, to himself, to Dr Sheafe, and to Dr Mundy, and to their relations and others named in their copies.

It was resolved that Mr Nicholas Dowthwayte should examine the records of the dean and chapter for certain information sought by Mrs [ ] Butts.

The next day being Good Friday, the chapter was continued and adjourned to April 6.

April 6 In the chapter house between 8 am and 12 noon. Present: Peirs, Selleck, and Sheafe, who continued and adjourned the chapter to April 9.

April 9 In the chapter house between 1 pm and 4 pm. Present: Holt, Selleck, and Sheafe, who adjourned the chapter to the next morning.

April 10 In the chapter house between 8 am and 12 noon. Present: Holt and Selleck, who continued and adjourned the chapter to the afternoon.

p31 In the chapter house between 3 pm and 6 pm. Present: Peirs, Holt, Selleck, and Sheafe; Harrison in attendance.

Walter Hungerford, S.T.D., was installed by Dr Sheafe and Dr Selleck in the prebend or canonry of Wedmore II, vacant by the death of Roger Nicholls.

p32 The chapter was continued and adjourned to the next afternoon.

April 11 In the chapter house between 2 pm and 6 pm. Present: Peirs (proxy for Smythe) and Holt (proxy for Busby); Harrison in attendance.

It was enacted as follows [no further entry].

pp33–40 blank

p41–p42 **April 15** In the chapter house between 8 am and 10 am. Present: Peirs and prebendaries Hungerford and Thirlby; Harrison in attendance.

Christopher Sadbery, M.A., was installed by Dr Hungerford and Mr Thirlby in the prebend or canonry of Timberscombe, vacant by the cession of Robert Creyghtone.

p43 **July 1** In the chapter house between 9 am and 11 am. Present: Peirs, Selleck, Sheafe, and Fane; Harrison in attendance.

The following vicars choral of the New Close appeared: Benford and Thomas Standish (principals), Alderly, Francis Standish, Beaumont, Davis, Clarke, Edmonds, Hobbs, and Browne. Absent: Moss, excused.

p44 Because the clerks of the cathedral are negligent in performing their respective duties in and about the church, or even do not perform them at all, the communar would withold their salaries.

The chapter was adjourned to the afternoon.

In the chapter house between 2 pm and 5 pm. Present: Peirs, Holt, Selleck, Sheafe, and Fane, who continued and adjourned the chapter to the next morning.

July 2 In the chapter house between 8 am and 12 noon. Present: Peirs, Holt, Selleck, Sheafe, and Fane, who continued and adjourned the chapter to the afternoon.

In the chapter house between 2 pm and 6 pm. Present: Peirs, Holt, Selleck, Sheafe, and Fane, who continued and adjourned the chapter to the next morning.

July 3 In the chapter house between 10 am and 12 noon. Present: Peirs, Holt, Selleck, Sheafe, and Fane, who adjourned the chapter to the afternoon.

In the chapter house between 2 pm and 5 pm. Present: Peirs, Holt, Selleck, Sheafe, and Fane, who adjourned the chapter to the next morning.

p45 **July 4** Between 10 am and 12 noon, place not stated, Peirs, Holt, Selleck, Sheafe, and Fane adjourned the chapter to the afternoon.

In the chapter house between 2 pm and 5 pm. Present: Peirs, Holt, Selleck, Sheafe, and Fane, who adjourned the chapter to the next morning.

July 5 In the chapter house between 10 am and 12 noon. Present: Peirs, Holt, Selleck, Sheafe, and Fane, who continued and adjourned the chapter to the afternoon.

In the chapter house between 2 pm and 6 pm. Present: Peirs, Holt, Selleck, Sheafe, and Fane, who adjourned the chapter to the next morning between 10 am and 12 noon. [There is no record of this meeting].

pp46–48 blank

p49 **Oct 1** In the chapter house between 10 am and 12 noon. Present: Peirs and Holt.

[Roll-call of vicars choral; the names are listed, but there is no record of attendance

or absence]. Benford and Thomas Standish (principals), Alderly, Francis Standish, Moss, Beaumont, Davis, Clarke, Edmonds, Hobbs, and Browne.
The chapter was continued and adjourned to the next morning.

p50 In the chapter house between 10 am and 12 noon. Present: Peirs, Holt, Selleck, Sheafe, and Fane, who adjourned the chapter to the afternoon.
No place or time stated; Holt, Selleck, Sheafe, and Fane adjourned the chapter to the next morning.

Oct 3 In the chapter house between 10 am and 12 noon. Present: Peirs, Holt, Sheafe, and Fane; Harrison in attendance.

p51 The dean and chapter and Mr Tristram Towse of Wells, merchant, both agreed to submit to the arbitration and determination of Thomas White esq., for settlement before Oct 23, the case now depending between them in the chancery court.
Tabellar: Mr Daniel Davis.
Escheator: the vicars choral nominated Messrs Alderly and Clarke, and the chapter elected Mr Alderly.

p52 **Oct 5** In the chapter house between 10 am and 12 noon. Present: Peirs, Holt, Sheafe, and Fane; Harrison in attendance.

p53 An indenture was sealed, granting to Thomas Bower of North Curry for three lives a messuage or tenement with orchard and garden, and two fields of arable land called Greenewayes Close and Sheepefields Close.[1]
Another indenture was sealed, granting to Thomas Bower for three lives eight fields of arable and pasture land called Woodbreach and Nythewood, situate in West Hatch.[2]

p54 blank

p55 **Oct 26** In the chapter house between 10 am and 1 pm. Present: Peirs, Holt, Selleck, Sheafe, and Fane; Harrison in attendance.
An indenture was sealed, granting to Thomas White for three lives various parcels of land [in Lymekill (*sic*) Close] in the parish of St Cuthbert's, Wells.[3]
Another indenture was sealed, granting to Thomas Stephens, "inholder", for forty years 'The Three Horsloaves', now commonly called 'The Globe', in New Street, Wells.[4]

p56 blank

p57 *1667-8*

Jan 2 In the chapter house between 10 am and 12 noon. Present: Creyghtone, Peirs, Holt, Selleck, Sheafe, and Fane; Harrison in attendance.

[1] See W.C.L., Ledger G, 584. [2] See ibid. 587. [3] See ibid. 592.

[4] See ibid. 590. Horse-loaves were "a kind of bread, formerly given to horses. It was anciently a common phrase to say that a diminutive person was no higher than three horse-loaves. A phrase still current says such a one must stand on three penny loaves to look over the back of a goat, or, sometimes, a duck", J. O. Halliday, *Dictionary of Archaic and Provincial Words*. London, 1901, i. 460.

Confirmation by the chapter that, as directed by the king,[1] they will elect to the next vacant residentiary canonry Mr Robert Creyghtone, professor of Greek at *p58* Cambridge and canon and prebendary of Wells; and lest there should be the slightest suspicion of fraud or malpractice, they subscribe their names:

"Rob: Creyghtone Dec.W.
Guil: Peirs: Archinus Taunton
Tho: Holt Cancellarius
J: Selleck Archinus Bathon
Grindall Sheafe Archi-D. Wellen.
Willm Fane Resident."

p59 [Officers for the ensuing year]: Steward, Dr Sheafe; Baron of the exchequer, Dr Peirs; Auditors, Dr Holt and Dr Fane; Communar, Dr Selleck; Master of the fabric, Dr Fane; Overseers of the houses, Dr Peirs and Dr Holt.

[Roll-call of vicars choral]. Present: Benford (principal), Alderly, Clarke, Francis Standish, Moss, Beaumont, Davis, Edmonds, Hobbs, and Browne. Absent: Thomas Standish (principal), sick.

p60 The chapter was continued and adjourned to the next morning.

Jan 3 In the chapter house between 10 am and 12 noon. Present: Creyghtone, Peirs, Holt, Selleck, Sheafe, and Fane; Harrison in attendance. [Space left, but no further entry].

p61 The chapter was adjourned to the afternoon.

In the chapter house between 2 pm and 4 pm. Present: Creyghtone, Peirs, Holt, Selleck, Sheafe, and Fane, who adjourned the chapter to the next morning.

Jan 4 In the chapter house between 10 am and 12 noon. Present: Creyghtone, Peirs, Holt, Selleck, Sheafe, and Fane; Harrison in attendance.

It was resolved that daily distributions should be given to the canons for as many days as they had omitted to attend the cathedral.

p62 **Jan 9** In the chapter house between 10 am and 12 noon. Present: Creyghtone, Peirs, Holt, and Sheafe; Harrison in attendance.

An indenture was confirmed by which Mr John Peirs, prebendary of Dultingcote or Thinghurst, granted to Mary, widow of Thomas Ferrar or Turner, late of Thinghurst or Fingest, the whole manor of Thinghurst with all and sundry its appurtenances.[2]

Letters patent were sealed, granting to Dr Sheafe the officialty of the dean and chapter, and appointing him to act in all causes within the peculiar jurisdiction of the dean and chapter, except those relating to its jurisdiction within the Liberties.

The chapter was then adjourned to the afternoon.

p63 In the chapter house between 2 pm and 5 pm. Present: Creyghtone, Peirs, Holt, Sheafe, and prebendary Thirlby; Harrison in attendance.

John Randall, B.A., was installed by Dr Holt and Dr Sheafe in the prebend or canonry of Combe VIII, vacant by the death of Roger Ley.

[1] In a letter dated from Whitehall, 14th November 1667, enjoining the election of Robert Creyghton, "notwithstanding any other persons pretencion that Wee have or shall recommend unto you for that place", and ordering that "att the next Chapter after the Receipt of these Our Letters, you make an Act for his Title of Election thereunto, and that every one of the present Residentiaryes attest his consent to the said Act by subscribing his hand to the same"; see W.C.L. Parfitt papers, No. 3.

[2] See W.C.L., Ledger G, 595.

p64 The chapter was adjourned to Jan. 11.

Jan 11 In the chapter house between 2 pm and 5 pm; no attendances recorded.
The chapter was adjourned to Jan. 13.

Jan 13 In the chapter house between 10 am and 12 noon. Present: Creyghtone, Peirs, Selleck, Sheafe, and Fane; Harrison in attendance.

It was resolved that the money belonging to Mr Bridge, now in the hands of Dr Sheafe, should be paid over to Dr Peirs for him to hold in like manner.[1]

Then the chapter was continued and adjourned day by day until the afternoon of Jan. 17.

p65 **Jan 17** In the chapter house between 2 pm and 5 pm. Present: Creyghtone, Peirs, Holt, Selleck, Sheafe, and Fane; Harrison in attendance.

Letters patent were confirmed, appointing Dr Henry Deane as vicar general and official principal of the bishop of Bath and Wells for life.[2]

The chapter was adjourned to the next morning.

Jan 18 Between 10 am and 12 noon; no place or attendances recorded—only the adjournment of the chapter to the afternoon.

In the chapter house between 3 pm and 6 pm. Present: Creyghtone, Holt, Selleck, and Sheafe; Harrison in attendance.

It was resolved that sufficient security for Mr Bridge's money should be deposited and paid to the communar.

p66 Within the next month the master of the fabric and the overseers of the houses were to inspect the choristers' house[3] and make provision for such repairs as might seem necessary.

March 6 In the chapter house between 3 pm and 5 pm. Present: Peirs, Holt, Selleck, Sheafe, and prebendary Thirlby; Harrison in attendance.

James Douch, B.A., was installed by Dr Selleck and Dr Sheafe in the prebend or canonry of Timberscombe, vacant by the death of Christopher Sadbery.

p67 **March 12** In the chapter house between 3 pm and 5 pm. Present: Peirs, Sheafe, Fane, and prebendary Creyghtone; Harrison in attendance.

p68 Hamnett Ward, M.D., was installed by Dr Sheafe and Mr Creyghtone in the prebend or canonry of Combe I, vacant by the death of John Carhele.

[1] See also the entry below for 18th January 1667–8. Nothing is known about Bridge's money, though a letter to the dean and chapter from a certain Roger Walker (probably the brother of Dr Thomas Walker, canon residentiary, who died in 1665) dated 6th August 1670 may have some bearing upon it, as there are two references to "Bridges mony"; see Appendix I, p.xxxix for the letter—original in W.C.L., Documents, series III, box 3, 170.

[2] See W.C.L., Ledger G, 600.

[3] The choristers' house stood on land donated by bishop Bekynton adjoining the west cloister at the south-east corner of the Cathedral Green (*Reg. Bekynton*, (Som. Rec. Soc.49), p. 318). It became increasingly dilapidated during the 19th century and finally collapsed in April 1870 (E. A. Freeman, op.cit., 184), leaving only the north gable wall of the hall, which is still standing. For a description of the house, which had latterly been assigned to the organist as a residence, see J. H. Parker in *Trans. Som. Arch. and Nat. Hist. Soc.*, vol. XII (1863), ii. 31 and plate IV; also the same author's *Architectural Antiquities of the City of Wells*, Oxford, 1866, 22–3. See also, on repairs to this house, the entry below for 1st April 1671.

1668

p69 **April 1** In the chapter house between 10 am and 12 noon. Present: Peirs, Holt, Selleck, and Sheafe; Harrison in attendance.

[Roll-call of vicars choral]. Present: Benford, Alderly, Francis Standish, Mosse, Beaumont, Davis, Edmonds, Hobbs, Browne, Willis, and Willmott. Absent: Clarke and Horsey, sick.

A stall and an *auscultor* were assigned to each of three probationer vicars choral: to Peter Horsey, Combe I and Mr Benford; to Thomas Willis, Combe II and Mr Standish; to James Willmott, Combe III and Mr Alderly.

p70 Mr [ ] Williams was admitted as schoolmaster of the cathedral grammar school on the nomination of the chancellor, Dr Holt, in place of Mr Thirlby; the appointment was for one quarter, after which it would be reviewed.[1]

Dr Holt, Dr Selleck, and Dr Sheafe continued and adjourned the chapter to the next day.

April 2 In the chapter house between 10 am and 12 noon. Present: Peirs, Holt, Selleck, Sheafe, and Fane, who adjourned the chapter to the afternoon of April 3, when Peirs, Holt, and Sheafe adjourned it to the morning of April 4.

April 4 In the chapter house between 10 am and 12 noon. Present: Peirs, Holt, Selleck, Sheafe, and Fane; Harrison in attendance.

It was decreed that an order be made by the steward, Arthur Weaver, for taking possession of trees felled by the widow of [ ] Hearne on a certain tenement situated in West Hatch.

The chapter was adjourned to the afternoon.

p71 In the chapter house between 2 pm and 5 pm. Present: Peirs, Selleck, Sheafe, and Fane, who adjourned the chapter to April 6.

April 6 In the chapter house between 10 am and 12 noon. Present: Peirs, Holt, Selleck, Sheafe, and Fane; Westley in attendance. The chapter was adjourned to the next day.

April 7 In the chapter house between 10 am and 12 noon. Present: Peirs, Holt, and Sheafe; Clynton in attendance. The chapter was adjourned to the next day.

April 8 In the chapter house between 10 am and 12 noon. Present: Peirs, Holt, Selleck, Sheafe, and Fane; Harrison in attendance. The chapter was continued and adjourned to the afternoon.

In the chapter house between 2 pm and 5 pm. Present: Peirs, Holt, Selleck, Sheafe, and Fane; Harrison in attendance.

Letters patent were sealed and confirmed, appointing Arthur Mattock jnr the bishop's auditor general for life.[2]

p72 Nicholas Painter and Christopher Brawdripp of Wells appeared and undertook to

[1] Either Williams resigned or he was found to be unsuitable, for a further appointment to the mastership of the grammar school was made three months later: see the entry below for 2nd July.

[2] See W.C.L., Ledger G, 605.

return to Mr [Thomas] Romman, silversmith, of Wells by the feast of Pentecost next following a silver communion chalice handed to them by Mr Arthur Alderly.

April 23 In the chapter house between 9 am and 11 am. Present: Peirs, Selleck, Sheafe, and prebendary Thirlby; Harrison in attendance.

Henry Dutton, S.T.B., was installed by Dr Sheafe and Mr Thirlby in the prebend or canonry of Whitelackington, vacant by the death of Alexander Huish.

p73–p74 **April 25** In the chapter house between 3 pm and 5 pm. Present: Peirs, Fane, and prebendary Thirlby; Harrison in attendance.

Robert Collier, M.A., was installed by Dr Fane and Mr Thirlby in the prebend or canonry of East Harptree, vacant by the resignation of Henry Dutton.

p75 **July 1** In the chapter house between 10 am and 12 noon. Present: Creyghtone, Peirs, and Sheafe; Harrison in attendance.

[Roll-call of vicars choral]. Present: Benford, Alderly, Clarke, Standish, Moss, Beaumont, Davis, Edmonds, Hobbs, [Horsey and Willmott not marked as present or absent]. Absent: Browne (excused) and Willis.

The chapter was continued and adjourned to the afternoon.

p76 In the chapter house between 3 pm and 5 pm. Present: Creyghtone, Peirs, Holt, and Sheafe; Harrison in attendance.

James Aston, M.A., was installed by Dr Peirs and Dr Holt in the prebend or canonry of Buckland Dinham, vacant by the resignation of John Duncombe.

The chapter was continued and adjourned to the next morning.

p77 **July 2** In the chapter house between 10 am and 12 noon. Present: Creyghtone, Peirs, Holt, Selleck, and Sheafe, who adjourned the chapter to the afternoon.

In the chapter house between 4 pm and 6 pm. Present: Creyghtone, Peirs, Holt, Selleck, Sheafe, and Fane; Harrison in attendance.

Mr John Pottinger, clerk, admitted on the nomination of Dr Holt, chancellor, to the mastership of the cathedral grammar school, vacant by the cession of Mr Charles Thirlby.

p78 The chapter was continued and adjourned to the next day.

July 3 In the chapter house between 10 am and 12 noon. Present: Creyghtone, Peirs, Holt, Selleck, Sheafe, and Fane, who adjourned the chapter to the afternoon.

Between 4 pm and 6 pm; place not stated. Present: Creyghtone, Holt, Selleck, Sheafe, and Fane; Harrison in attendance.

An indenture was sealed, granting a lease of 'The Katherine Wheele' in High Street, Wells, to Thomas Nixon for forty years.[1]

The chapter was continued and adjourned to the next morning.

July 4 In the chapter house between 9 am and 12 noon. Present: Creyghtone, Selleck, and Sheafe, who adjourned the chapter to July 13.

p79 **July 13** In the chapter house between 10 am and 12 noon. Present: Creyghtone, Peirs, Holt, Sheafe, and Fane, who adjourned the chapter to the afternoon, between 5 pm and 7 pm. [There is no record of a meeting then].

[1] See ibid. 608.

p80 **Sept 30** In the chapter house between 9 am and 11 am. Present: Creyghtone, Holt, Selleck, Sheafe, and Fane; Harrison in attendance.

[Officers for the ensuing year]: Baron of the exchequer, Dr Peirs; Auditors, Dr Holt and Dr Fane; Communar, Dr Selleck; Master of the fabric, Dr Fane; Overseers of the houses, Dr Peirs and Dr Holt; Tabellar, Mr Moss; Escheator, the vicars *p81* choral nominated Messrs Edmonds and Hobbs and the chapter elected Mr Hobbs; Bailiff of the grange and *cursor ecclesiae*, John Gray.

Oct 1 In the chapter house between 10 am and 12 noon. Present: Creyghtone, Holt, Selleck, Sheafe, and Fane; Harrison in attendance.

[Roll-call of vicars choral]. Present: Moss, Beaumont, Benford, Alderly, Clarke, Standish, Davis, Edmonds, Hobbs, Browne, Willis, and Willmott.

p82 Mrs Anne Clynton (wife of Mr Guy Clynton) and Mrs Margaret Neblett (wife of Mr Nicholas Neblett) were given permission to sit in the second seat from the south entrance to the quire during the pleasure of the chapter.[1]

The chapter was adjourned to the afternoon, and from then to the next morning.

Oct 2 In the chapter house between 10 am and 12 noon. Present: Creyghtone, Holt, Selleck, Sheafe, and Fane, who adjourned the chapter to the afternoon.

Between 4 pm and 6 pm, place not stated. Present: Creyghtone, Holt, Selleck, Sheafe, and Fane. [Incomplete entry].

It was decreed that no chorister might sleep at night out of the choristers' house without first obtaining permission, on pain of losing his place; this rule would operate from Nov 1 next, and Mr Browne, master of the choristers, was ordered to make it known to the boys and their friends.

The chapter was adjourned to the next morning between 10 am and 12 noon and then, in the chapter house, to the afternoon.

Oct 3 In the chapter house between 2 pm and 4 pm. Present: Creyghtone, Selleck, Sheafe, and Fane, who adjourned the chapter to Oct 5.

p83 **Oct 5** In the chapter house between 10 am and 12 noon. Present: Creyghtone and Sheafe, who adjourned the chapter to the afternoon.

In the chapter house between 4 pm and 6 pm. Present: Creyghtone, Sheafe, and Fane, who adjourned the chapter to the next morning.

Oct 6 In the chapter house between 10 am and 12 noon. Present: Creyghtone, Selleck, Sheafe, and Fane; Westley in attendance. The chapter was adjourned to the afternoon.

In the chapter house between 4 pm and 6 pm. Present: Creyghtone, Holt, Selleck, Sheafe, and Fane.

It was decided that the dean should pay to the vicars the salaries for the prebends of Wedmore I and Combe VIII in perpetuity; and that the two other Combe stalls assigned to Thomas Willis and James Willmot should be taken from them. In their place, Mr Willis would have the stall of Worminster and Mr Willmott the stall of Litton from Michaelmas next.

The chapter was adjourned to the next morning.

[1] This permission was withdrawn three years later: see the entry below for 9th October 1671.

Oct 7 In the chapter house between 10 am and 12 noon. Present: Creyghtone, Holt, Selleck, and Fane.

The present steward and communar of the chapter were empowered to enter into contract with any person or persons whatsoever for the sale of property in Congresbury belonging to the dean and chapter, and to propose and accept whatever fine they should judge to be appropriate; this would be confirmed by the chapter.

It was ordered that a notice be affixed to the stall of Dinder, citing Mr Lanfire to attend upon the dean and chapter on Oct 6 [*sic*] between 10 am and 12 noon.

p84 blank

p85 **Nov 11** In the chapter house between 3 pm and 5 pm. Present: Creyghtone, Sheafe, and prebendary Thirlby; in attendance [ ] chapter clerk.

Edward Hitchman, LL.B., was installed by Dr Sheafe and Mr Thirlby in the prebend or canonry of Combe XIII, vacant by the death of Thomas Stanniford.

1668-9

p86 **Jan 1** In the chapter house between 10 am and 12 noon. Present: Holt and Sheafe; Westley in attendance. The chapter was adjourned to the next day.

Jan 2 In the chapter house between 10 am and 12 noon. Present: Creyghtone, Peirs, and Sheafe; Westley in attendance.

[Roll-call of vicars choral]. Present: Moss and Beaumont (principals), Benford, Alderley, Standish, Clarke, Hobbs, Browne, Willis, and Willmott. Absent: Edmonds (sick), and Davis.

p87 Messrs Willis and Willmot, having completed their year of probation, were approved for perpetuation by the vicars.

The chapter was adjourned to the afternoon, in Dr Selleck's house.[1]

In Dr Selleck's house between 3 pm and 5 pm. Present: Creyghtone, Selleck, and Sheafe; Westley in attendance. [There is a marginal heading, *Negocium*, but no business is recorded; a large blank space is left, before the final entry on the page.]

The chapter was adjourned to the chapter house in the afternoon of Jan. 4.

p88 **Jan 4** In the chapter house between 2 pm and 5 pm. Present: Peirs, Selleck, and Sheafe, who immediately adjourned the chapter to the audit room, where they were joined by the dean; Westley in attendance.

In all future copies the amount payable in respect of heriot on anyone's death must be clearly stated.

Every tenant of the manor of East Curry seeking to buy property registered in the court rolls of the dean and chapter shall, in his application to them, state how many lives are specified in the copy or copies furnished to him.

Memorandum: the bishop had sent his chancellor to intimate to the dean his gratitude to the chapter for stating to him in writing the reasons for not confirming

[1] Dr Selleck lived in the house which was later converted into the present No. 21, The Liberty.

the lease of the parsonage of Ashbury;[1] he accepted those reasons; and thanked them for their concern on behalf of the Church, the bishopric, and his own interests.

Dr Sheafe moved that with the agreement of the chapter this should be entered in the chapter's books; Dr Holt had also consented to these three acts; and the whole chapter decreed that their humble thanks should be conveyed to the bishop through his chancellor.

p89 **Jan 9** In the audit room between 10 am and 12 noon. Present: Peirs, Holt, Selleck, and Sheafe; Westley in attendance.

Permission was given to the widow of Amos Walrond to place a stone above the monument to her late husband in the cathedral, with an inscription in English or Latin, and to fix on the wall such emblems (*vexilla*) and insignia as seemed to her appropriate.[2]

The chapter was adjourned to Jan. 11.

Jan 11 In the audit room between 10 am and 12 noon. Present: Peirs, Selleck, and Sheafe, who adjourned the chapter to the afternoon of Jan. 12.

Jan 12 In the audit room between 2 pm and 5 pm. Present: Peirs, Selleck, and Sheafe; Westley in attendance.

p90 Letters patent were sealed, granting to George Creyghtone the office of registrar to the dean and deanery of Wells.[3]

An indenture was sealed, granting to Nathaniel Selleck, son of Dr Selleck, the lease of a parcel of land at Wick St Lawrence containing 24 acres.[4]

p91 **Feb 6** In the chapter house between 2 pm and 5 pm. Present: Creyghtone, Selleck, Sheafe, and prebendary Thirlby; Harrison in attendance.

John Potinger was installed by Dr Selleck and Dr Sheafe in the prebend or canonry of Wedmore IV, vacant by the death of Jonathan Palmer.

p92

1669

April 1 In the chapter house between 10 am and 12 noon. Present: Creyghtone, Peirs, Selleck, Sheafe, and Fane; Harrison in attendance.

[Roll-call of vicars choral]. Present: Mosse, Beaumont, Benford, Alderley, Clarke, Standish, Davis, Edmonds, Hobbs, Browne, Willis, and Willmott.

p93 The chapter was adjourned to the next day.

April 2 In the chapter house between 10 am and 12 noon. Present: Creyghtone, Peirs, Holt, Selleck, Sheafe, and Fane; Harrison in attendance.

[1] See 'The Reasons of the Deane and Chapter . . . tendered to . . . William Lord Bishop of Bath and Wells to stop the Confirmacion of Ashbury Lease', W.C.L., Documents, series III, box 4, 172; and also the discussion of this matter, pp.xxx ff.

[2] Amos Walrond died 11th November 1668, and was buried 15th November. He is commemorated by a floor-slab at the entrance to St John Baptist chapel in the cathedral, but there is no evidence that any other memorial was erected; see A. J. Jewers, *Wells Cathedral, its Monumental Inscriptions and Heraldry*, 91–2—but the transcription of the wording on the floor-slab contains many errors.

[3] See W.C.L., Ledger G, 610. [4] See ibid. 613.

It was decreed that an action should be commenced in the chancellor's court against Mr Augustine Benford in the matter of a house in Chamberlain Street, Wells.[1]
The chapter was adjourned to the afternoon between 2 pm and 4 pm, and then by Creyghtone, Peirs, Holt, Selleck, Sheafe, and Fane to the next day.

April 3 In the chapter house between 10 am and 12 noon. Present: Peirs, Holt, Selleck, Sheafe, and Fane, who adjourned the chapter to April 5.

April 5 In the chapter house between 10 am and 12 noon. Present: Peirs, Holt, Selleck, Sheafe, and Fane, with Westley in attendance, who adjourned the chapter to the afternoon.
In the chapter house between 2 pm and 6 pm. Present: Creyghtone, Peirs, Holt, Selleck, Sheafe, and Fane; Harrison in attendance.
p94 A capitular visitation was fixed for June 3 next.
John Potenger was installed by Dr Holt and Dr Selleck in the prebend or canonry of Warminster or Luxville, vacant by the death of Richard Merry.
The chapter was adjourned to the next morning.

p95 **April 6** In the chapter house between 10 am and 12 noon. Present: Peirs, Holt, Selleck, Sheafe, and Fane; Harrison in attendance.
It was decreed that the communar should allocate to Mr George Bisse for the revenue of the rectory of St Cuthbert's, Wells, 31*l.* in respect of royal aid for the years 1665, 1666 plus supplement, 1667 plus supplement, and 1668 (ending at Michaelmas last) plus supplement—eleven months for king Charles and one month for the duke of York; provided always that the communar should not allocate this sum of 31*l.* unless Mr Bisse paid such rents and sums of money as were now due to the dean and chapter.

p96 **April 12** In the chapter house between 9 am and 11 am. Present: Creyghtone, Selleck, and prebendaries Creyghtone jnr and Thirlby; Harrison in attendance.
John Wood, S.T.B., was installed by Mr Creyghtone and Mr Thirlby in the prebend or canonry of Compton Dundon, vacant by the resignation of Henry Byam.

p97 **April 26** In the chapter house between 3 pm and 5 pm. Present: Creyghtone, Peirs, Selleck, and prebendaries Thirlby and Potenger; Harrison in attendance.
Robert Gale, M.A., was installed by Mr. Thirlby and Mr Potenger in the prebend or canonry of Wedmore IV, vacant by the cession of John Potenger.

pp98–102 blank

p103 **July 1** In the chapter house between 9 am and 11 am. Present: Creyghtone, Peirs, and Holt; Harrison in attendance.
The dean and Dr Selleck nominated and elected Dr Sheafe as steward for the ensuing two years—Dr Peirs, Dr Holt, and Dr Fane dissenting; and Dr Piers and

[1] The point at issue is not known. On 31st December 1662 Augustine Benford, a lay vicar choral, had asked for a 40-year lease of a cottage with garden and well situated on the south side of Chamberlain street, Wells, vacant by the death of Margaret Packer, widow, to whom it had passed on the death of her husband Thomas Packer. See W.C.L., Documents, series III, box 3, 152.

Dr Holt nominated and elected Dr Fane as steward—the dean, Dr Selleck, and Dr Sheafe similarly dissenting.

Then the vicars choral were summoned for their roll-call, Dr Peirs being absent. Present: Moss and Beaumont (principals), Alderley, Standish, Benford, Clarke, Davis, Edmonds, Browne, Willis, and Wilmott. Absent: Hobbs.

p104 It was ordered that on Lord's Days and festivals morning prayer would be read publicly in the Lady Chapel according to ancient usage, and that the Book of Common Prayer or liturgy of the Church, and the Testament, would be prepared for this purpose.[1]

The chapter was adjourned to the afternoon.

In the chapter house between 2 pm and 5 pm. Present: Creyghtone, Peirs, Holt, Selleck, Sheafe, and Fane. [No business is recorded, and a blank space follows, at the end of which is the entry]:

Dr Holt, Dr Selleck, and Dr Sheafe adjourned the chapter to the next morning.

July 2 In the chapter house between 10 am and 12 noon. Present: Peirs, Holt, Selleck, Sheafe, and Fane, who adjourned the chapter to the afternoon.

p105 In the chapter house between 3 pm and 6 pm. Present: Peirs, Holt, and Selleck (proxy for Creyghtone). [It appears from the minutes of the proceedings that Dr Sheafe was also present]

Dr Peirs exhibited a proxy in writing from Dr Sebastian Smythe, precentor; Dr Selleck and Dr Sheafe protested that the proxy was null and void, and that Dr Smythe should receive no quotidians or dividend on account of his non-residence.

Dr Peirs and Dr Holt proposed and elected Dr Fane as steward for the ensuing two years; but Dr Selleck and Dr Sheafe protested that the election was null and void because the time for electing a steward had passed, and Dr Sheafe had been elected on the previous day.

The chapter was adjourned to the next morning.

July 3 In the chapter house between 9 am and 12 noon. Present: Creyghtone, Peirs, Holt, Selleck, Sheafe, and Fane; Harrison in attendance.

Dr Peirs presented a written protestation which he had drawn up, and which Dr Holt and Dr Fane had signed.

Then the dean, Dr Selleck, and Dr Sheafe adjourned the chapter to the deanery, where they again adjourned it to the afternoon, to meet in the deanery for convenience.

In the deanery between 2 pm and 5 pm. Present: Creyghtone, Selleck, and Sheafe.

p106 The sacrist was ordered to close the outer doors of the cathedral, except at the times of divine service and when the ecclesiastical courts were in session, when one door only would be open.

The chapter was adjourned to July 5 in the deanery for convenience.

July 5 In the deanery between 10 am and 12 noon. Present: Creyghtone, Selleck, and Sheafe.

An indenture dated Oct. 5, 1668, was sealed, granting to Mr William Andrews a lease of the first house from the east in the New Works for a term of 40 years.[2]

[1] See also the entry for 5th July 1670.

[2] See W.C.L., Ledger G, 615. The New Works was the row of houses on the north side of the present Market Place, Wells, built by bishop Bekynton between 1451 and c.1460.

pp107–112 blank

p113 **Aug 28** In the chapter house. [Spaces are left for the insertion of the times and the signature of the chapter clerk, but these details have not been entered]. Present: Sheafe and prebendaries Creyghtone and Potenger.

Thomas Cartwright, S.T.D., was installed by Messrs Creyghtone and Potenger in the prebend or canonry of Scanford or Shalford, vacant by the death of Henry Osbaston.

p114 **Sept 10** In the chapter house between 2 pm and 5 pm. Present: Sheafe and prebendaries Creyghtone, Thirlby, and Potenger; Harrison in attendance.

John Lonsdale, B.A., was installed by Messrs Creyghtone and Thirlby in the prebend or canonry of Combe VII, vacant by the cession of Thomas Cartwright.

p115 **Sept 30** In the chapter house between 9 am and 12 noon. Present: Creyghtone, Selleck, and Sheafe; Harrison in attendance.

[Officers for the ensuing year]: Baron of the exchequer, Dr Creyghtone; Auditor, Dr Sheafe; Communar, Dr Selleck; Master of the fabric, Dr Selleck; Overseers of the houses, Dr Selleck and Dr Sheafe; Tabellar, Mr Moss; Escheator, the vicars choral nominated Messrs Alderly and Edmonds and the chapter elected Mr Edmonds; Bailiff of the grange and *cursor ecclesiae*, John Gray.

p116 **Oct 1** In the chapter house between 9 am and 11 am. Present: Creyghtone, Selleck, and Sheafe; Harrison in attendance. The chapter was adjourned to the deanery.

[Roll-call of vicars choral] Present: Beaumont and Mosse (principals), Standish, Alderly, Benford, Davis, Clarke, Edmonds, Hobbs, Brown, and Willmott. Absent: Willis.

The chapter was adjourned to the afternoon in the deanery for convenience.

In the deanery between 1 pm and 3 pm. Present: Creyghtone, Selleck, and Sheafe, who adjourned the chapter to the next morning.

p117 **Oct 2** In the deanery between 10 am and 12 noon. Present: Creyghtone, Selleck, and Sheafe, who adjourned the chapter to the afternoon.

In the deanery between 1 pm and 4 pm. Present: Creyghtone, Selleck, and Sheafe, who adjourned the chapter to Oct. 4.

Oct 4 In the deanery between 10 am and 12 noon. Present: Creyghtone, Selleck, and Sheafe, who adjourned the chapter to the afternoon.

In the deanery between 4 pm and 6 pm. Present: Creyghtone, Selleck, and Sheafe, who adjourned the chapter to the next afternoon.

Oct 5 In the deanery between 1 pm and 5 pm [4 pm deleted]. Present: Creyghtone, Selleck, and Sheafe, who adjourned the chapter to the next afternoon.

Oct 6 In the deanery between 4 pm and 6 pm. Present: Creyghtone, Selleck, and Sheafe, who adjourned the chapter to the next morning.

Oct 7 In the deanery between 10 am and 12 noon. Present: Creyghtone, Selleck, and Sheafe, who adjourned the chapter to the next morning.

Oct 8 In the deanery between 10 am and 12 noon. Present: Creyghtone, Selleck, and Sheafe.

Alexander Harrison, deputy chapter clerk, was appointed to represent the dean and chapter in a case concerning the pension from Chew Magna, in which Mr Crosse was the plaintiff.[1]

The chapter was adjourned to the afternoon between 4 pm and 6 pm. [It is doubtful whether it was held at this hour].

p118 blank

1669-70

p119 **Jan 1** In the chapter house between 10 am and 12 noon. Present: Holt, Selleck, Sheafe, and Fane; Harrison in attendance. The chapter was adjourned to Jan 3.

Jan 3 In the chapter house between 10 am and 12 noon. Present: Creyghtone, Holt, Selleck, Sheafe, and Fane; Harrison in attendance.

[Roll-call of vicars choral; the names are listed, but there is no indication of attendances or absences]. Beaumont, Moss, Standish, Alderly, Davis, Clarke, Edmonds, Hobbs, Browne, Willis, and Willmott.

p120 Mr Nicholas Dowthwaite was instructed to make available to the vicars choral the records pertaining to them which were in his custody; Dr Selleck and Dr Fane were to be present in the audit room to witness the handing over of these records.[2]

The chapter was adjourned to the afternoon.

In the chapter house between 2 pm and 4 pm. Present: Creyghtone, Holt, Selleck, Sheafe, and Fane; Harrison in attendance.

The dean and chapter proposed that the vicars choral should withdraw the petition they had laid before the archbishop of Canterbury and concisely disclose their case. The chapter would likewise make its own case known; and both cases, being thus brought together, could be laid before those most skilled in the law for their opinions, so that the controversy between the two parties might be ended and rooted out. Further, for the sake of peace and quiet and for no other reason, the chapter offered to pay counsels' fees in this matter.

The chapter was adjourned to Jan 5.

Jan 5 In the chapter house between 10 am and 12 noon. Present: Creyghtone, Holt, Selleck, Sheafe, and Fane; Harrison in attendance.

p121 In future no residentiary canon would receive anything by way of quotidians or dividend unless he had completed his residence according to the charter, and members

[1] The chapter claimed three pensions from the vicar of Chew Magna under a royal warrant and a grant from bishop Ralph of Shrewsbury in 1349: *6l. 13s. 4d.* payable to the vicars choral, *3l. 6s. 8d.* to the choristers, and *3l. 6s. 8d.* to the escheator—the last sum originally being due to the prior and convent of Bath. Mr Crosse argued that all such payments were abolished by the act 1 Edward 6, ch 14, while the chapter contended that notwithstanding any such enactment the pensions were confirmed by the Elizabethan charter. See S.R.O., DD/CC 110026, 13–17 and 36 for the few documents relating to this case which have survived.

[2] These records were presumably required in connexion with the controversy between the chapter and the vicars choral over escheatory revenues; see also the entry for the afternoon of 3rd January, and for a general discussion of the matter, pp. xxxii ff.

of the chapter were to declare that they had complied with the act made to this end.
The chapter was adjourned to the afternoon.

In the chapter house between 1 pm and 3 pm. Present: Creyghtone, Holt, Selleck, Sheafe, and Fane, who adjourned the chapter to the deanery, to meet the same evening.

In the deanery between 6 pm and 8 pm. Present: Creyghtone, Holt, Selleck, Sheafe, and Fane; Harrison in attendance.

Any money due to the communar should be received only by him, or by the dean and chapter in full chapter assembled, and not by any other person whatsoever.

An indenture was sealed, granting to Mr [ ] Sealy [entry incomplete][1]

The dean, Dr Selleck, and Dr Sheafe decreed that no canon might appoint a proxy unless such canon had completed his residence for the preceding year according to the charter.

p122 **Jan 7** In the chapter house between 10 am and 12 noon. Present: Creyghtone, Holt, Selleck, Sheafe, and Fane; Harrison in attendance.

It was decreed that Thomas and George Mattock, sons of Arthur Mattock, should by agreement be made parties to the decree against Reginald Dight; and that a caution or security for the dean and chapter entered against the said Thomas and George should be remitted; also that the sum of 200*l.* awarded in judgement should be divided equally between the dean and chapter and Dr Holt.

In the deanery between 3 pm and 6 pm. Present: Creyghtone, Holt, Selleck, Sheafe, and Fane; Harrison in attendance.

Letters patent were sealed, appointing Dr Fane to the officialty of the dean and chapter within its peculiar jurisdiction.

p123 **March 3** In the deanery between 10 am and 12 noon. Present: Creyghtone, Holt, Selleck, Sheafe, and Fane; Harrison in attendance.

Out of the fine accruing from Buckland Abbas, 100*l.* was granted by the dean and chapter to Colonel Francis Wyndham as a favour, without regard to any other person, on account of the full and prompt payment of the fine.

A further 100*l.* from the same fine was lodged with the present master of the fabric for the three following good uses: 1. The casting of the larger bells;[2] 2. The restoration of the library; and 3. The repair of the south cloister. And if this sum proved to be insufficient for all these works, the communar was authorized to pay to the master of the fabric whatever he spent in excess thereof.

p124 **March 4** In Mr Francis Poulett's house in the Liberty[3] between 1 pm and 4 pm. Present: Creyghtone, Holt, Selleck, Sheafe, and Fane; Harrison in attendance.

An indenture was sealed, granting the rectory of Buckland Abbas in the county of Dorset to John, Lord Poulett, for his life and the lives of his daughters Catherine and Letitia.

pp125–130 blank

[1] See W.C.L., Ledger G, 617: a lease of Meare Court to William Sealy for three lives.

[2] The largest bell, called 'Harewell', had been repaired in 1634 (*Cal.* ii. 419) and in 1638 (*Cal.* ii. 419), and in 1668 had been recast by Thomas Purdy (Reynolds, op.cit., lxii); see also the entry for 5th July 1670, and the entry and note for the afternoon of 2nd January 1670–1.

[3] This was the house which was virtually rebuilt at the beginning of the 18th century by Dr Claver Morris, and is now numbered 19, The Liberty.

1670

p131 **April 1** In the chapter house between 10 am and 12 noon. Present: Creyghtone, Holt, Selleck, Sheafe, and Fane; Harrison in attendance. The chapter was continued and adjourned to the next day.

April 2 In the chapter house between 10 am and 12 noon. Present: Creyghtone, Holt, Selleck, Sheafe, and Fane, who adjourned the chapter to April 4.

April 4 In the chapter house between 10 am and 12 noon. Present: Creyghtone, Selleck, Sheafe, and Fane.

[Roll-call of vicars choral] Present: Beaumont, Moss, Alderly, Clarke, Edmonds, Hobbs, and Browne. Absent: Standish (sick), Davis, Willis, and Wilmott.

p132 The deputy chapter clerk was instructed to write to Mr Francis Atkins, prebendary of Compton Bishop, requiring him to pay the stall wages due to Mr Moss; if he then failed to pay, a citation would be affixed to his stall.

Immediately the fine for the rectory of Buckland Abbas was received from Lord Poulett, it was divided severally between the residentiaries by order of the chapter.

It was now resolved that anything done in chapter, by act or decree or otherwise,[1] to deprive Dr Smyth and Dr Busby of their portions or dividends should be revoked, so far as the fine was concerned, but should continue in force so as to prevent their receiving any dividend at the end of the year, unless they had completed their residence.

Dr Selleck protested that it was contrary to the charter for anyone to receive any dividend who had not completed his residence; and that Lord Poulett's fine was not divided by the chapter in chapter assembled, according to ancient tradition and custom and the practice of the cathedral.

The chapter was adjourned to the afternoon.

Between 2 pm and 4 pm; place not stated. Present: Creyghtone, Peirs, Holt, Sheafe, and Fane; Harrison in attendance.

The chapter remitted to Mr Charles Thirlby, vicar of St Cuthbert's, Wells, all past arrears of pension due to be paid from the vicarage of St Cuthbert's, provided that Mr Thirlby paid to the choristers[2] and to Dr Walker's executor the sums justly due to them.[3] Mr Thirlby promised to do this, and to pay the pension in future.

p133 It was resolved that Mr Francis Poulett should allocate 40*s.* to the steward of the dean and chapter when he came to hold the courts at Pucklechurch, in lieu of the accustomed hospitality shown to the steward.

Then the chapter was adjourned to the next morning.

[1] The reference, presumably, is to the act made in the morning of 5th January 1669–70.

[2] On 4th December 1434 bishop Stafford decreed that an annual pension of 20*l.* should be paid to the dean and chapter for the use of the choristers out of the fruits and profits of St Cuthbert's, Wells: *Reg. Stafford* (Som. Rec.Soc. 32), 168–9. The 20*l.* was part of a total pension of 34*l.* 1*d.* due from the vicarage of St Cuthbert's to the dean and chapter. Mr Thirlby denied any knowledge of such a pension; he asserted that his predecessor for 32 years prior to the civil war had never paid it, and that it had not been demanded of him until 1665. Further, he stated that the income of the benefice was not more than 50*l.*, although the rectory, let out to farm, yielded 300*l.* from which the dean and chapter already derived 40*l.* for old rents. See S.R.O., DD/CC 110026a, 6, 8 and 11 for the few surviving documents bearing on this matter.

[3] There is nothing to indicate whether the debt due to Dr Walker's executor was in any way connected with the subject of Roger Walker's letter to the chapter, see Appendix I, p.xxxix; also the entries for 7th July and 6th Oct. 1670.

April 5 In the chapter house between 10 am and 12 noon. Present: Peirs, Holt, and Fane (proxy for Creyghtone); Harrison in attendance. The chapter was adjourned to the afternoon between 2 pm and 5 pm. but afterwards to between 2 pm and 6 pm. In the chapter house between 2 pm and 6 pm. Present: Peirs, Holt, and Fane, who adjourned the chapter to the next morning.

April 6 In the chapter house between 10 am and 12 noon. Present: Peirs, Holt, Sheafe, and Fane, who adjourned the chapter to the afternoon.
In the chapter house between 3 pm and 6 pm. Present: Peirs, Holt, Sheafe, and Fane, who adjourned the chapter to the next morning.

April 7 In the chapter house between 10 am and 12 noon. Present: Peirs, Holt, Sheafe, and Fane (proxies for Creyghtone), who adjourned the chapter to the next morning.

p134 **April 8** In the chapter house between 10 am and 12 noon. Present: Peirs, Holt, and Fane (proxies for Creyghtone); Harrison in attendance.

Since Mr Charles Thirlby had asked to be fully released from all arrears of pension due from the vicarage of St Cuthbert's, Wells, according to the tenor of the chapter act made on April 4, it was resolved that at the next chapter he should have a discharge, such as legal opinion deemed to be satisfactory to him; and that the terms of the said chapter act should be confirmed and established by the same legal advice.

p135–p136 **May 20** In the chapter house between 10 am and 12 noon. Present: Holt, Selleck, Sheafe, and Fane (proxies for Creyghtone); Harrison in attendance.

A mandate was received for the election of a bishop to the vacant see of Bath and Wells, and May 25 between 10 am and 12 noon was appointed for this purpose.

p137–p138 **May 25** In the chapter house between 9 am and 11 am [and not as previously arranged]. Present: Holt, Selleck, Sheafe, Fane, and prebendaries Vannam, Hitchman, Potenger, and Standish; Harrison in attendance.

Robert Creyghtone, S.T.D., dean of Wells, was elected bishop of Bath and Wells.

pp139–140 blank

p141–p142 **June 28** In the chapter house between 8 am and 11 am. Present: Peirs, Selleck, and prebendaries Thirlby, Barker, Douch, Coward, Potenger, and Standish; Harrison in attendance.

Ralph Bathurst, M.D., represented by his proxy Dr Selleck, was installed by Messrs Thirlby and Barker as dean of Wells.

pp143–146 blank

p147 **July 1** In the chapter house between 9 am and 11 am. Present: Holt, Selleck, Sheafe, and Fane; Harrison in attendance.

[Roll-call of vicars choral]. Present: Beaumont and Mosse (principals), Standish, Alderly, Clarke, Edmonds, Hobbs, Browne, Willis, and Willmott. Absent: Davis. The chapter was adjourned to the next day, Dr Peirs being present and consenting to this.

p148 **July 2** In the chapter house between 10 am and 12 noon. Present: Bathurst, Peirs, Busby, Holt, Selleck, Sheafe, and Fane; Harrison in attendance.
Dr Bathurst applied for admission as a canon residentiary, and undertook to pay his caution of 100*l.*; his application was accepted. [There follows an entry recording business done on Oct 8 relative to the dean's caution, for which see under that date.]

p149 Dr Busby nominated Mr Samuel Tilly for presentation to the rectory of East Lambrook; this was accepted by the chapter, and it was resolved that the deed of presentation should be sealed.
The chapter was adjourned to July 4.

July 4 In the chapter house between 10 am and 12 noon. Present: Bathurst, Peirs (proxy for Smith), Busby, Holt, Selleck, Sheafe, and Fane; Harrison in attendance.

p150 Lots were cast for benefices:
The dean—the vicarages of Winscombe and Bishop's Lydiard.
Dr Smythe—the vicarages of Burnham and Mudford.
Dr Peirs—the vicarage of Cheddar and the rectory of Shipham.
Dr Busby—the vicarages of Long Sutton and St Cuthbert's, Wells.
Dr Holt—the vicarage of Buckland Abbas.
Dr Selleck—the vicarages of Stogumber and Dulverton.
Dr Sheafe—the rectory of Allerton and the vicarage of North Curry.
Dr Fane—the vicarage of Pucklechurch and the rectory of East Lambrook.
The capitular books and the individual manuscripts pertaining to the cathedral were to be brought as soon as possible to the audit room while the archives were being repaired with all speed to receive them.
It was resolved that the steward, Dr Fane, with such help as he might desire, should bestow the books and manuscripts in suitable locations according to an orderly system, and should produce for the chapter a catalogue of them; and that his assistants should be paid such remuneration as Dr Fane proposed and the chapter

p151 deemed suitable. The books and manuscripts, both in the audit room and in the archives, were to be kept in the care and custody of Mr Nicholas Dowthwaite, and the key of the outer door of the audit room was to be handed over to the dean for his use. Also, Mr Dowthwaite and Mr Westley the chapter clerk were to have different keys, both to the outer doors and to the cabinets in which the books and manuscripts entrusted to their respective custody were lodged. If Mr Dowthwaite or Mr Westley happened to be absent for any reason, he must first hand his key to the dean or the senior canon then in the city. No book or manuscript might be removed from the audit room or the archives unless the borrowers first wrote their names in the public book provided for this purpose, and books or manuscripts so taken out must be returned to their proper places within seven days, unless the dean and chapter should decide otherwise.
The power granted to Dr Selleck and Dr Sheafe to summon any persons to law in the name of the dean and chapter was to cease and expire.[1]
The deed of presentation of Mr Samuel Tilly to the rectory of East Lambrook was sealed.
The chapter was adjourned to the afternoon.

[1] On 6th February 1666 power of attorney had been granted to Dr Selleck and Dr Sheafe to sue and implead all persons in arrears with their rents due to the dean and chapter; see charter 844, *Cal.* ii. 715.

In the chapter house between 4 pm and 6 pm. Present: Bathurst, Peirs (proxy for Smyth), Busby, Holt, Selleck, Sheafe, and Fane; Harrison in attendance.

p152 It was decreed that the proxy of any residentiary should have the same force, and should be equally valid for all acts of the chapter, as if that residentiary were present personally in chapter.

Further, it was decreed that all acts or constitutions depriving residentiaries of their quotidians or dividends should be absolutely cancelled.[1]

It was also decreed that no act of the chapter might be rescinded, save by the authority of persons equal in number to those who had passed it.[2]

The chapter was adjourned to the next morning.

p153–p156 **July 5** In the cathedral [hour not stated]. Present: Bathurst, Peirs, Busby, Holt, Selleck, Sheafe, and prebendary Thirlby; Harrison in attendance.

Robert Creyghtone, represented by his proxy Dr Holt, was enthroned in the quire as bishop of Bath and Wells, and after morning prayer was also assigned and installed in the place in the chapter customarily allotted to the bishop [*locum in Capitulo Episcopo . . . assignari consuetum . . .*].[3]

p157 In the chapter house between 8 am and 12 noon. Present: Bathurst, Peirs (proxy for Smyth), Busby, Holt, Selleck, Sheafe, and Fane; Harrison in attendance.

The priest vicars who read morning prayer publicly in the Lady chapel at the hours of 6 or 7 on Sundays and festivals would receive four nobles annually *ex gratia* from the dean and chapter in augmentation of their former stipends.

The chapter was continued and adjourned to the afternoon.

In the chapter house between 4 pm and 6 pm. Present: Bathurst, Peirs (proxy for Smyth), Busby, Holt, Sheafe, and Fane; Harrison in attendance. The steward was asked to complete the rental of all his manors before the next audit, and to call upon the help of Mr Dowthwaite and Mr Westley for this purpose; they were promised a just and fitting remuneration for their labours.

In the presence of Dr Selleck: the chapter gave full approval to the agreement between Dr Selleck and Thomas Purde the bellfounder which had been laid before it, signed by both parties.

p158 The chapter was continued and adjourned to the next morning.

July 6 In the chapter house between 10 am and 12 noon. Present: Bathurst, Peirs (proxy for Smythe), Busby, Holt, Sheafe, and Fane; Harrison in attendance.

Memorandum: Dr Busby explained to the dean and chapter that his absences were due to the following reasons—first, that he served as proctor and clerk for the chapter in the Convocation; second, that he laboured under frequent and severe bodily infirmities; and third, that he served the king continually in his royal school at Westminster. This explanation was fully accepted.

It was resolved that copies should be delivered to Dr Busby of the ordinances or decrees of the dean and chapter by which all sums of money, whether due to him and retained by Dr Selleck the communar or to be received hereafter by Dr Selleck for his benefit, were to be fully paid to him before the next feast of the Annunciation

[1] For a qualification of this act made on 8th July, see p. 104.

[2] This act was annulled on 19th July 1672; see below.

[3] On the installation of the bishop in chapter, see p. xxii.

of the Blessed Virgin Mary. Also that copies of the ordinances touching Dr Smyth and his moneys should be delivered to him.[1]

p159 The chapter was continued and adjourned to the afternoon.

In the chapter house between 2 pm and 6 pm. Present: Bathurst, Peirs (proxy for Smythe), Busby, Holt, Sheafe, and Fane; Harrison in attendance.

The chapter was continued and adjourned to the next morning.

July 7 In the chapter house between 10 am and 12 noon. Present: Bathurst, Peirs (proxy for Smyth), Busby, Holt, Sheafe, and Fane; Harrison in attendance.

Dr Busby would obtain from legal experts a general form of proxy, and would send a copy as soon as possible to the dean and chapter. After approval, it would be inscribed in the register, and would be the one form for common use by all residentiaries in case of absence.

p160 Mr Dowthwaite was asked to collect together in writing all the acts, statutes, or precedents concerning the right of visitation, either by the dean alone or by the dean and chapter, and to seek permission to search the books and manuscripts in the bishop's registry in which anything relating to visitation by the dean or the dean and chapter might be entered. Everything thus collected was to be prepared before Oct. 1 next.[2]

The chapter was continued and adjourned to the afternoon.

In the chapter house between 1 pm and 4 pm. Present: Bathurst, Peirs (proxy for Smyth), Busby, Holt, Sheafe, and Fane; Harrison in attendance.

When Dr Selleck was about to set out on his journey, he had been reminded to leave behind the key of the cabinet in which the seal was kept. Since he did not leave the key the chapter, compelled by the necessities of business, ordered that the bar be broken.

Memorandum: Dr Peirs, on behalf and in the absence of Mr Charles Thirlby, promised and bound himself to the chapter to guarantee everything owed by Mr Thirlby to the choristers and to the executor of Dr Walker that had accrued after the last payment made by the communar, according to the act made in chapter; on this understanding, and not otherwise, the release granted to Mr Thirlby was sealed.

An indenture in the name of Samuel Clarke was sealed, relating to a certain house in Wells in which he then dwelt.[3]

[In the dean's handwriting]. The acts of this chapter held in the month of July 1670 as here set down are sanctioned and approved by us.

"Rad. Bathurst Decan^{s}."

p161 **Sept 30** In the chapter house between 10 am and 12 noon. Present: Bathurst, Peirs, Holt, Sheafe, and Fane; Harrison in attendance.

[Officers for the ensuing year]: Baron of the exchequer, Dr Peirs; Auditors, Dr Holt and Dr Fane; Communar, Dr Smythe; Master of the fabric, Dr Sheafe;

[1] In this connexion cf. the complaint lodged against Dr Selleck on 15th December 1670 (W.C.L., Documents, series III, box 4, 174) following a resolution of the chapter on the previous day; see p.xxvii.

[2] See also W.C.L., Documents, series III, box 4, 173.

[3] See W.C.L., Ledger G, 623: lease to Samuel Clarke "thelder" for the lives of his children John, Samuel, and Anne of a house with shop, backside, and garden situated in East Wells (now St Thomas street) between a tenement on the east held by James Williams and one on the west in the occupation of Mary Standish, widow.

Overseers of the houses, Dr Holt and Dr Fane; Tabellar, Mr Clarke; Escheator, the vicars choral nominated Messrs Browne and Willis and the chapter elected Mr Browne; Bailiff of the grange and *cursor ecclesiae*, John Gray.

p162 **Oct 1** In the chapter house between 9 am and 12 noon. Present: Bathurst, Peirs, Holt, Selleck, Sheafe, and Fane; Harrison in attendance.

[Roll-call of vicars choral]. Present: Standish, Alderly, Beaumont, Moss, Davis, Edmonds, Clarke, Hobbs, Browne, Willis, and Willmott.

The chapter was adjourned to Oct. 3.

Oct 3 In the chapter house between 10 am and 12 noon. Present: Bathurst, Peirs, Holt, Selleck, Sheafe, and Fane; Harrison in attendance.

p163 Mr Anthony Walkely was admitted a vicar choral on probation for one year, with the stall of Combe IX and Mr Alderly as his *auscultor*.

The chapter was adjourned to the next morning.

Oct 4 Between 10 am and 12 noon, place not stated. Dr Holt and Dr Sheafe adjourned the chapter to the afternoon.

In the chapter house between 2 pm and 5 pm. Present: Bathurst, Holt, Selleck, Sheafe, and Fane; Harrison in attendance.

In all the manors of the dean and chapter, lives were to be nominated at the time grants of leases were made.

The chapter was adjourned to the next morning.

Oct 5 In the chapter house between 10 am and 12 noon. Present: Bathurst, Peirs, Holt, Selleck, Sheafe, and Fane; Harrison in attendance.

p164 The dean proposed and the chapter agreed to the presentation of Mr William Crofts, B.A., to the vicarage of Winscombe, vacant by the cession of Mr Stuckey; the deed of presentation was then sealed.

The chapter was adjourned to between 3 pm and 6 pm, and then by Holt and Sheafe to Oct. 6.

Oct 6 Between 10 am and 12 noon, place not stated. Bathurst, Peirs, Holt, Sheafe, and Fane adjourned the chapter to between 4 pm and 6 pm, and then to Oct. 7.

Oct 7 Between 10 am and 12 noon, place not stated. Bathurst, Peirs, Holt, Sheafe, and Fane adjourned the chapter to between 4 pm and 6 pm. when Peirs and Sheafe again adjourned it to Oct. 8.

p148 **Oct 8** Between 10 am and 12 noon, place not stated. Present: Bathurst, Peirs, Holt, Sheafe, and Fane; Harrison in attendance.

p149 The dean's caution was divided, the vicars choral receiving 10*l*. and the fabric 10*l*., and the remainder being distributed between seven canons residentiary (the dean excepted); the usual arrangement was made regarding the refunding of the caution money in the event of the dean's death before his entry upon residence.

The chapter was adjourned to between 4 pm and 6 pm. when the same residentiaries adjourned it to Oct. 10.

p164 **Oct 10** In the chapter house between 10 am and 12 noon. Present: Bathurst, Peirs, Holt, Sheafe, and Fane; Harrison in attendance.

Dr Fane's term of office as steward having come to an end, it was resolved that the heriots be divided, as formerly, between the whole chapter and computed with the other dividends.

The chapter was adjourned to the afternoon.

In the chapter house between 4 pm and 6 pm. Present: Bathurst, Peirs, Holt, Sheafe, and Fane.

It was resolved that Dr Fane and Mr Dowthwaite should receive 50*l.* paid by Reginald Dight, and that Mr Dight's lives be published.

The chapter was adjourned to Oct. 12.

p165 **Oct 12** Between 8 am and 12 noon, place not stated. Bathurst, Peirs, Holt, and Fane adjourned the chapter to between 4 pm and 6 pm, and then Bathurst, Peirs, and Holt (having Fane's vote) again adjourned it to Oct. 13.

Oct 13 In the chapter house between 10 am and 12 noon Bathurst, Peirs, and Holt adjourned the chapter to Oct. 14.

Oct 14 Between 10 am and 12 noon, place not stated. Bathurst, Peirs, and Holt adjourned the chapter to Oct. 15.

Oct 15 In the chapter house between 10 am and 12 noon Bathurst, Peirs, and Holt adjourned the chapter to Oct. 17.

Oct 17 In the chapter house between 10 am and 12 noon. Present: Bathurst, Peirs, Holt, and Sheafe; Harrison in attendance.

It was resolved that Dr Sheafe should receive for the fabric 10*l.* from the moneys reserved out of the dean's caution.

For his pains in examining the records of the dean and chapter and writing various extracts therefrom, Mr Nicholas Dowthwaite was given 8*l.*

p166 blank

p167 Since it is laid down in canon 44 that the canons of a cathedral church shall always divide between themselves the periods of residence for the whole year, so that their church is never wholly destitute at least of some residentiaries; and since in recent times the fullest ecclesiastical discipline has been neglected, so that all the canons have assembled for their residences together in the earlier months, while the rest of the year has been too much neglected; and since, finally, having completed their terms of residence (of whatever duration), they have taken entire and undiminished the profits and emoluments for the whole of the following year: We, in order that the authority of so laudable an ordinance may be vindicated and regard paid to the greater honour and advantage of this church for the future, do enact and decree:

1. That at the beginning of the year, that is, within the octave of the feast of St Michael, the dean and canons assembled in chapter shall so ordain and arrange their times of residence for the ensuing year that two at least of them shall keep residence continually during each quarter of the year.

2. That each canon, according to the precedence of the dignity which he holds in the cathedral, shall be free to designate in which quarter of the year he prefers to take his turn.

p168 3. Those canons to whom the duty of four months residence falls shall be free to devote the extra fourth month to the cathedral at any time of the year, either continuously or intermittently [*sive continue, sive interpolatim*].

4. Lest this statute should be detrimental to those to whom the later turns of residence fall, all stipends, dividends, revenues, and any other kinds of profit or emolument shall be due and paid, not only to those who have actually completed their residences in the first quarter of the year, but also to those who are prepared to do so, even though their turn has been postponed to the later months, so that they have not been able to complete their actual residences, or even to begin them.

5. Whenever the canons are in residence each of them, and particularly the dean, shall attend to the relief of the poor and to the provision of a more worthy hospitality; but above all they shall sedulously take care to see that public prayers are duly and canonically conducted, and are attended particularly by those chiefly concerned, that is, the vicars and choristers. Nor shall they themselves heedlessly be absent, but only if prevented by pressing business, or by some other critical, most urgent, or most serious cause.[1]

We have therefore allocated to each one of us the following quarters for the ensuing year:

To Dr Peirs and Dr Selleck—October, November, December.
To Dr Fane and Dr Sheafe—January, February, March.
To Dr Smythe and Dr Holt—April, May, June.
To the Dean and Dr Busby—July, August, September.

"Rad. Bathurst Dec.
Guil: Peirs: Archinus Taunton
Tho Holt Cancillarius
Gr. Sheafe Archi.D.Wel."

p169 [In the dean's handwriting] I, Ralph Bathurst, publicly testify, and desire it to be known to all present by the following reckoning [*computus*], that I have accepted five pounds paid by Dr Selleck the communar as nothing other than the quotidians due to me at the feast of St John Baptist last past by virtue of my deanery; I have already declared this in a statement which I handed to the communar privately.

"Rad. Bathurst. Dec."

p170 **Oct 19** In the chapter house between 3 pm and 5 pm. Present: Peirs, Holt, Sheafe, and prebendaries Creyghtone and Potenger; Harrison in attendance.

Edward Burgh, M.A., was installed by Dr Holt and Mr Creyghtone in the prebend or canonry of Wedmore V, vacant by the death of Thomas Potman.

p171 **Dec 15**[2] In the chapter house between 3 pm and 5 pm. Present: Peirs, Holt, Sheafe, Fane, and prebendaries Thirlby and Potenger; Harrison in attendance.

Gabriel Thistlethwaite, M.A., was installed by Dr Holt and Mr Thirlby in the prebend or canonry of Dultingcote or Thinghurst, vacant by the death of John Peirs.

[1] This act was approved and ratified by Charles II in a letter dated 10th May 1683: see *Cal.* ii. 449.

[2] There is no reference in the act book at this point to the business of the petition against Dr Selleck which had occupied the chapter on the morning of the 14th. See pp.xxvii and 104, and W.C.L., Documents, series III, box 4, 174.

1670-1

p172 **Jan 2** In the chapter house between 10 am and 12 noon. Present: Peirs, Holt, Sheafe, and Fane; Harrison in attendance.

[Roll-call of vicars choral; only the names are listed—there is no note of attendance or absence]. Alderly, Standish, Mosse, Beaumont, Davis, Edmonds, Clarke, Hobbs, Browne, Willis, Willmott, Walkely.

Mr Henry Duvall was admitted a vicar choral for one year on probation; he was assigned the stall of Wiveliscombe, and Mr Beaumont as *auscultor*.

The chapter was adjourned to the afternoon.

p173 Between 4 pm and 6 pm; place not stated. Present: Peirs, Holt, Sheafe, and Fane; Harrison in attendance.

The chapter stated that the bell hung in the small steeple was taken down because the steeple was unsafe, the irons holding the bell were rusty, and the bell itself was very much corroded by the copper rust adhering to it.[1]

The chapter was adjourned to Jan. 3, between 10 am and 12 noon.

Jan 3 Dr Holt adjourned the chapter to Jan. 4.

Jan 4 Between 10 am and 12 noon Peirs, Holt, Sheafe, and Fane adjourned the chapter to Jan. 5.

Jan 5 In the chapter house between 10 am and 12 noon. Present: Peirs, Holt, Sheafe, and Fane; Harrison in attendance.

p174 It was resolved and decreed that what remained of the copper from the bell belonging to the clock should be offered for sale, and that the money received should be expended in restoring the tower and meeting the cost of casting a new bell; any sum left over should be retained in the hands of the master of the fabric for the use of the cathedral.

The chapter was adjourned to Jan. 7.

[1] It appears from an entry for 5th January (see below) that the bell in question was the hour bell of the clock. The "small steeple", therefore, must have been the turret which once rose from the middle of the roof of the central tower, and not the north-east pinnacle where this bell is now hung. The turret is not shown on W. Hollar's drawing of the cathedral from the south, engraved by Daniel King and published in Dugdale's *Monasticon*, 1655 (?), but it appears in Ford's drawing, engraved by Toms, *temp*. Matthew Brailsford, dean 1713–34, and in William Simes's map of Wells, 1735. It also appears on John Carter's drawing of a cross-section of the central tower (BM Add.MS 29943, f.141) preparatory to his large and detailed drawings for the Society of Antiquaries. This sketch clearly shows the hour-bell and striker, and the elaborate wind-vanes on top of the turret, and probably belongs to the beginning of 1794. On the final drawing, however, completed before the end of that year (BM Add.MS 29932, f.64), the turret seems to have been erased, though its very faint outline can be detected—suggesting that it was removed sometime during 1794.
It is not clear what happened to the bell. On 24th May (see below) Dr Fane was asked to settle accounts with Mr Purdy the brassfounder, but this may refer to work done on 'Harewell', the great bell in the south-western tower. Another payment was made to Purdy on 3rd July 1672, and on 5th July 1672 arrangements were concluded for casting a bell (see below on those dates). Among later references there is a payment of 7*l*. 6*s*. to Edward Bilbie in the accounts of the master of the fabric 1706–7 for "new casting the little bell in the great middle tower" (*Cal*. ii. 489)—evidently the hour-bell, since the clock was repaired at the same time. On 15th May 1714 it was ordered that 'Harewell', cracked again, should be recast, and that "the bell used to a clock hanging in one of the pinnacles of the tower over the Church" should be melted down with 'Harewell' as "an addition to her mettle" (*Cal*. ii. 513). In 1725 a new bell was provided for the pinnacle (*Cal*. ii. 513), and it appears that the pinnacle itself was rebuilt about that time (*Cal*. ii. 515—extracts from the accounts of the master of the fabric for 1725–6).

Jan 7 In the chapter house between 9 am and 12 noon. Present: Peirs, Holt, Sheafe, and Fane, who adjourned the chapter to Jan. 9.

Jan 9 Between 10 am and 12 noon Peirs, Holt, Sheafe, and Fane adjourned the chapter to Jan. 10.

Jan 10 Sheafe and Fane adjourned the chapter to Jan. 11, between 2 pm and 5 pm.

Jan 11 Sheafe adjourned the chapter to Jan. 12, between 10 am and 12 noon.

Jan 12 Sheafe again adjourned the chapter to Jan. 13, between 10 am and 12 noon.

Jan 13 Peirs, Sheafe, and Fane adjourned the chapter to Jan. 14.

Jan 14 Between 10 am and 12 noon Peirs, Holt, Sheafe, and Fane adjourned the chapter to between 4 pm and 6 pm, when Peirs and Sheafe concluded it.

1671

p175 **April 1** In the chapter house between 10 am and 12 noon. Present: Peirs (proxy for Bathurst and Smythe), Holt (proxy for Busby), Sheafe, and Fane; Harrison in attendance.

[Roll-call of vicars choral]. Present: Standish, Moss, Beaumont, Davis, Edmonds, Hobbs, Browne, Willis, Willmott, Walkely, and Duvall. Absent, sick: Alderly and Clarke.

Dr Holt and Dr Fane exhibited a proxy from Dr Busby dated March 1 last.

p176 It was decreed that the supervisors of the houses should go to inspect the dilapidations of the choristers' house and inquire carefully who was competent to repair it, so that the roof might be put in order immediately, and the bishop might be fully satisfied.

The chapter was adjourned to April 3.

April 3 In the chapter house between 10 am and 12 noon. Present: Holt (proxy for Bathurst and Busby), and Sheafe, who adjourned the chapter to between 2 pm and 6 pm, when Peirs (proxy for Bathurst and Smith), Holt (proxy for Busby), Sheafe, and Fane adjourned it to the next morning.

April 4 In the chapter house between 10 am and 12 noon, Peirs, Holt, and Sheafe adjourned the chapter to between 2 pm and 6 pm, when Peirs (proxy for Bathurst and Smythe), Holt (proxy for Busby), Sheafe, and Fane adjourned it to the next morning.

April 5 In the chapter house between 9 am and 12 noon, Peirs (proxy for Bathurst and Smyth), Holt (proxy for Busby), Sheafe, and Fane adjourned the chapter to between 3 pm and 6 pm, when they adjourned it to the next morning.

April 6 In the chapter house between 8 am and 10 am, Peirs, Holt, Sheafe, and Fane adjourned the chapter to April 7.

p177 **April 7** In the chapter house between 9 am and 11 am. Present: Peirs (proxy for Bathurst and Smythe), Holt (proxy for Busby), Sheafe, and Fane; Harrison in attendance.

Mr Willis was to be cited to appear before the chapter between 4 pm and 6 pm.[1]

Mr Walkely's stall was changed from Combe IX to Combe XIII.

The chapter was adjourned to the afternoon.

In the chapter house between 4 pm and 6 pm. Present: Peirs, Holt, Sheafe, and Fane; Harrison in attendance.

An indenture was sealed, granting the rectory of St Cuthbert's, Wells, to Edward Bisse for his life and the lives of his wife Jane and his son George.[2]

The chapter was adjourned to the next morning.

April 8 In the chapter house between 8 am and 12 noon. Present: Peirs, Holt, Sheafe, and Fane; Harrison in attendance.

An indenture was sealed, granting a messuage at North Curry to Thomas Bower for his life and the lives of William and Anne his children.[3]

Another indenture was sealed, granting a tenement in East Wells to James Williams for forty years.[4]

p178 **May 24** In the chapter house between 5 pm and 7 pm. Present: Peirs (proxy for Bathurst and Smyth), Holt (proxy for Busby), Selleck, Sheafe, and Fane; Harrison in attendance.

A grant of the prebend of Wiveliscombe by Mr Thirlby to Ralph Stawell was confirmed.[5]

Dr Fane was asked to settle with Mr Purdy the brassfounder; if Dr Fane approved his bill, Dr Selleck would pay it.

p179 **July 1** In the chapter house between 8 am and 12 noon. Present: Peirs (proxy for Bathurst and Smythe), Holt (proxy for Busby), Selleck, Sheafe, and Fane; Harrison in attendance. The chapter was adjourned to between 4 pm and 6 pm, present as in the morning.

[Roll-call of vicars choral]. Present: Standish, Mosse, Beaumont, Edmonds, Clarke, Browne, Wilmott, Walkely, and Duvall. Absent: Alderly (sick) and Hobbs.

Dr Smythe was elected to the stewardship on condition that his deputy was appointed *ex ordine capituli*; otherwise the former steward would continue in office.

p180 The chapter was adjourned to July 3.

July 3 In the chapter house between 10 am and 12 noon, Peirs, Holt, Sheafe, and Fane adjourned the chapter to between 4 pm and 6 pm, when they again adjourned it to the next morning.

July 4 Between 10 am and 12 noon, Peirs, Holt, Sheafe, and Fane adjourned the chapter to the afternoon.

[1] There is no record of Thomas Willis's appearance at the time stated, nor of the reason for the summons, but from the omission of his name at the next roll-call of vicars choral on 1st July it may be inferred that he had been dismissed for some offence, such as insubordination.

[2] See W.C.L., Ledger G, 628. [3] See ibid. 624. [4] See ibid. 627.

[5] See ibid. 643 and the entry below for 2nd July 1672.

In the chapter house between 4 pm and 6 pm. Present: Peirs, Holt, Sheafe, and Fane; Harrison in attendance.

It was resolved that a letter of attorney should be drafted to enter again the estate of the widow Henborow of Knapp in Curry.

The chapter was adjourned to the next morning.

July 5 In the chapter house between 10 am and 12 noon. Present: Peirs, Holt, Sheafe, and Fane; Harrison in attendance.

Letters of attorney were sealed, addressed to John Gray, Henry Exon, Thomas Braily, and others.

p181 The chapter was adjourned to the next morning.

July 6 In the chapter house between 10 am and 12 noon, Peirs, Holt, Sheafe, and Fane adjourned the chapter to July 7.

July 7 In the chapter house between 10 am and 12 noon, Peirs (proxy for Bathurst and Smythe), Holt (proxy for Busby), Sheafe, and Fane concluded the chapter.

p182 **Sept 12** In the chapter house between 8 am and 11 am. Present: Bathurst, Peirs (proxy for Smythe), Holt (proxy for Busby), and Fane; Harrison in attendance.

Daniel Mew, M.A., admitted a vicar choral for one year on probation; he was assigned the stall of Yatton, and Mr Standish as *auscultor*.

p183 **Sept 30** In the chapter house, hour not stated. Present: Bathurst, Peirs, Holt, Sheafe, and Fane; Harrison in attendance.

[Officers for the ensuing year]: Baron of the exchequer, Dr Holt; Auditors, Dr Holt and Dr Sheafe; Communar, Dr Fane; Master of the fabric, Dr Sheafe; Overseers of the houses, Dr Holt and Dr Fane; Tabellar, Mr Beaumont; Escheator, the vicars nominated Messrs Clarke and Willmott and the chapter elected Mr Willmott; Bailiff of the grange and *cursor ecclesiae*, John Gray.

p184 **Oct 2** In the chapter house between 9 am and 12 noon. Present: Bathurst, Holt, and Sheafe; Harrison in attendance.

Mr Anthony Walkley was perpetuated.

The chapter was adjourned to the next morning.

p185 **Oct 3** In the chapter house between 10 am and 12 noon. Present: Bathurst, Peirs, Holt, Sheafe, and Fane. [Harrison's signature is omitted, but he was probably in attendance].

Residences for the ensuing year were settled as follows:

Dr Peirs and Dr Fane—October, November, December.

Dr Selleck and Dr Sheafe—January, February, March.

Dr Smith and Dr Holt—April, May, June.

The dean and Dr Busby—July, August, September.

It was ordered that a sum of 10*l*. expended by Dr Peirs in prosecuting the appeal against Mr Cross should be repaid.[1]

The best pulpit cloth and cushion were to be provided for doctors of divinity, chaplains to the king, and chaplains to the bishop—and for no one else.

The chapter was adjourned to the afternoon.

[1] See also the entry for 11th April 1672.

In the chapter house between 4 pm and 6 pm. Present: Bathurst, Peirs, Holt, Sheafe, and Fane; Harrison in attendance.

It was decreed that letters requisitory [*litteras requisitoriales*] and a writ of Significavit against George Crane [should be issued?]

The chapter was adjourned to the next morning.

Oct 4 In the chapter house between 10 am and 12 noon Bathurst, Peirs, Holt, Sheafe, and Fane adjourned the chapter to Oct 5.

p186 **Oct 5** In the chapter house between 10 am and 12 noon Bathurst, Peirs, Holt, Sheafe, and Fane adjourned the chapter to the afternoon.

In the chapter house between 3 pm and 5 pm. Present: Bathurst, Peirs, Holt, Sheafe, and Fane; in attendance [ ], chapter clerk.

An indenture was sealed, granting to David Harris the tenancy of a house and garden in Mill Lane, Wells, for forty years.

The chapter was adjourned to the next morning

Oct 6 In the chapter house between 10 am and 12 noon. Present: Bathurst, Peirs, Holt, Sheafe, and Fane; in attendance [ ], chapter clerk.

An official document (*instrumentum officiale*] directed to Dr Smith was sealed, and was handed to Dr Fane for the use of Dr Smith.

All prebendaries having corpses of land pertaining to their prebends who neglected their respective preaching turns in the cathedral would be fined 40*s*. for each turn so neglected, and the prebendaries of Combe and Wedmore[1] would be fined 30*s*. for each like offence.

Of the 40*s*. thus exacted, 20*s*. would be paid to the priest who on that occasion preached the Gospel, and the remainder would be applied for the use of the fabric; but if any turn were not supplied, the whole sum exacted would be used for that purpose.

Memorandum: Dr Peirs, on behalf and in the absence of Mr Charles Thirlby, vicar of St Cuthbert's, Wells, promised and pledged himself to the dean and chapter to pay the pension of 34*l*. 1*d*. due to them, and Mr Thirlby's arrears due to the choristers and to the executors of Dr Walker, lately canon residentiary of the cathedral, as the series of previous chapter acts more fully showed; since all this was transacted for Mr Thirlby by Dr Peirs, the latter was relieved of the obligation he had undertaken.

p187 Memorandum: Mr Thirlby attended for the purpose of paying immediately the whole pension of 34*l*. 1*d*. due to the dean and chapter from the vicarage of St Cuthbert's; but because of the great labour incurred by Mr Thirlby in discharging the care of this vicarage, the dean and chapter were pleased to receive from him only that part of the pension (i.e., 20*l*.) which they paid annually to the choristers, and the remaining 14*l*. 1*d*. would be refunded to him for this time only.

The chapter was adjourned to Oct. 9 between 10 am and 12 noon.

Oct 9 Bathurst, Peirs, and Fane assembled [here the entry breaks off, and a space is left—apparently for an insertion which was not made].

[1] These prebendaries (19 in all) shared the revenues derived from the two large prebends of Combe St Nicholas and Wedmore, but did not personally possess any lands therein.

It was also resolved that the chapter act[1] permitting the wives of Mr Clinton and Mr Neblett to sit in the second seat from the south entrance to the quire [*ab ostio Australi Colubri*] be annulled, and that hereafter the seat be free to all persons of quality.

Mr Willmott's stall was changed to that of Old Cleeve,[2] vacant by the death of Francis Standish.

The steward of the dean and chapter would inspect the rectory of the parish church of Cheddar and report upon its condition.

p188 The chapter was adjourned to between 4 pm and 6 pm, when Bathurst and Peirs again adjourned it to Oct. 10.

Oct 10 Between 3 pm and 5 pm Bathurst adjourned the chapter to Oct. 11.

Oct 11 Between 10 am and 12 noon Peirs adjourned the chapter to Oct. 12.

Oct 12 Between 10 am and 12 noon Bathurst and Peirs adjourned the chapter to Oct. 14.

Oct 14 In the chapter house between 10 am and 12 noon Bathurst adjourned the chapter to Oct. 16. [No meeting on that day is recorded].

p189 **Nov 25**[3] In the chapter house between 2 pm and 5 pm. Present: Fane and prebendaries Thirlby and Creyghton.

Daniel Mew, M.A., was installed by Messrs Thirlby and Creyghton in the prebend or canonry of Wedmore III, vacant by the death of Francis Standish.

1671-2

p190 **Jan 1** In the chapter house between 9 am and 12 noon. Present: Peirs (proxy for Bathurst and Smith), Holt (proxy for Busby), Selleck, Sheafe, and Fane; in attendance [ ]. The chapter was adjourned to Jan. 2.

Jan 2 In the chapter house between 9 am and 12 noon. Present: Peirs, Holt, Selleck, Sheafe, and Fane; in attendance [ ].

[Roll-call of vicars choral]. Present: Beaumont, Hobbs, Willmot, Walkley, Mew, and Duvall. Absent, sick: Aulderly, Mosse, Edmonds, Clarke, and Browne.

p191 Mr Beaumont was appointed *auscultor* to Mr Mew.

Mr Guy Clinton, registrar to the bishop, entered and brought from the bishop, with other documents, three letters relating to confirmation of the lease of Ashbury rectory, one from the king, another from Mr Cooke, and a third from Dr Mundy.[4] Mr Westley was holding these letters, and the bishop was to be given an answer to them on Thursday next [Jan. 4].

[1] See the entry above for 1st October 1668.

[2] The prebend of Cleeve was granted by bishop Savaric to the abbot of Bec, and was leased by the monks of Bec in 1199 to the abbot and monks of Cleeve. It was abolished at the dissolution of the monasteries, but revenue from Cleeve continued to provide stall wages for one vicar.

[3] The act book does not record the bishop's proceedings against Dr Peirs on 16th and 18th November; see W.C.L., Documents, series III, box 4, 177 (dup.178) and 179, and also p.xxviii.

[4] None of these letters seem to have survived. See W.C.L., Documents, series III, box 4, 172.

The chapter was adjourned to the audit room, where Peirs, Holt, and Fane further adjourned it to the audit room between 2 pm and 5 pm, when Peirs, Holt, Selleck, Sheafe, and Fane adjourned it to the next morning.

Jan 3 In the audit room between 9 am and 12 noon. Present: Peirs, Holt, Selleck, Sheafe, and Fane; Quirke in attendance.

In the presence of Messrs Mosse, Beaumont, Hobbs, Willmott, and Walkley, *p192* Mr Henry Duvall was perpetuated.

The chapter was adjourned to the afternoon.

In the audit room between 2 pm and 5 pm. Present: Peirs, Holt, Selleck, Sheafe, and Fane; in attendance [ ].

It was ordered that all tenants of the dean and chapter contracting with them in future for [leases of] lands must nominate their lives for the copies according to the contract; otherwise a penalty [*mulctam*] of 5*s*. for every pound of their fines [*mulctarum*] would be imposed on the respective Acceptavits.

The chapter was adjourned to the next morning.

Jan 4 In the audit room between 9 am and 12 noon. Present: Peirs, Holt, Selleck, Sheafe, and Fane.

An indenture in the name of Thomas Buncombe was sealed.

The chapter was adjourned to the afternoon between 3 pm and 6 pm in the audit room, when the same residentiaries adjourned it to the next morning.

p193 **Jan 5** In the audit room between 9 am and 12 noon the same residentiaries adjourned the chapter to the afternoon.

In the audit room between 2 pm and 6 pm. Present: Peirs, Holt, Selleck, Sheafe, and Fane.

An indenture was sealed, granting to John Saunders a messuage in Knappfee for his life and the lives of Elizabeth his wife and Elizabeth his daughter.

The chapter was adjourned to the following day, between 2 pm and 6 pm. [There is no record of a meeting then, but the rest of the page and the beginning of the next page are blank.]

p194 **Jan 8** In the audit room in the morning, hours not stated; Peirs, Holt, Selleck, Sheafe, and Fane adjourned the chapter to between 2 pm and 6 pm. when they again adjourned it to the next day.

Jan 9 In the audit room between 9 am and 12 noon Peirs and Sheafe adjourned the chapter to the audit room between 3 pm and 6 pm, when Peirs, Holt, Sheafe, and Fane again adjourned it to the following afternoon.

Jan 10 In the audit room between 3 pm and 6 pm Peirs (proxy for Bathurst and Smith), Holt, and Fane adjourned the chapter to the next morning.

Jan 11 In the audit room between 9 am and 12 noon; Peirs was present and adjourned the chapter to the afternoon.

p195 In the audit room between 2 pm and 6 pm. Present: Peirs (proxy for Bathurst and Smith), Holt, and Fane; in attendance [ ].

Dr Peirs exhibited a proxy from the dean.

The letters and other documents relating to the Ashbury lease,[1] lately received from the bishop by the hand of Mr Clinton, were returned with the following written reply:

"To the . . . Bishop of Bath and Wells.

Wee the Deane and Chapter of . . . Wells upon the first day of our Chapter received from your Lordship by Mr Guydo Clynton Pub. Notary and Deputy Register to your Lordship your . . . Comands concerning the Confirmation of Ashbury Lease. And in obedience thereunto wee held our selves in duty bound to reveiw the Reasons formerly presented to the late . . . Bishop . . . to stopp the confirmation thereof, and with our greatest care and diligence have examined the weight and force of the Answer to those Reasons,[2] and upon the whole matter do find That the said Reasons are not at all answered. For:

First, the Rectory of Ashbury is a Rectory with cure of souls and not a *Sine Cura*, as in the Answer is suggested; The Rector thereof being Instituted by the Bishop, and the Bishop in the Instrument of Institution doth commit to him *Curam et*

p196 *Regimen omnium Animarum Parochianorum*.

Secondly, supposing Ashbury to bee a *Sina* [*sic*] *Cura*, it doth not follow that it may bee Leased because wee know of no Sine Cure with Institution that ever was so, for Sine Cures are not demisable as Sine Cures.

Thirdly, although there is a Vicarage endowed at Ashbury, and that the Vicar hath also the Cure of Soules, yet that is no Argument that the Rector hath not, For there are some places where the Cure of Soules is committed both to Rector and Vicar, as at Blackwell in your Lordshipp's Diocesse, and also other places where the Cure is Committed to three persons, as at Tiverton in the Diocese of Exon, and at Bampton in the Diocess of Oxon; and the Vicar hath no where soley the Cure of Soules but where the Parsonage is either Impropriate or Appropriate. And wee think it a very great absurdity to say that there are Vicarages endowed where there are sine Cures, because every Vicarage hath a Cure of soules.

Fourthly, whereas it is sayd in the first paragraph of the said Answer, That the Vicarage of Ashbury is better endowed than many Parsonages, wee are credibly informed that the same is not *Communibus annis* worth forty pounds.

But the Answer to the seaventh Reason hath less weight in it; for one or two Presidents are not enough to prove the lawfullnesse and Conveniency for Clergy men to grant Leases of Rectories presentative. For one Clergy man may too little consider the interest of the Church and another may consider his owne too much,

p197 and Bishops may bee surprised and confirme such Leases when the case is not truely stated to them, as this of Ashbury—whatever hath beene of Wootton, which tis said is confirmed by the Patron Bishop and Diocesan: but that is but *gratis dictum*, and there needs other proofe besides the Answerers saying so. But sure the answerer hath not many Instances more, supposing this to bee true; for if hee had any other hee would never have brought in Wm Cheshire for one, who (hee sayes) granted a Lease to Queene Eliz: the 23rd of her Reigne, which was ten yeares after the first restrayning Statute—a very good Law and to the joy of all good Churchmen, the Revenue of the Church being thereby so far preserved, which would otherwise have been distroyed, as the Answerer well observes. And hee might as well have

[1] On the Ashbury lease, see pp.xxx ff.

[2] See 'An Answere to the Reasons offered to the late . . . Bishopp of Bath and Wells by the Deane and Chapter . . . against the Confirmacion of the lease of Ashbury parsonage', in W.C.L., Documents, series III, box 4, 172.

observed, That Mr Cheshire's Lease (if there were any for 99 years to Comence ten yeares after the date of it) was not for the preservacion of the Rights of the Church of Ashbury, nor did answer, but rather evade, the end of that statute. For although Mr Cheshire did grant it to the Crowne, yet it was never intended that the Crowne should have any benefitt by it, but that it should bee the better vested in Doctor Baily. Tis strange that a Clergyman should grant such a Lease for such an end, but not more strange then that it should bee drawne into a president. But suppose there was such a Lease granted, and that it was not to the detriment of the Church, then there is Nineteene yeares yet to come. If so, why so much adoe for another Lease? Why is the King troubled for his Letter and the Bishop for his Confirmacion?—

p198 for Church and Colledge Leases for the most part are but for one and twenty years. If there bee noe such Lease or that this bee not good, then it can bee noe president. Nor hath there beene any other at Ashbury these eighty yeares, and then the Reason doth not universally hold against all Church and Colledge Leases which have beene usually granted.

In the fifth Reason the Answerer thinks hee hath discovered a strange mistake, telling us that it is notorious That the Church hath from time to time lett long Leases for one hundred years, sometimes for two hundred and more, but doth not prove it by any one Instance, which certainly hee would have done if hee had either heard or found it in his Reading. Nor indeed was there any such of Demeasne or Tythes for any long terme before the Reigne of King Henry the 8th, there being no reason for it as there was afterwards. And the too great liberty thence taken occasioned the restrayning Statutes which required a reservacion of the antient Rent to the Church, that being surely now no good support for a Clergy man who is bound to Hospitality and Charity. For tis seldome knowne that the Clergy man makes more than one Fine (sometimes none) during his life, and that, too, so small that it doth not amount to the one halfe of what a lay man would make in the like case. And then there is no equality betweene the life of a Churchman and three Tenants' lives.

Wee shall not now looke into the designes against the Church which the Answerer suggests, but onely at present of this of Ashbury, which is as bad as the greatest enemies of the Church can contrive against it, and from whence any man may very well conclude the great benefitt the Church will have by such a defender as the

p199 Answerer or Lessor is, who looke upon Ashbury as a fatt morsell and therefore in prudence think it fitt to be swallow'd. And for the honour and dignity of the Rector would have two Chambers reserved by endorsement, wherein wee cannot but againe observe the Answerer's prudence, for two Roomes will bee enough to spend the remainder of thirty five pounds a year, when Tenths, Subsidies, and other rates and Taxes are discharged. And wee would faine know of the Answerer how the poore Parson shall live and have that good support hee speaks off, when hee payes first fruits which, as wee are informed, are thirty pounds besides charges.

And as the Deane and Chapter were not mistaken in their seaventh reason, so tis as evident that they are not in their third and fourth, as that the Answerer sayes nothing of weight or Argument against them, unless that the Presentacion of the Vicarage of Ashbury, the Chappell of Wycke, and the Parson's Wood are not to bee excepted in this Lease as they were in that made in the 29th Henry 8th, because the Farmers of this Rectory have beyond memory Presented every other turne to it. And because the Chappell of Wycke, for want of a better support than thirty pound a yeare, is utterly demolished, and because the Parson's Wood grubbd up and layd common, which wee conceive ought to have beene reserved in the last Lease made to the Crowne, if any such Lease as the Answerer sayes was made, otherwise wee suppose that pretended Lease cannot bee good.

p200 And if the Deane and Chapter are mistaken in the yearly value of the Parsonage of Ashbury, so are all the Countrey both Clergy and Laity that live in or about that place. And the Deane and Chapter in their fifth Reason onely affirme it to bee worth three hundred pounds per annum from the Comon report given them of it's value. Many other things may bee said against the Confirmacion of the Lease of Ashbury, but wee feare wee have been too large already and humbly conceive these bee a sufficient reply and Argument against the Confirmacion desired, which must necessarily prove so prejudiciall to your Lordshipp's Rights, and to the Rights of your Lordshipp's Successors . . . aswell as to the Rights of the Succeeding Rectors of Ashbury; yet saving alwayes to our selves libertie of giving your Lordshipp further satisfaction in this affaire when occasion shall require."

The chapter was adjourned to the following afternoon.

Jan 12 In the audit room between 2 pm and 6 pm. Present: Peirs (proxy for Bathurst and Smith), Holt, and Fane; in attendance [ ].

Licence was given to the dean, Dr Peirs, Dr Holt, Dr Selleck, Dr Sheafe, and Dr Fane, or any three of them, to hold a court in the almshouse in Wells.

An indenture was sealed, granting to Francis Standish for forty years a house and garden in the New Works.

p201 The presentation of Henry Batten, M.A., to the vicarage of Long Sutton was sealed.

The presentation of Mr Alderson to the vicarage of Winscombe was sealed.

The chapter was adjourned to the next afternoon.

Jan 13 In the audit room between 3 pm and 6 pm. Present: Peirs, Holt, Sheafe, and Fane; in attendance [ ]. The chapter was adjourned to Jan. 15.

Jan 15 In the audit room between 8 am and 12 noon. Present: Peirs, Holt, Sheafe, and Fane; in attendance [ ]. The chapter was concluded.

Feb 17 In the chapter house between 2 pm and 5 pm. Present: Peirs, Sheafe, and prebendaries Creyghton and Thirlby; Quirke in attendance.

p202 Edwin Sandys was installed by Messrs Creyghton and Thirlby in the prebend or canonry of Wedmore IV, vacant by the death of Robert Gale.

p203 **March 6** In the chapter house between 2 pm and 5 pm. Present: Holt, Sheafe, and prebendaries Creyghton, Thirlby, and Sandys; Quirke in attendance.

The Hon. William Fane, S.T.D., was installed by Dr Sheafe and Mr Creyghton in the prebend or canonry of Dinder, vacant by the death of Samuel Lanfire.

1672

p204 **March 30** In the chapter house between 2 pm and 5 pm. Present: Holt, Sheafe, Fane, and prebendaries Thirlby, Potenger, and Sandys; Quirk in attendance.

George Brush, M.A., was installed by Messrs Thirlby and Sandys in the prebend or canonry of Taunton, vacant by the cession of William Fane.

p205 **April 1** In the chapter house between 10 am and 12 noon. Present: Holt, Selleck, and Sheafe; Quirke in attendance.

[Roll-call of vicars choral]. Present: Alderley, Mosse, Beaumont, Edmonds, Hobbs, Browne, Walkley, Duvoll, and Mew. Absent: Clarke (sick), and Willmott.

p206 The chapter was adjourned to between 5 pm and 7 pm, when Holt, Selleck, Sheafe, and Fane again adjourned it to the next morning.

April 2 In the chapter house between 10 am and 12 noon. Present: Holt, Selleck, Sheafe, and Fane; Quirke in attendance. The chapter was adjourned to between 4 pm and 7 pm, when the same residentiaries again adjourned it to the next morning.

April 3 In the chapter house between 10 am and 12 noon. Present: Peirs, Holt, Selleck, Sheafe, and Fane; Quirke in attendance.

Memorandum: The nomination of a rector to the parish church of Allerton would be deferred to the next chapter on July 1; meanwhile all rents, fees, and fruits pertaining to the rectory would be sequestrated for the use of the next incumbent.

p207 Memorandum: Dr Holt had the nomination of a registrar to the registry of the dean and chapter by virtue of his right as chancellor, and proposed him to the dean and chapter.

The chapter was adjourned to the afternoon.

In the chapter house between 2 pm and 5 pm. Present: Holt, Selleck, and Fane; Quirke in attendance.

The presentation of John Ball, B.A., to the vicarage of Mudford was sealed.

The chapter was adjourned to the next morning.

April 4 In the chapter house between 10 am and 12 noon. Present: Peirs, Holt, Selleck, and Fane; Quirke in attendance.

The chapter was adjourned to the afternoon.

In the chapter house between 2 pm and 5 pm. Present: Peirs, Holt, Selleck, and Fane; Quirke in attendance.

An indenture was sealed, granting to Robert Thomas a house and garden in the New Works, Wells, for forty years.

p208 An indenture was also sealed, granting to Robert Thomas for forty years the house near the cross in Wells where he now dwells.

The chapter was adjourned to April 10.

April 10 In the chapter house between 10 am and 12 noon. Present: Holt, Selleck, and Fane, who adjourned the chapter to between 3 pm and 6 pm, and then to the next morning.

April 11 In the chapter house between 9 am and 12 noon. Present: Holt, Selleck, and Fane; Quirke in attendance.

Memorandum: The dean and chapter and Mr Cross, vicar of Chew Magna, have agreed together that Mr Cross will pay all the pensions due to the dean and chapter in the future from the vicarage of Chew Magna, and all the remaining moneys due for the last twelve years, the royal aid taxed in the same taxation excepted; also that the costs and expenses incurred in the suit concerning the said pensions would be referred to Dr Henry Deane and Dr Alexander Dyke for determination and

settlement. This agreement was made in the presence of William Westley, chapter clerk; Guy Clynton, notary public; and Robert Quirke, notary public.
The chapter was then concluded.

p209 **May 23** In the chapter house between 2 pm and 5 pm. Present: Peirs, Holt, Selleck, and prebendaries Thirlby, Creyghton, Mattock, and Mew; Quirke in attendance.
p210 Robert Collyer, M.A., was installed by Mr Creyghton and [ ] in the prebend or canonry of Compton Bishop, vacant by the death of Francis Atkins.

p211 **May 25** In the chapter house between 9 am and 11 am. Present: Holt, Selleck, and prebendary Creyghton; Quirke in attendance.
Anthony Prowse, B.A., was installed by Mr Creyghton and [ ] in the prebend or canonry of East Harptree, vacant by the cession of Robert Collyer.

p212 **July 1** In the chapter house between 10 am and 12 noon. Present: Bathurst, Holt, Sheafe, and Fane; Quirke in attendance.
[Roll-call of vicars choral]. Present: Alderly, Beaumont, Edmonds, Hobbs, Browne, Willmot, Walkley, Duvall, and Mew. Absent, sick: Mosse and Clarke.
p213 Samuel Wootson was admitted a vicar choral for one year on probation; he was assigned the stall of [ ] and Mr Edmonds as *auscultor*.
The chapter was adjourned to the afternoon.
In the chapter house between 3 pm and 6 pm. Present: Bathurst, Holt, Sheafe, and Fane; Quirke in attendance.
Dr Holt and Dr Fane exhibited a proxy from Dr Busby; this done, the chapter was full,[1] and Dr Holt was elected steward for the current year and that following.[2]
The chapter was adjourned to the next morning.[3]

July 2 In the chapter house between 9 am and 12 noon. Present: Bathurst, Holt, Selleck, Sheafe, and Fane; Quirke in attendance.
p214 The chapter confirmed the grant by Mr Thirlby to Ralph Stowell of the prebend of Wiveliscombe.
The chapter was adjourned to the next day.

July 3 In the chapter house between 10 am and 12 noon. Present: Bathurst, Holt, Selleck, Sheafe, and Fane; Quirke in attendance.
On the presentation of the chancellor, Dr Holt, Robert Quirke, notary public, was admitted deputy chapter clerk during the life of William Westley, chapter clerk.
p215 The chapter was adjourned to the afternoon.
In the chapter house between 3 pm and 6 pm. Present: Bathurst, Holt, Selleck, Sheafe, and Fane, who adjourned the chapter to between 4 pm and 6 pm, when they met again.
It was decreed that nothing of moment concerning the dean and chapter should be done or made without an act of the chapter passed in the chapter house.

[1] *Plenum fuit capitulum*—this may mean that a quorum was present; Drs Smith, Peirs, and Selleck were absent and had not appointed proxies.

[2] This act was rescinded on 9th July, see below.

[3] Correctly dated 2nd July (a Tuesday), but described in error as *dies Mercurii* (Wednesday).

Dr Selleck was asked to pay to Mr Purdy the brassfounder a sum of 5*l.* which he was holding for that purpose.[1]

The chapter was adjourned to July 5.[2]

p216 **July 5** In the chapter house between 9 am and 12 noon. Present: Bathurst, Holt, Selleck, Sheafe, and Fane.

When the mould and furnace for the bell were finished and completed by the brassfounder, James Williams, sacrist, would have the bell despatched and weighed, and would go to the foundry.[1]

The chapter was adjourned and continued to July 8.

July 8 In the chapter house between 9 am and 12 noon. Present: Bathurst, Peirs, Holt, Selleck, Sheafe, and Fane; Quirke in attendance.

p217 Gabriel Greene was admitted a vicar choral on probation for one year; he was assigned the stall of [ ] and Mr Duvoll as *auscultor.*

The matters at issue between the dean and chapter and the vicars choral of the cathedral and the New Close concerning the fines from the escheatory land would be defined, set forth, and at an early date laid before counsel on both sides, in order to avoid a lawsuit.[3]

The chapter was adjourned and continued to the afternoon.

In the chapter house between 4 pm and 6 pm. Present: Bathurst, Peirs, Holt, Selleck, Sheafe, and Fane.

p218 Memorandum: Dr Sheafe had assigned and donated to the dean the rectory of Allerton or Allverton, the gift of which had fallen to him by lot.

A certain building below or next to the house of Mr Marsh,[4] belonging to the cathedral, was granted to Mr Frycker for the purpose of melting lead.

The chapter was adjourned to the next morning.

July 9 In the chapter house between 9 am and 12 noon Bathurst, Peirs, Holt, Selleck, Sheafe, and Fane adjourned and continued the chapter to the afternoon.

In the chapter house between 4 pm and 6 pm. Present: Bathurst, Holt, Peirs, Selleck, Sheafe, and Fane; Quirke in attendance.

The act of July 1 electing Dr Holt as steward was rescinded, and Dr Peirs was elected in his place for the current year and for 1673.

The chapter was adjourned to the next morning.

July 10 In the chapter house between 10 am and 12 noon. Present: Bathurst, Peirs, Holt, Selleck, Sheafe, and Fane; Quirke in attendance.

[1] See note 1, p.28.

[2] Described correctly as *dies Veneris* (Friday), but incorrectly as the next (*crastinus*) day.

[3] See pp.xxxii ff.

[4] On 4th January 1661 Humphrey Marsh, sexton, purchased "at a Deare rate" the remainder of a 40 years lease to Augustine Benford, vicar choral, of a house with a plot of ground adjoining, and was granted a new lease for the same period (W.C.L., Bargain Book 1, 20a). This house lay to the north-east of the undercroft or treasury of the cathedral and, with its ground, was situated between the undercroft and the canonical house in the bishop's gift, and until recently the residence of the Principal of the Theological College. Benford obtained the house and land from John Atwell and a lease was granted to him on 20th March 1634 (W.C.L., Ledger G, 213 and *Cal.* ii. 406. The descriptions of the location in these documents is far from clear, but they indicate that a casting house lay on the south side of the property. William Simes's map of 1735, John Carter's map of 1794, and W. Byrne's engraving of T. Hearne's illustration of the Lady chapel viewed from the wells (1802), all show a house in the place stated, but it seems to have been demolished soon after 1802.

p219 Dr Sheafe nominated Dr Bathurst for presentation to the rectory of Allerton or Allverton, vacant by the death of Matthew Laws, and the chapter confirmed the presentation under seal.[1]

Memorandum: "That the said Worshipful Deane did first take the Oathes of Allegiance and Supremicy, And did Subscribe to the three Articles, which Subscription was Subscribed and Oathes of Allegience and Supremacy taken *die predicto*."

Guy Clynton, notary public, was appointed to the office of registrar to the dean and chapter for its peculiar jurisdictions—North Curry, Stoke St Gregory, West Hatch, Cheddar, Long Sutton, Bishop's Lydiard, Combe St Nicholas, Winsham, Lovington, and South Barrow.

p220 The chapter was adjourned and continued to between 1 pm and 4 pm, in the chapter house, when Bathurst, Peirs, Holt, Selleck, and Fane again adjourned and continued it to the next morning.

July 11 In the chapter house between 9 am and 12 noon Bathurst, Peirs, Holt, Selleck, and Fane adjourned and continued the chapter to July 18.

July 18 In the chapter house between 3 pm and 6 pm Bathurst, Holt, Selleck, and Sheafe adjourned the chapter to the next morning.

July 19 In the chapter house between 9 am and 12 noon. Present: Bathurst, Peirs, Holt, Selleck, and Sheafe; Quirke in attendance.

The decree of July 4, 1670, that no act of the chapter might be rescinded, save by the authority of persons equal in number to those who had passed it, was abrogated and excised.

p221 The chapter was adjourned to the afternoon.

In the chapter house between 2 pm and 6 pm. Present: Bathurst, Peirs, Holt, Selleck, and Sheafe; Quirke in attendance.

An indenture was sealed, granting the rectory of Bishop's Lydiard to John, Earl of Rochester, for his life and those of his wife Elizabeth and his son Lord Charles Willmott.[2]

The chapter was adjourned to the next morning.

July 20 In the chapter house between 9 am and 12 noon. Present: Bathurst, Peirs, Holt, Selleck, and Sheafe; Quirke in attendance.

The chapter discussed and sealed leases to Francis Paulet of the rectory of Pucklechurch,[3] and of his house in Mount Roy Lane or College Lane within the Liberties of St Andrew.[4]

The three-monthly terms [of residence] for the ensuing year were to be arranged as in the year now ending.

The chapter was concluded.

p222 **Aug 20** In the chapter house between 9 am and 11 am. Present: Bathurst, Holt, and prebendaries Thirlby and Mew; Quirke in attendance.

[1] See W.C.L., Ledger G, 647.

[2] For the surrender of the previous lease, see W.C.L., Ledger G, 663.

[3] See W.C.L., Ledger, 653. [4] See ibid. 655, and for the house, note 3, p.19

Joseph Shallett was admitted a vicar choral on probation for one year; he was assigned the stall of [ ] and Mr Edmonds as *auscultor*.

p223 **Sept 20** In the chapter house between 4 pm and 6 pm. Present: Bathurst, Peirs, Holt, Sheafe, and Fane; Quirke in attendance.

Mr Daniel Mew, vicar choral, was perpetuated.

p224 **Sept 30** In the chapter house between 9 am and 12 noon. Present: Bathurst, Peirs, Holt, Sheafe, and Fane; Quirke in attendance.

All the vicars choral attended, except Messrs Mew, Green, and Shallet.

[Officers for the ensuing year]: Baron of the exchequer, Dr Selleck; Auditors, Dr Holt and Dr Sheafe; Communar, Dr Fane; Master of the fabric, Dr Sheafe; Overseers of the houses, Dr Peirs and Dr Selleck; Tabellar, Mr Duvall; Escheator, the vicars nominated Messrs Moss and Beaumont and the chapter elected Mr Beaumont; Bailiff of the grange and *cursor ecclesiae*, John Gray.

p225 The master of the fabric would requisition and receive from the communar the moneys which he needed for expenditure on the cathedral.

Mr Daniel Mew's perpetuation was confirmed.

Oct 1 In the chapter house between 9 am and 12 noon. Present: Bathurst, Holt, and Fane; Quirke in attendance.

[The names of the vicars choral are listed without indication of attendance or absence, and it is not clear whether the roll-call was made on this occasion or on the previous morning.]

The chapter was adjourned to the next day.

p226 **Oct 2** In the chapter house between 9 am and 12 noon. Present: Bathurst, Peirs, Holt, Sheafe, and Fane; Quirke in attendance.

The communar was instructed to contribute in the name of the dean and chapter the sum of 40*s*. for the use of certain Londoners who had lost their homes in the fire.

The chapter was adjourned to between 4 pm and 6 pm, when Bathurst, Peirs, Holt, Sheafe, and Fane again adjourned it to the next morning.

Oct 3 In the chapter house between 9 am and 12 noon Bathurst, Peirs, Holt, Selleck, and Sheafe continued and adjourned the chapter to the afternoon.

Between 4 pm and 6 pm; place not stated. Present: Bathurst, Peirs, Holt, Selleck, Sheafe, and Fane; Quirke in attendance.

At the next court all tenants must state the names of their lives if these had not previously been named, or the steward must give an assurance upon this point to the dean and chapter.

p227 The chapter was continued and adjourned to the next morning.

Oct 4 In the chapter house between 10 am and 12 noon the chapter was continued and adjourned *per eosdem venerabiles et Honorabilem virum Guilielmum Fane* to the afternoon.

Then an indenture in the name of Mrs Morgan was confirmed.

In the chapter house between 4 pm and 6 pm *per eosdem venerabiles* the chapter was adjourned to the next morning.

Oct 5 In the chapter house between 10 am and 12 noon, *coram venerabilibus viris predictis*, Quirke in attendance, the chapter was adjourned and continued to Oct 7.

Oct 7 In the chapter house between 10 am and 12 noon. Present: Bathurst, Peirs, Holt, Selleck, and Fane; Guy Clynton jnr in attendance. The chapter was continued and adjourned to the next morning.

Oct 8 In the chapter house between 10 am and 12 noon. Present: Bathurst, Peirs, Holt, Selleck, and Fane; Guy Clynton in attendance. The chapter was continued and *p228* adjourned to between 4 pm and 6 pm, when the same members again continued and adjourned it to the next morning.

Oct 9 In the chapter house between 10 am and 12 noon. Present: Bathurst, Peirs, Holt, Selleck, and Fane; Guy Clynton jnr in attendance. The chapter was continued and adjourned to between 4 pm and 6 pm, when Bathurst, Peirs, Holt, and Selleck, with Guy Clynton in attendance, again continued and adjourned it to the next morning.

Oct 10 In the chapter house between 10 am and 11 am. Present: Bathurst, Piers, Holt, Selleck, and Fane; Guy Clynton jnr in attendance. The chapter was continued and adjourned to between 4 pm and 6 pm, when Bathurst and Holt, with Quirke in attendance, again continued and adjourned the chapter to the next morning.

p229 **Oct 11** In the chapter house between 10 am and 12 noon. Present: Bathurst, Holt, Selleck, Sheafe, and Fane; Quirk in attendance. The chapter was continued and adjourned to the next day.

Oct 12 In the chapter house between 10 am and 12 noon. Present: Bathurst, Peirs, Holt, Selleck, Sheafe, and Fane; Quirke in attendance.

An indenture was sealed, granting to Mr Bampfield the lease of his house in Mount Roy Lane.[1]

The chapter was adjourned and continued to the afternoon.

In the chapter house between 4 pm and 6 pm. Present: Bathurst, Holt, Selleck, Sheafe, and Fane; Quirke in attendance.

The stall of Compton Bishop was assigned to Mr Woodson, and the stall of Yatton to Mr Shallet.

The chapter was continued and adjourned to Oct. 14.

p230 **Oct 14** In the chapter house between 10 am and 12 noon. Present: Bathurst, Peirs, Holt, Selleck, Sheafe, and Fane, who continued and adjourned the chapter to the afternoon, when they met between 4 pm and 6 pm.

An indenture was sealed, granting the rectory of Cheddar to Mr Dodington.[2]

The chapter was adjourned and continued to Oct. 16.

Oct 16 Between 9 am and 12 noon. [No record of place or attendance].

On the last day of his annual audit, the auditor was to draw up and write out plainly and fairly on parchment the accounts of the reeves [*prepositi*] and bailiffs of the dean and chapter, and also his own accounts and those of the communar.

[1] See W.C.L., Ledger G, 664; the house is the one now numbered 25, The Liberty.

[2] See W.C.L., Ledger G, 675 and 676.

The steward should not publish any copies of court rolls before they had been shown to, and approved by, the dean and chapter, in accordance with his agreement and pursuant to the ancient custom obtaining in this matter.

At the end of every chapter, the chapter clerk or his deputy should produce in the chapter house all the acts made by that chapter, in order that the chapter might approve them before they were written up in the register.

p231 Mr Duvall, to whom had been committed by order of the dean and chapter the care and instruction of three choristers, would receive from the communar *6l.* for his pains.

The chapter was adjourned and continued to Oct. 21.

Oct 21 In the chapter house between 10 am and 12 noon. Present: Bathurst, Peirs, Holt, Selleck, Sheafe, and Fane; Quirke in attendance.

The wives and daughters of both the gentry and the clergy dwelling within the Liberties of the cathedral may be allowed to occupy the stalls and seats which are usually assigned to persons of their rank; but to others outside [the Liberties] this privilege is denied. Nevertheless, as often as it shall be in their minds to attend common prayer in the cathedral they are to be treated according to their rank with the courtesy that imparts greater lustre to the Christian religion.

The chapter was adjourned and continued to Oct. 24.

Oct 24 In the chapter house between 10 am and 12 noon Holt, Selleck, and Sheafe adjourned the chapter to the next day.

Oct 25 In the chapter house between 10 am and 12 noon Peirs, Holt, Selleck, and Sheafe adjourned the chapter to between 4 pm and 6 pm, when Peirs, Holt, Selleck, *p232* Sheafe, and Fane again adjourned it to the next morning.

Oct 26 In the chapter house between 10 am and 12 noon. Present: Peirs, Holt, Selleck, Sheafe, and Fane; Quirke in attendance.

Memorandum: Mr Dowthwaight was to send forthwith to all reeves threatening letters [*Litteras minarum plenas*], requiring them to bring in their returns and make statements of their accounts.

The chapter was adjourned to Oct. 28.

Oct 28 In the chapter house between 9 am and 12 noon Peirs, Holt, Selleck, and Fane adjourned the chapter to Oct. 30.

Oct 30 In the chapter house between 10 am and 12 noon Peirs, Holt, Selleck, and Sheafe adjourned the chapter to Nov. 4.

p233 **Nov 4** In the chapter house between 10 am and 12 noon Peirs, Holt, Selleck, and Sheafe adjourned the chapter to the afternoon.

In the chapter house between 4 pm and 6 pm. Present: Peirs, Holt, Selleck, and Sheafe.

The stall of St Decumans was assigned to Mr Green.

The chapter was adjourned to Nov. 6.

Nov 6 In the chapter house between 9 am and 12 noon Peirs, Holt, Selleck, and Sheafe adjourned the chapter to the afternoon.

In the chapter house between 3 pm and 5 pm. Present: Peirs, Holt, Selleck, Sheafe, Fane, and prebendary Creyghton; Quirke in attendance.

p234 Abraham Allen, S.T.P., was installed by Dr Holt and Mr Creyghton in the prebend or canonry of Combe XIII,[1] vacant by the death of Edward Hitchman.

The chapter was concluded.

p235 **Dec 12** In the chapter house between 8 am and 12 noon. Present: Peirs, Holt, Selleck, Sheafe, and prebendary Sandys; Quirke in attendance.

p236–p237 A mandate[2] was received for the election of a bishop to the vacant see of Bath and Wells, and Dec. 19 between 9 am and 12 noon was appointed for this purpose.

p238 **Dec 19** In the chapter house between 9 am and 12 noon. Present: Peirs, Holt, Selleck, Sheafe, and prebendaries Thirlby, Creyghton, Sandys, and Potenger; Quirke in attendance.

p239 Peter Mew, LL.D., dean of Rochester and vice-chancellor of the university of Oxford was elected bishop of Bath and Wells.[3]

1672-3

p240 **Jan 1** In the chapter house between 10 am and 12 noon Holt, Selleck, and Sheafe, with Quirke in attendance, met and adjourned the chapter to Jan. 2.

Jan 2 In the chapter house between 10 am and 12 noon Holt, Selleck, and Sheafe adjourned and continued the chapter to Jan. 3.

Jan 3 In the chapter house between 10 am and 12 noon Holt, Selleck, and Sheafe adjourned and continued the chapter to between 4 pm and 6 pm, when they again *p241* adjourned and continued it to the next morning.

Jan 4 In the chapter house between 10 am and 12 noon. Present: Holt, Selleck, and Sheafe; Quirke in attendance.

James Gilbert was appointed bailiff of the Liberty and *cursor ecclesiae*, and swore to discharge his office faithfully and diligently.

The chapter was adjourned and continued to between 4 pm and 6 pm, when Holt, Selleck, Sheafe, and Fane adjourned and continued it to Jan. 7.

Jan 7 In the chapter house between 10 am and 12 noon Holt, Selleck, and Sheafe adjourned and continued the chapter to Jan. 8.

p242 **Jan 8** In the chapter house between 10 am and 12 noon Holt, Selleck, and Sheafe adjourned the chapter to between 4 pm and 6 pm, when Holt, Selleck, Sheafe, and Fane again adjourned and continued it to the next morning.

[1] This act contains two scribe's errors: in the heading the prebend is shown as "Comba 14ª" (there is a marginal correction, "Combe 13"), and in the act itself the prebend is shown as "Comba 4ª".

[2] For the nomination of Dr Mews to the chapter on 25th November 1672 see W.C.L., Documents, series III, box 4, 180.

[3] Dr Bathurst, considering his consent to be more important than his presence, had already written to signify his full concurrence: W.C.L., Documents, series III, box 4, 181.

Jan 9 In the chapter house between 10 am and 12 noon Holt, Selleck, Sheafe, and Fane adjourned and continued the chapter to the next morning.

Jan 10 In the chapter house between 10 am and 12 noon Holt and Sheafe adjourned and continued the chapter to the next morning.

Jan 11 In the chapter house between 10 am and 12 noon Holt and Sheafe adjourned and continued the chapter to Jan. 13.

Jan 13 In the chapter house between 10 am and 12 noon. Present: Peirs, Holt, Selleck, and Sheafe; Quirke in attendance.

p243 Two indentures[1] in the name of Francis, Lord Hawley, were sealed.

The chapter was adjourned and continued to the next morning.

Jan 14 In the chapter house between 10 am and 12 noon Peirs adjourned and continued the chapter to between 4 pm and 6 pm, when Selleck and Sheafe again adjourned and continued it to the next morning.

Jan 15 In the chapter house between 10 am and 12 noon Peirs adjourned and continued the chapter to between 4 pm and 6 pm, when Peirs, Selleck, and Sheafe again adjourned and continued it to the next morning.

p244 **Jan 16** In the chapter house between 10 am and 12 noon Peirs, Selleck, and Sheafe adjourned and continued the chapter to the next morning.

Jan 17 In the chapter house between 10 am and 12 noon Peirs and Sheafe adjourned and continued the chapter to between 4 pm and 6 pm, when Peirs, Holt, Selleck, and Sheafe again adjourned and continued it to the next morning.

Jan 18 In the chapter house between 10 am and 12 noon Peirs, Holt, and Sheafe adjourned and continued the chapter to the afternoon.

In the chapter house between 4 pm and 6 pm. Present: Peirs, Holt, Selleck, and Sheafe; Quirke in attendance.

p245 An assignment [*deputatio*] was sealed for holding courts at the old almshouse in Wells.

The chapter was adjourned to Jan. 20.

Jan 20 In the chapter house between 10 am and 12 noon, Holt and Sheafe adjourned and continued the chapter to between 4 pm and 6 pm, when Peirs, Holt, Selleck, and Sheafe again adjourned it to the next morning.

Jan 21 In the chapter house between 10 am and 12 noon. Present: Peirs, Holt, Selleck, and Sheafe; Quirke in attendance.

p246 Since Dr Busby made it clear, by a letter under his own hand and seal, that he had given 100*l*. for the restoration of our common library, and that this sum was coming from him into the funds of the cathedral this year, we desire and decree that a like sum be paid by the communar to Dr Sheafe, who has requisitioned and urgently

[1] See W.C.L., Ledger G, 679: grant of fishing, fowling, and hunting rights in the hundred of North Curry; and ibid. 681: grant of Ham Mills on the river Tone, near North Curry.

asked for it, having expended on the library not less than this amount from his own resources as master of the fabric.

The sum of 43*s*. which Robert Quirke had paid to the dean and chapter was to be refunded by the communar.

The chapter was adjourned and continued to the next morning.

Jan 22 In the chapter house between 10 am and 12 noon. Present: Peirs, Holt, Selleck, and Sheafe; Quirke in attendance.

p247 Dr Peirs, Dr Selleck, and Dr Sheafe each declared that he had now completed his residence according to the charter of the cathedral for the year beginning on Oct. 1 last.

Dr Holt declared that he had completed one hundred days towards his residence in the year beginning on Oct. 1 last.

p248–p251 **Feb 28** In the cathedral between 9 am and 12 noon. Present: Peirs and Holt (with proxies for Bathurst, Busby, and Smith), and prebendaries Creyghton, Thirlby, Potenger, Sandys, and Mattock; Quirke in attendance.

Peter Mew, represented by his proxy Dr Holt, was enthroned in the quire as bishop of Bath and Wells, and after morning prayer was also assigned and installed in the place in the chapter customarily allotted to the bishop.

1673

p252 **April 1** In the chapter house between 9 am and 12 noon. Present: Peirs, Selleck, and Sheafe; Quirke in attendance. The chapter was adjourned and continued to the next morning.

April 2 In the chapter house between 10 am and 12 noon Peirs, Holt, Selleck, and Sheafe adjourned and continued the chapter to the next morning.

p253 **April 3** In the chapter house between 10 am and 12 noon Holt, Selleck, and Sheafe adjourned and continued the chapter to the next morning.

April 4 In the chapter house between 9 am and 12 noon. Present: Peirs, Holt, Selleck, and Sheafe; Quirke in attendance.

An indenture in the name of Thomas Smith of West Hatch was sealed. The chapter was adjourned and continued to the next morning.[1]

April 5 In the chapter house between 10 am and 12 noon Holt and Sheafe adjourned and continued the chapter to April 7.

April 7 In the chapter house between 10 am and 12 noon. Present: Peirs, Holt, Selleck, Sheafe, and Fane; Quirke in attendance.

p254 Dr Holt declared that he had completed his residence according to the charter of the cathedral for the year beginning on Oct. 1 last.

The chapter was adjourned and continued to the next morning.

[1] This is stated in error to be the morning *crastini diei diei Veneris* (Friday); 5th April was a Saturday.

April 8 In the chapter house between 10 am and 12 noon Peirs, Holt, Selleck, Sheafe, and Fane adjourned and continued the chapter to the next morning.

April 9 In the chapter house between 10 am and 12 noon. Present: Peirs, Holt, Selleck, Sheafe, and Fane; Quirke in attendance.

An indenture was sealed in the name of Timothy Rivet of the parish of St Cuthbert's, Wells.

The chapter was concluded.

p255 **May 7** In the chapter house between 10 am and 12 noon. Present: Holt, Selleck, and Sheafe; Quirke in attendance.

A document was sealed for holding a court at Bubwith's almshouse.

May 13 In the chapter house between 10 am and 12 noon. Present: Peirs, Holt, Selleck, and Sheafe; Quirke in attendance.

Joshua Lasher was admitted a vicar choral for one year on probation; he was assigned the stall of [ ] and Mr Mew as *auscultor*.

p256 **July 1** In the chapter house between 9 am and 12 noon. Present: Peirs, Holt, Sheafe, and Fane; Quirke in attendance.

p257 Mr Samuel Woodson was perpetuated.

The stall of Warminster or Luxville was assigned to Mr Lasher.

The chapter was adjourned and continued to between 3 pm and 5 pm, when Peirs, Holt, and Sheafe again adjourned and continued it to the next morning.

p258 **July 2** In the chapter house between 9 am and 12 noon Peirs, Holt, Sheafe, and Fane adjourned and continued the chapter to between 3 pm and 4 pm, when Peirs and Sheafe again adjourned and continued it to the next morning.

July 3 In the chapter house between 9 am and 12 noon Peirs, Holt, Sheafe, and Fane adjourned and continued the chapter to between 3 pm and 5 pm, when they again adjourned and continued it to the next morning.

July 4 In the chapter house between 10 am and 12 noon. Present: Peirs, Holt, Sheafe, and Fane. [Space left, but no record of anyone in attendance].

It was decreed that Thomas Comer and his wife Mary should immediately be taken to court about the felling of trees at Winscombe.

p259 The chapter was adjourned and continued to between 3 pm and 6 pm, when Piers, Holt, Sheafe, and Fane again adjourned and continued it to the next morning.

July 5 In the chapter house between 9 am and 12 noon Peirs, Holt, Sheafe, and Fane adjourned and continued the chapter to July 7.

July 7 In the chapter house between 9 am and 12 noon. Present: Peirs, Holt, Sheafe, and Fane; Quirke in attendance.

Memorandum: Mr [ ] Stacy appeared and in answer to questioning stated "That he, when he contracted with the Vicars Chorall . . . for their Phisick Garden, was to pay 2 shillings per annum to the Deane and Chapter . . . if demanded."

The chapter was adjourned and continued to between 3 pm and 6 pm, when the same residentiaries again adjourned and continued it to the next morning.

p260

July 8 In the chapter house between 9 am and 12 noon. Present: Peirs, Holt, Sheafe, and Fane; Quirke in attendance.

Gabriel Greene, vicar choral, was perpetuated.

An indenture in the name of Thomas Rush was sealed.

p261 The chapter was adjourned and continued to the next morning.

July 9 In the chapter house between 9 am and 12 noon. Present: Peirs, Holt, Sheafe, and Fane.

Memorandum: "The Deane and Chapter agreed with Mr Tanton to mend the Organs and make a Cornet Stopp in them, all to be done before the Feast of St Michaell next for Twenty pounds to be paid at the next Audite."

The chapter was adjourned to the afternoon.

In the chapter house between 3 pm and 6 pm. Present: Peirs, Holt, Sheafe, and Fane.

It was decreed that Dr Fane should pay one part of the choristers' money, due to Mr Duvall, but the other part to Mr Browne if he would accept it; otherwise he was to retain the money in his own hands to the end of the next chapter.

The dean's stall wages were to be paid to Mr Mew from the time they were not paid to the fabric.

p262 Mr Lasher would receive the stall wages of Warminster or Luxville from Mr Potenger at the feast of St John Baptist.

The chapter was concluded.

Aug 18 In the chapter house between 4 pm and 6 pm. Present: Bathurst, Fane, and prebendary Creyghton; Quirke in attendance.

Joseph Shallett, vicar choral, was perpetuated.

p263 **Sept 30**[1] In the chapter house between 10 am and 12 noon. Present: Holt and Sheafe; Guy Clynton jnr in attendance.

All the vicars choral appeared, except Messrs Mew and Woodson.

[Officers for the ensuing year]: Baron of the exchequer, Dr Holt; Auditors, Dr Selleck and Dr Fane; Communar, Dr Sheafe; Master of the fabric, Dr Sheafe; Overseers of the houses, Dr Peirs and Dr Holt; Tabellar, Mr Greene; Escheator, Mr Walkley; Bailiff of the grange and *cursor ecclesiae*, James Gilbert.

p264 **Oct 1**[2] In the chapter house between 9 am and 11 am. Present: Holt and Sheafe; Guy Clynton jnr in attendance. The chapter was adjourned and continued to the next morning.

Oct 2 In the chapter house between 10 am and 12 noon Peirs, Holt, and Sheafe, with Quirke in attendance, adjourned and continued the chapter to between 4 pm and 6 pm, when they again continued and adjourned it to the next morning.

[1] No reference is made in the act book to bishop Mews's primary visitation of the dean and chapter held in the chapter house on 6th September 1673. For the orders and injunctions then exhibited, see p.xli.

[2] A paper bearing this date and entitled 'A full answer to the desires of the Deane left with Dr Peirs to be communicated to the chapter' (W.C.L., Documents, series III, box 4, 184), refers to business transacted at this quarterly chapter; see p.xliii.

Oct 3 In the chapter house between 10 am and 12 noon Peirs and Holt continued the chapter to the next morning.

p265 **Oct 4** In the chapter house between 10 am and 12 noon Peirs and Holt adjourned and continued the chapter to Oct. 6.

Oct 6 In the chapter house between 10 am and 12 noon. Present: Peirs, Holt, Sheafe, and Fane; Quirke in attendance.

An indenture was sealed in respect of John Prickman's house in the New Works—the fifth, numbering from the east.

Letters patent were confirmed, appointing Guy Clynton to the office of registrar to the dean.

The chapter was adjourned and continued to between 4 pm and 6 pm, when Piers, Holt, Sheafe, and Fane again adjourned and continued it to the next morning.

Oct 7 In the chapter house between 9 am and 12 noon. Present: Peirs, Holt, Sheafe, and Fane; Quirke in attendance.

p266 "I, Charles Thirlby, Clerke, Master of Arts, Vicar of the Vicaridge of St Cuthberts in Wells . . . now to be admitted to the Grammer Schole within the Liberty of St Andrews . . . doe voluntaryly and *ex animo* Subscribe to the Three Articles mencioned and contained in the 36th Canon . . . and to all things therein contained.
Charles Thirlby."

Mr Potenger, master of the grammar school, appeared and resigned his office into the hands of Dr Holt.

The chapter was adjourned and continued to between 4 pm and 6 pm, when Piers, Holt, Sheafe, and Fane again adjourned and continued it to the next morning.

p267 **Oct 8** In the chapter house between 10 am and 12 noon. Present: Peirs, Holt, and Sheafe; Quirke in attendance.

Charles Thirlby, M.A., was admitted master of the cathedral grammar school on the nomination of the chancellor, Dr Holt.

The chapter was adjourned and continued to the afternoon.

p268 In the chapter house between 4 pm and 6 pm. Present: Peirs, Holt, Sheafe, and Fane; Quirke in attendance.

After discussion, it was decided to remit arrears of pension amounting to 17*l.* ½*d.* and 14*l.* 1*d.* due to the dean and chapter by Mr Thirlby from the vicarage of St Cuthbert's Wells.

p269 The chapter was adjourned and continued to the next morning.

Oct 9 In the chapter house between 10 am and 12 noon. Present: Peirs, Holt, Sheafe, and Fane; Quirke in attendance.

Letters of attorney were sealed, addressed to Mr Dowthwaight, Mr Cannington, and Allen Law, for receiving the rents due from the rectory of Mudford.[1]

The chapter was adjourned and continued to Oct. 20.

Oct 20 In the chapter house between 10 am and 12 noon Peirs, Sheafe, and Fane, with Thomas Heath in attendance, adjourned and continued the chapter to the next morning.

[1] See charters 846 and 851, *Cal.* ii. 716; also p.xlv.

p270 **Oct 21** In the chapter house between 10 am and 12 noon Peirs, Holt, Sheafe, and Fane, with Heath in attendance, adjourned the chapter to the next morning in the audit room.

Oct 22 In the audit room between 10 am and 12 noon Peirs, Holt, Sheafe, and Fane adjourned the chapter to between 4 pm and 6 pm when, with Quirke in attendance, they again adjourned and continued it to the next morning.

Oct 23 In the audit room between 10 am and 12 noon Peirs, Holt, Sheafe, and Fane adjourned the chapter to between 4 pm and 6 pm, when they again adjourned and continued it to the next morning.

p271 **Oct 24** In the audit room between 10 am and 12 noon Peirs, Holt, Sheafe, and Fane adjourned and continued the chapter to Oct. 27.

Oct 27 In the audit room between 10 am and 12 noon Peirs, Holt, Sheafe, and Fane adjourned the chapter to between 4 pm and 6 pm, when they again adjourned it to the next morning.

Oct 28 In the audit room between 10 am and 12 noon Peirs, Holt, Sheafe, and Fane, with Guy Clynton jnr in attendance, adjourned the chapter to the afternoon.
In the audit room between 4 pm and 6 pm. Present: Peirs, Holt, Sheafe, and Fane; Guy Clynton jnr in attendance.

Mr Nicholas Dowthwaight was empowered to collect the Martin's wheat[1] and the arrears due at the last feast of St Martin.

The communar was to pay Mr Nicholas Dowthwaite a sum of 20*l.* against his bill.

The chapter was adjourned and continued to Dec. 5 in the audit room.

p272 **Dec 5** In the audit room between 10 am and 12 noon Peirs, Holt, Selleck, Sheafe, and Fane, with Quirke in attendance, adjourned and continued the chapter to the afternoon.
In the audit room between 3 pm and 6 pm. Present: Peirs, Holt, Selleck, Sheafe, and Fane.

Mr John Davis was appointed steward of the old almshouse.

1673-4

p273 **Jan 1** In the chapter house between [ ]. Present [ ]; Westley in attendance. [No business recorded].

[1] In an undated document of about this time 'Martin's wheat' is defined as "Severall quantyties and measures of Corne called Churchels, otherwise Martins wheate, yearely payable on St Martins day . . ." The payment was due from tenants of land on various manors belonging to the dean and chapter. In the document mentioned, the dean and chapter ask for the issue of a writ of subpoena against certain defaulters holding lands in Easton, East and West Horrington, Binegar, Litton, and Worminster yielding in all 54½ bushels of wheat; it is asserted that this payment has been made time out of mind, but ceased "ever since the beginninge of the late troubles" (see W.C.L., Documents, series III, box 4, 182). An earlier document (W.C.L., Documents, series III, box 3, 155) states the case for the dean and chapter against one of the defaulters named in the application for a writ, Philip Ball, who denied "takinge advantage of the late troubles" and claimed that neither he nor his predecessors had paid Martin's wheat, and that they were under no liability to do so. See also the entries below for 1st and 22nd October 1680.

p274 **Jan 3** Between 9 am and 12 noon, [place not stated], Peirs, Holt, and Selleck, with Quirke in attendance, adjourned and continued the chapter to Jan. 5.

Jan 5 In the chapter house between 10 am and 12 noon Holt adjourned and continued the chapter to Jan. 7.

Jan 7 In the chapter house between 8 am and 12 noon Peirs, Holt, and Selleck, with Quirke in attendance, adjourned and continued the chapter to the next morning.

Jan 8 In the chapter house between 10 am and 12 noon Peirs, Holt, and Selleck adjourned and continued the chapter to the next morning.

p275 **Jan 9** In the chapter house between 10 am and 12 noon Peirs, Holt, and Selleck adjourned and continued the chapter to the next morning.

Jan 10 In the chapter house between 10 am and 12 noon. Present: Peirs, Holt, Selleck, and Sheafe; Quirke in attendance. It was enacted as follows [no further entry].

p276 blank

1674

p277 **April 3** In the chapter house between 10 am and 12 noon. Present: Peirs, Holt, Selleck, and Sheafe; Quirke in attendance.

The four members present affirmed that they had all completed their residences for the year beginning Oct. 1 last.

They adjourned and continued the chapter to between 4 pm and 6 pm, and then to the next morning.

p278 **April 4** In the chapter house between 10 am and 12 noon. Present: Holt, Selleck, and Sheafe; Quirke in attendance.

It was decreed "That Mr Westley as Chapter Clerke and Mr Dowthwaight as Auditor should examine and State the Accompt betweene Dr Holt and Dr Smith, and make reporte thereof to the Chapter; and when my Lord Bishopp shall require it, they the said Mr Westley and Mr Dowthwaight to state it to him".

The chapter was adjourned and continued to April 7.

April 7 In the chapter house between 10 am and 12 noon. Present: Peirs, Holt, Selleck, and Sheafe; Quirke in attendance.

A sum of 5*l.* would be paid to Mr Edmonds for the labours and attention of his son, and it ought to be considered at the next chapter whether anything more was due to him.

p279 The chapter was adjourned and continued to the next morning.

April 8 In the chapter house between 10 am and 12 noon Holt, Selleck, and Sheafe adjourned and continued the chapter to the next morning.

April 9 In the chapter house between 10 am and 12 noon Holt, Selleck, and Sheafe adjourned and continued the chapter to April 13.

April 13 In the chapter house between 10 am and 12 noon Peirs and Sheafe adjourned the chapter to Dr Selleck's canonical house between 2 pm and 4 pm, where Peirs, Holt, and Selleck adjourned the chapter at that time to the next morning in the chapter house.

p280 **April 14** In the chapter house between 10 am and 12 noon Peirs and Sheafe adjourned and continued the chapter to the next morning.

April 15 In the chapter house between 10 am and 12 noon Sheafe adjourned and continued the chapter to the next morning between 10 am and 12 noon. [Entry incomplete, and no further entries for this chapter.]

p281–p282 **May 2** In the chapter house between 3 pm and 6 pm. Present: Holt, Sheafe, and prebendaries Thirlby, Pottenger, and Mew; Quirke in attendance.

Robert Creyghton, S.T.B., was installed by Dr Sheafe and Mr Thirlby as precentor.

p283 Robert Creyghton, M.A. [*sic*], sought election as a canon residentiary in accordance with the king's letter of Jan. 2, 1667, and deposited his caution of 100*l.* He was elected and admitted, and took the usual oaths. His caution was divided, 10*l.* going to the vicars choral, 10*l.* to the fabric, and the rest to the members of the chapter. [There follows a record of the confirmation of this election on July 10, for which see that date.]

p284 **May 4** In the chapter house between 3 pm and 5 pm. Present: Sheafe, Creyghton, and prebendaries Thirlby, Potenger, Willan, and Knowles; Quirke in attendance.

Edwin Sandys was installed by Mr Creyghton and Mr Thirlby in the prebend or canonry of Wanstrow, vacant by the death of Arthur Mattock.

p285 Daniel Mew, M.A., was installed by Mr Creyghton and Mr Thirlby in the prebend or canonry of Haselbury Plucknett, vacant by the death of John Head.

p286 Joseph Shallet, M.A., was installed by Mr Creyghton and Mr Thirlby in the prebend or canonry of Combe VII, vacant by the death of John Lonsdale.

p287 Joshua Lasher, M.A., was installed by Mr Creyghton and Mr Thirlby in the prebend or canonry of Wedmore IV, vacant by the cession of Edwin Sandys.

p288 **May 30** In the chapter house between 10 am and 12 noon. Present: Peirs, Holt, and Sheafe; Quirke in attendance.

Letters patent were confirmed, granting to Mr William Westley the office of registrar to the archdeacon of Wells for the lives of Francis Keene, Nicholas Neblet, and Guy Clynton jnr.[1]

p289 blank

p290 **July 1** In the chapter house between 10 am and 12 noon. Present: Peirs, Holt, Sheafe, Fane, and Creyghton; Clynton in attendance.

Lots were cast for benefices:

The dean—Buckland Abbas.

[1] See W.C.L., Ledger G, 667.

Dr Peirs—Stogumber and Dulverton.
Dr Busby—Burnham and Mudford.
Dr Holt—Winscombe and Bishop's Lydiard.
Dr Selleck—Cheddar and Shipham.
Dr Sheafe—Long Sutton and St Cuthbert's [Wells].
p291 Dr Fane—Allerton and North Curry.
Mr Creyghton—Pucklechurch and East Lambrook.
The chapter was adjourned to the next morning.

July 2 In the chapter house between 10 am and 12 noon Peirs, Holt, Sheafe, and Creyghton, with Quirke in attendance, adjourned and continued the chapter to the next morning.

July 3 In the chapter house between 10 am and 12 noon. Present: Peirs, Holt, Sheafe, and Creyghton; Quirke in attendance.

Memorandum: Dr Fane declared that he had completed his residence for the current year beginning on Oct. 1 last.

The chapter was adjourned and continued to between 4 pm and 6 pm, when the same residentiaries again adjourned and continued it to the next morning.

p292 **July 4** In the chapter house between 10 am and 12 noon Peirs, Holt, Sheafe, and Creyghton adjourned and continued the chapter to July 6.

July 6 In the chapter house between 9 am and 12 noon Peirs, Holt, Sheafe, and Creyghton adjourned the chapter to between 4 pm and 6 pm, when they again adjourned and continued it to the next morning.

July 7 In the chapter house between 10 am and 12 noon. Present: Peirs, Holt, Sheafe, Fane, and Creyghton.

The presentation of Thomas Hansom, M.A., to the rectory of Shipham was sealed.

The chapter was adjourned to between 4 pm and 6 pm, when the same members again adjourned and continued it to the next morning.

p293 **July 8** In the chapter house between 10 am and 12 noon Holt, Sheafe, and Creyghton adjourned and continued the chapter to the next morning.

July 9 In the chapter house between 9 am and 12 noon Peirs, Holt, Sheafe, Fane, and Creyghton adjourned the chapter to between 4 pm and 6 pm, when Peirs, Holt, Sheafe, and Fane adjourned and continued it to the next morning.

July 10 In the chapter house between 10 am and 12 noon. Present: Holt [(proxy for Busby)], Sheafe, Fane, and Creyghton; [Quirke in attendance].

The chapter confirmed the election of Mr Creyghton to the residentiary canonry vacant by the death of Dr Smith, according to the chapter act of May 2 last. [He *p283* was to commence residence on Oct. 1 next, and was not to receive any emoluments before that date. If he should die before Oct. 1, his caution of 100*l.* would be repaid to his executor.]

p293 The chapter was adjourned and continued to July 13.

p294 **July 13** In the chapter house between 10 am and 12 noon Peirs, Sheafe, and Creyghton adjourned and continued the chapter to the next morning.

July 14 In the chapter house between 10 am and 12 noon Peirs, Sheafe, Fane, and Creyghton adjourned and continued the chapter to between 2 pm and 4 pm, when they again adjourned it to July 27.

July 27 In the chapter house between 10 am and 12 noon Holt and Creyghton adjourned and continued the chapter to between 4 pm and 6 pm, and then to the next morning.

July 28 In the chapter house between 10 am and 12 noon Peirs, Holt, and Creyghton adjourned the chapter to between 4 pm and 6 pm. [There is no record of a meeting at that time].

p295 **Sept 9** In the chapter house between 10 am and 12 noon. Present: Bathurst, Peirs, Holt, and Sheafe, with the consent of Fane; Quirke in attendance.

Although the dean had not resided that year [and he would not be prejudiced on that account][1] his emoluments would not be affected.

The chapter was adjourned and continued to the afternoon.

In the chapter house between 4 pm and 6 pm. Present: Bathurst, Peirs, Holt, and Sheafe, with the consent of Fane; Quirke in attendance.

John Jackson was appointed organist and vicar choral for one year on probation; he p296 was assigned the stall of [ ] and Mr Mew as *auscultor*.

For this year only the stipend of the organist and the emolument due to him as vicar choral would be 50*l*.

The chapter was adjourned and continued to the next morning.

Sept 10 In the chapter house between 10 am and 12 noon. Present: Bathurst, Peirs, Holt, and Sheafe, with the consent of Fane.

It was decreed: "That Doctor Smith's widdow and his Son to have an Hundred pounds *in fine anni*, so they joyne in giveing a Discharge to the Chapter for the claime of the year *post mortem*."

p297 "... whereas there was a presentation of The Rectory of Shipham Sealed to Mr Hansom, it is decreed to be cancelled and is cancelled accordingly."

Sept 12 In the chapter house between 10 am and 12 noon. Present: Bathurst, Peirs, Holt, Selleck, and Sheafe; Quirke in attendance.

Memorandum: "It is ordered That Davis his wife have half a Crowne a weeke to be paid from the Chapter dureing their pleasure."

The chapter was adjourned and continued to between 5 pm and 7 pm, at which time Bathurst, Peirs, Holt, Selleck, and Sheafe concluded it.

p298 blank

p299 **Sept 30** In the chapter house between 10 am and 12 noon. Present: Holt and Sheafe; Quirke in attendance.

All the vicars choral appeared.

[1] The words in brackets have been deleted.

[Officers for the ensuing year]: Baron of the exchequer, Dr Selleck; Auditors, Dr Peirs and Dr Fane; Communar, Dr Sheafe; Master of the fabric, Dr Sheafe; Overseers of the houses, Dr Fane and Mr Creyghton; Tabellar, Mr Walkley; Escheator, Mr Duvall; Bailiff of the grange and *cursor ecclesiae*, James Gilbert.

p300 **Oct 1** In the chapter house between 9 am and 11 am. Present: Holt, Sheafe, and Creyghton; Quirke in attendance.

The chapter was adjourned to the next morning.

Oct 2 In the chapter house between 9 am and 12 noon Peirs, Holt, Sheafe, and Creyghton adjourned the chapter to between 4 pm and 6 pm, and then to the next morning.

Oct 3 In the chapter house between 10 am and 12 noon. Present: Peirs, Holt, Sheafe, and Creyghton.

A presentation to the rectory of Shipham was sealed.[1]

The chapter was adjourned to the afternoon.

p301 Between 4 pm and 6 pm [No record of place or attendance]

An instrument of officialty was sealed.

The chapter was adjourned to Oct. 5.

Oct 5 In the chapter house between 10 am and 12 noon Peirs, Holt, Sheafe, and Creyghton adjourned the chapter to between 4 pm and 6 pm, when Holt, Sheafe, and Creyghton again adjourned it to the next morning.

Oct 6 In the chapter house between 10 am and 12 noon. Present: Peirs, Holt, Selleck, Sheafe, and Creyghton; Quirke in attendance.

Nathaniel Chiles Esq. appeared and presented on behalf of the king a private letter under the royal privy seal in favour of the election of Edwin Sandys to the next residentiary canonry in the cathedral. The letter was received with respect, and the *p302* chapter unanimously professed their readiness to comply with the royal will; it was decreed that the letter should be registered in the archives.[2]

An indenture in the name of John Martin relating to South Barrow was sealed.[3]

Mr Robert Creyghton was admitted into residence from Oct. 1.

The chapter was adjourned to between 4 pm and 6 pm, and then, by the same residentiaries, to the next morning.

Oct 7 In the chapter house between 10 am and 12 noon. Present: Holt, Selleck, and Creyghton.

An indenture in the name of Mr Pope was sealed.[4]

The chapter was adjourned to the next morning.

p303 **Oct 8** In the chapter house between 10 am and 12 noon Peirs, Holt, Selleck, and Creyghton adjourned the chapter to Oct. 13.

[1] See W.C.L., Ledger G, 687.

[2] Sandys had already been recommended for a residentiary's place in a letter dated 31st August 1674, W.C.L., Documents, series III, box 4, 186.

[3] See W.C.L., Ledger G, 687. [4] See ibid. 689: 30 acres of land in Bradenhurst, Allerton manor.

Oct 13 In the chapter house between 10 am and 12 noon Peirs and Selleck adjourned the chapter to Oct. 19.

Oct 19 In the chapter house between 9 am and 12 noon Holt, Sheafe, and Creyghton adjourned the chapter to between 4 pm and 6 pm, when Selleck, Sheafe, and Creyghton again adjourned it to the next morning.

Oct 20 In the chapter house between 10 am and 12 noon Peirs, Holt, Selleck, Sheafe, Fane, and Creyghton adjourned the chapter to the next morning.

Oct 21 In the chapter house between 10 am and 12 noon Peirs, Holt, Selleck, Sheafe, and Creyghton adjourned the chapter to the next morning.

p304 **Oct 22** In the chapter house between 10 am and 12 noon *coram Doctoribus praedictis* the chapter was adjourned to the next morning.

Oct 23 In the chapter house between 10 am and 12 noon Peirs, Holt, Selleck, Sheafe, Fane, and Creyghton adjourned the chapter to between 9 am and 12 noon on Dec. 4. [There is no record of a meeting on that day]

pp305–310 blank

1675

p311 **July 7** In the chapter house between 10 am and 12 noon. Present: Peirs, Holt, Selleck, Sheafe, Fane, and Creyghton; Quirke in attendance.

Joseph Barker appeared and presented a royal letter directed to the dean and chapter, which was received with fitting respect and obedience, and was deposited in the archives.[1]

The chapter was adjourned to the afternoon of the next day.

p312 **July 8** In the chapter house between 4 pm and 6 pm. Peirs, Selleck, Sheafe, and Creyghton adjourned the chapter to the next morning.

July 9 Between 9 am and 12 noon [place not stated] Peirs, Selleck, Holt, Sheafe, and Creyghton adjourned the chapter to between 4 pm and 6 pm, and then to the next[2] morning.

July 10 Between 9 am and 12 noon [place not stated] Peirs, Holt, Selleck, Sheafe, and Creyghton adjourned the chapter to July 12.

July 12 Between 9 am and 12 noon [place not stated] Peirs, Holt, Selleck, and Creyghton adjourned the chapter to July 19.

[1] A letter had already been received, dated 16th June 1675, commending Joseph Barker, chaplain to the Speaker of the House of Commons (W.C.L., Documents, series III, box 4, 187), and it was followed by another dated 18th July to the effect that Edwyn Sandys's election was in no way to be prejudiced (ibid. 188).

[2] The entry erroneously has *antemeridiem eiusdem diei*.

July 19 In the chapter house between 9 am and 12 noon Bathurst, Holt, Selleck, Sheafe, and Creyghton adjourned the chapter to Aug. 2.

p313 **Aug 2** Between 10 am and 12 noon [place not stated] Bathurst, Holt, Selleck, Sheafe, and Creyghton adjourned the chapter to between 4 pm and 6 pm, and then to the next morning.

Aug 3 Between 10 am and 12 noon [place not stated] Bathurst, Holt, Selleck, Sheafe, and Creyghton adjourned the chapter to between 10 am and 12 noon on the next day. [There is no record of a meeting on Aug. 4]

p314 **Sept 4** In the chapter house between 7 am and 9 am. Present: Bathurst, Peirs, and Sheafe; Quirke in attendance.

Mr [ ] Macy was admitted a vicar choral for one year on probation; he was assigned Mr Aulderly as *auscultator* [*sic*], but no stall.

p315 **Sept 30** In the chapter house between 10 am and 12 noon. Present: Peirs, Holt, Sheafe, and Creyghton; Quirke in attendance.

[Officers for the ensuing year]: Communar, Mr Creyghton; Baron of the exchequer, Dr Peirs; Auditors, Dr Holt and Mr Creyghton; Master of the fabric, Mr Creyghton; Overseers of the houses, Dr Selleck and Dr Sheafe; Escheator, the vicars nominated Messrs Shallet and Green and the chapter elected Mr Shallett; Tabellar, Mr Jackson; Bailiff of the grange, James Gilbert.

p316 **Oct 1** In the chapter house between 9 am and 12 noon. Present: Holt, Sheafe, and Creyghton; Quirke in attendance. The chapter was adjourned and continued to between 4 pm and 6 pm, when the same members adjourned and continued it to the next morning.

Oct 2 Between 9 am and 12 noon [place not stated] Holt, Sheafe, and Creyghton adjourned the chapter to Oct. 4.

p317 **Oct 4** Between 9 am and 12 noon [place not stated] Holt, Sheafe, and Creyghton adjourned and continued the chapter to the next morning.[1]

Oct 5 Between 9 am and 12 noon [place not stated] Holt, Selleck, Sheafe, and Creyghton adjourned the chapter to the next morning.

Oct 6 Between 9 am and 12 noon [place not stated] Holt, Selleck, Sheafe, and Creyghton adjourned the chapter to the afternoon.
In the chapter house between 3 pm and 6 pm [No record of attendance].

Edwin Sandys appeared and presented a letter under the royal seal addressed to the dean and chapter, which was received with obedience and respect and deposited in the archives.

pp318–319 blank

[1] The entry reads (in error) *antemeridiem crastini diei . . . quarti vizt diei mensis.*

1675-6

p320 **Jan 1** In the chapter house between 9 am and 12 noon. Present: Holt, Selleck, and Creyghton; Quirke in attendance. The chapter was adjourned and continued to Jan. 3.

Jan 3 In the chapter house between 9 am and 12 noon. Present: Holt, Selleck, and Sheafe; Quirke in attendance.

The stall of Old Cleeve was assigned to Mr Anthony Walkley.

A holy table would be set up in the eastern part of the Lady chapel.

p321[1] The chapter was adjourned and continued to between 2 pm and 6 pm, when Holt, Selleck, Sheafe, and Fane adjourned it to Jan. 5.[2]

Jan 5 Between 9 am and 12 noon [place not stated] Holt, Selleck, and Sheafe adjourned the chapter to Jan. 7.

Jan 7 Between 10 am and 12 noon [place not stated] Holt and Selleck adjourned the chapter to the next morning.

Jan 8 Between 9 am and 12 noon [place not stated] Holt, Selleck, Sheafe, [? Fane], and Creyghton adjourned the chapter to Jan. 10.

Jan 10 Between 10 am and 12 noon [place not stated] Creyghton adjourned the chapter to the next morning.

Jan 11 Between 9 am and 12 noon [place not stated] Sheafe and Creyghton adjourned the chapter to between 3 pm and 6 pm, when Holt, Sheafe, and Creyghton again p322[1] adjourned it to the next morning.

Jan 12 Between 9 am and 12 noon [place not stated] Holt, Selleck, Sheafe, Fane, and Creyghton adjourned and continued the chapter to the next morning.

Jan 13 Between 9 am and 12 noon [place not stated] Sheafe and Creyghton adjourned the chapter to the next morning.

Jan 14 Between 9 am and 12 noon [place not stated] Holt, Sheafe, and Creyghton adjourned the chapter to Jan. 17.[3]

Jan 17 Between 9 am and 12 noon [place not stated] [? Sheafe] adjourned the chapter to between [ ] in the afternoon, when it was again adjourned to the morning of Jan. 24.

Jan 24 Between 9 am and 12 noon [place not stated] Holt, Selleck, and Sheafe adjourned the chapter to between 9 am and 12 noon on the next day.

[There is no record of a meeting on Jan. 25]

[1] A large irregular round hole has been cut in the leaf for no obvious purpose, but fortunately the contents of the mutilated entries can easily be reconstructed; in two places it is uncertain who were at meetings.

[2] The entry reads (in error) *antemeridiem crastini diei*.

[3] The entry reads (in error) *antemeridiem diei Lunae 13^{m} vizt [diei] mensis*.

1676

p323 **April 1** In the chapter house between 10 am and 12 noon. Present: Holt, Selleck, Fane, and Creyghton; Quirke in attendance. The chapter was adjourned and continued to April 3.

April 3 Between 2 pm and 6 pm [place and attendance not stated] Dr Holt declared that he had completed his residence for the year which began on Oct. 1 last.

pp324–327 blank

p328 **July 1** In the chapter house between 9 am and 12 noon. Present: Holt and Creyghton; Quirke in attendance.

Dr Selleck was elected steward.

The chapter was adjourned to July 3.

July 3 Between 9 am and 12 noon [place not stated] Holt, Selleck, and Creyghton adjourned the chapter to between 3 pm and 5 pm, and then to the next morning.

July 4 Between 9 am and 12 noon [place not stated] Holt and Selleck adjourned the *p329* chapter to between 4 pm and 6 pm, and then to the next morning.

July 5 Between 10 am and 12 noon [place not stated] Holt, Selleck, and Creyghton adjourned the chapter to between 4 pm and 6 pm, and then to the next morning.

July 6 Between 10 am and 12 noon [place not stated] Holt, Selleck, and Creyghton adjourned the chapter to the afternoon.
Between 4 pm and 6 pm [place not stated]. Present: Holt, Selleck, and Creyghton.

An indenture in the name of John Sweeting was sealed.

The chapter was adjourned to the next morning.

p330 **July 7** Between 9 am and 12 noon [place not stated] Holt, Selleck, and Creyghton adjourned the chapter to between 4 pm and 6 pm, and then to the next morning.

July 8 Between 9 am and 12 noon [place not stated] Holt, Selleck, and Creyghton adjourned the chapter to between 3 pm and 6 pm, when Holt and Selleck again adjourned it to July 11.

July 11 Between 9 am and 12 noon [place not stated] Holt and Selleck adjourned the chapter to the next morning.

July 12 Between 9 am and 12 noon [place not stated] Holt and Selleck adjourned the chapter to July 21.

p331 **July 21** Between 9 am and 12 noon [place not stated] Creyghton adjourned the chapter to the next morning.

July 22 Between 10 am and 12 noon [place not stated] Holt, Sheafe, and Creyghton continued the chapter to July 24.

July 24 Between 9 am and 12 noon [place not stated] Bathurst, Holt, Sheafe, and Creyghton adjourned the chapter to July 31.

July 31 Between 9 am and 12 noon [place not stated] Bathurst, Holt, and Sheafe adjourned the chapter to Aug. 4.

Aug 4 Between 9 am and 12 noon [place not stated] Bathurst, Peirs, Holt, Sheafe, and Creyghton adjourned the chapter to Aug. 8.

p332 **Aug 8** Between 9 am and 12 noon [place not stated] Bathurst, Holt, Sheafe, and Creyghton adjourned the chapter to the afternoon.
Between 3 pm and 6 pm [place not stated]. Present: Holt, Sheafe, and Creyghton.
An indenture in the name of Mr Pine was sealed.
The chapter was then adjourned to between 4 pm and 6 pm, when it was again adjourned by Dr Peirs to the next afternoon.

Aug 9 Between 4 pm and 6 pm [place not stated]. Present: Bathurst, Holt, Sheafe, Fane, and Creyghton.
The dean and chapter resolved to contribute 10*l.* towards the repair of the town of Northampton, lately burnt.
The chapter was concluded.

p333 **Sept 30** In the chapter house between 9 am and 12 noon. Present: Holt and Sheafe; Quirke in attendance.
The following officers were elected: Baron of the exchequer, Dr Selleck; Auditors, Dr Holt and Dr Sheafe; Communar, Mr Creyghton; Master of the fabric, Mr Creyghton; Overseers of the houses, Dr Selleck and Dr Fane; Tabellar, Mr Macy; Escheator, the vicars choral nominated Messrs Lasher and Greene and the chapter elected Mr Lasher; Bailiff of the grange and *cursor ecclesiae*, James Gilbert.

p334 **Oct 2** In the chapter house between 9 am and 12 noon. Present: Holt, Selleck, and Sheafe; Quirke in attendance.
[Roll-call of vicars choral]. Present: Aulderly, Moss, Hobbs, Edmonds, Walkley, Lasher, Shallet, Greene, Winscombe, Jackson, and Macy; absent: Beaumont and Phipps (sick).
The chapter was adjourned to between 3 pm and 6 pm, when the same members again adjourned it to the next afternoon.

Oct 3 Between 3 pm and 6 pm [place not stated]. Holt, Selleck, Sheafe, and Creyghton adjourned the chapter to the next morning.

p335 **Oct 4** Between 9 am and 12 noon [place not stated] Holt, Selleck, Sheafe, and Creyghton adjourned the chapter to between 3 pm and 6 pm, when Holt, Selleck, and Creyghton adjourned it to the next morning.

Oct 5 Between 9 am and 12 noon [place not stated] Holt, Selleck, Sheafe, and Creyghton adjourned the chapter to between 3 pm and 6 pm, when they again adjourned it to Oct. 7.

Oct 7 Between 10 am and 12 noon [place not stated] Holt, Selleck, Sheafe, and Creyghton continued the chapter to the afternoon.
Between 3 pm and 6 pm [place not stated]. Present: Holt, Selleck, Sheafe, and Creyghton.

p336 All revenues due to William Hacker jnr would be received by Dr Selleck; and from them would be granted 10*l.* to William Hacker jnr in reimbursement of his expenditure, and 40*l.* to William Hacker snr for the use of William Hacker jnr.
The chapter was adjourned to Oct. 9.

Oct 9 Between 9 am and 12 noon [place not stated] Holt, Sheafe, and Creyghton adjourned the chapter to between 3 pm and 6 pm, and then to the next morning.

Oct 10 Between 9 am and 12 noon [place not stated] Holt, Sheafe, and Creyghton adjourned the chapter to Oct. 24 in the audit room.

Oct 24 In the audit room between 9 am and 12 noon Selleck and Creyghton *p337* adjourned the chapter to between 4 pm and 6 pm, when Holt, Selleck, Sheafe, and Creyghton adjourned it to the next day.

Oct 25 In the audit room between 9 am and 12 noon Holt, Selleck, Sheafe, Fane, and Creyghton adjourned the chapter to the next morning.

Oct 26 In the audit room between 8 am and 12 noon Holt, Selleck, Sheafe, Fane, and Creyghton adjourned the chapter to between 4 pm and 6 pm, and then to the next morning.

Oct 27 In the audit room between 9 am and 12 noon *coram Doctoribus et Selleck et Magistro Creyghton* the chapter was adjourned to between 4 pm and 6 pm, when Holt, Selleck, and Creyghton adjourned it to the next morning.

p338 **Oct 28** In the audit room between 8 am and 12 noon Holt, Selleck, Fane, and Creyghton adjourned the chapter to the next morning.

Oct 29[1] In the audit room between 9 am and 12 noon Peirs adjourned the chapter to the next morning.

Oct 30 In the audit room between 8 am and 12 noon Holt, Selleck, Sheafe, and Creyghton adjourned the chapter to Dec. 4.

Dec 4 In the audit room between 9 am and 12 noon Holt, Selleck, Sheafe, and Creyghton adjourned the chapter to between 3 pm and 6 pm, when Holt, Sheafe, Selleck, Fane, and Creyghton adjourned it to the next afternoon.

[1] This is one of the rare occasions when a chapter meeting on Sunday is recorded; another occurred on 1st October 1682 (see below). No business seems to have been done on either day, and the meeting may have been simply a formal one to deal with the adjournment.

p339 **Dec 5** In the audit room between 3 pm and 6 pm Holt, Selleck, Sheafe, Fane, and Creyghton adjourned the chapter to the next morning.

Dec 6 In the audit room between 9 am and 12 noon Holt, Selleck, Sheafe, Fane, and Creyghton adjourned the chapter to the next morning.

Dec 7 In the audit room between 9 am and 12 noon Holt, Selleck, Sheafe, Fane, and Creyghton adjourned the chapter to between 3 pm and 6 pm, and then to the next morning.

Dec 8 In the audit room between 9 am and 12 noon Holt, Selleck, Sheafe, Fane, and Creyghton adjourned the chapter to between 4 pm and 6 pm, and then to Dec. 11.

p340 **Dec 11** In the audit room between 9 am and 12 noon Holt, Selleck, Sheafe, Fane, and Creyghton adjourned the chapter to the afternoon.
In the audit room between 4 pm and 6 pm. Present: Holt, Selleck, Sheafe, Fane, and Creyghton.
Mr Hobbs was appointed tabellar in the place of Mr Macy, lately deceased.
The chapter was adjourned to the next afternoon.

Dec 12 In the audit room between 4 pm and 6 pm. Holt, Selleck, Sheafe, Fane, and Creyghton adjourned the chapter to the next morning.

Dec 13 In the audit room between 9 am and 12 noon Holt, Selleck, Sheafe, Fane, and Creyghton adjourned the chapter to between 3 pm and 6 pm, when the chapter was concluded.

1676-7

p341 **Jan 1** In the chapter house [no time stated]. Present: Holt, Selleck, Sheafe, and Creyghton; Quirke in attendance. The chapter was adjourned to the next morning.

Jan 2 Between 9 am and 12 noon [place not stated]. Present: Holt, Selleck, and Creyghton.
Thomas Webb was admitted a vicar choral for one year on probation; he was assigned the stall of [ ] and Mr Lasher as *auscultor*.
p342 From Michaelmas last the stall of Wiveliscombe was assigned to Mr Greene.
The chapter was adjourned and continued to between 2 pm and 6 pm in Dr Selleck's house, when Holt, Selleck, Sheafe, and Creyghton again adjourned it to Jan. 8 in the chapter house.

p343 **Jan 8** In the chapter house between 9 am and 12 noon Holt, Sheafe, and Creyghton adjourned the chapter to the next morning.

Jan 9 Between 9 am and 12 noon [place not stated] Selleck and Sheafe adjourned the chapter to between 3 pm and 6 pm, and then to the next morning.

Jan 10 Between 9 am and 12 noon [place not stated] Selleck, Sheafe, and Creyghton adjourned the chapter to the next morning.

Jan 11 Between 9 am and 12 noon [place not stated] Sheafe adjourned the chapter to the next morning.

Jan 12 Between 9 am and 12 noon [place not stated] Holt, Selleck, Sheafe, and Creyghton concluded the chapter.

1677

p344 **April 2** In the chapter house between 9 am and 12 noon. Present: Holt, Sheafe, and Creyghton; Quirke in attendance. The chapter was adjourned to the next morning.

April 3 Between 9 am and 12 noon [place not stated] Holt, Selleck, and Creyghton adjourned the chapter to the next day.

April 4 Between 9 am and 12 noon [place not stated] Holt, Selleck, and Creyghton adjourned the chapter to the next day.

p345 **April 5** Between 9 am and 12 noon [place not stated] Holt, Selleck, and Creyghton adjourned the chapter to the next morning.

April 6 Between 9 am and 12 noon [place not stated] Peirs, Holt, Selleck, and Creyghton adjourned the chapter to between [ ][1] in the afternoon, and then to the next morning.

April 7 Between 9 am and 12 noon [place not stated] Holt, Selleck, Sheafe, and Creyghton adjourned the chapter to April 9.

April 9 Between 9 am and 12 noon [place not stated] Peirs, Holt, Sheafe, and Creyghton adjourned the chapter to between 3 pm and 6 pm, and then to the next morning.

p346 **April 10** Between 9 am and 12 noon [place not stated] Peirs, Holt, Selleck, Sheafe, and Creyghton adjourned the chapter to the next morning.

April 11 Between 9 am and 12 noon [place not stated] Peirs, Holt, Selleck, Sheafe, and Creyghton adjourned the chapter to the next morning.

April 12 Between 9 am and 12 noon [place not stated] Peirs, Selleck, Sheafe, and Creyghton adjourned the chapter to the next morning.

April 13 Between 9 am and 12 noon [place and attendance not stated] the chapter was concluded.

[1] The actual entry reads *inter horas 9 et 12 postmeridiem.*

p347 **July 2** In the chapter house between 9 am and 12 noon. Present: Peirs, Holt, Selleck, and Creyghton; Quirke in attendance. The chapter was adjourned to the next morning.

July 3 Between 9 am and 12 noon [place not stated] Peirs, Holt, Selleck, and Creyghton adjourned the chapter to between 4 pm and 6 pm, when it was adjourned and continued to the next morning.

July 4 Between 9 am and 12 noon [place not stated]. Present: Peirs, Holt, Sheafe, Creyghton, and prebendaries Brigandine[1] and Dutton; Quirke in attendance.

p348 William Griffin, M.A., was installed by [ ] in the prebend or canonry of Barton St David, vacant by the death of Joseph Barker.

p349 The chapter was adjourned to between 2 pm and 6 pm, when Holt, Selleck, Sheafe, and Creyghton again adjourned the chapter for convenience to Dr Selleck's house between 6 pm and 8 pm when, with Quirk in attendance, an indenture was sealed granting to Giles Swetting for his life and the lives of his sons George and William a messuage or tenement in Bicknoller called the Wayfish.

The chapter was adjourned and continued to the next morning.

July 5 In the chapter house between 9 am and 12 noon Holt and Sheafe adjourned the chapter to July 9.

July 9 Between 9 am and 10 am [or 12 noon;[2] place not stated] Peirs, Holt, Sheafe, and Creyghton adjourned the chapter to the next morning.[3]

July 10 Between 9 am and 12 noon [place not stated] Holt, Sheafe, and Creyghton adjourned the chapter to the next morning.[3]

p350 **July 11** Between 9 am and 12 noon [place not stated] *coram doctoribus praedictis* the chapter was adjourned and continued to the next morning.

July 12 Between 9 am and 12 noon [place not stated]. Present: Peirs, Sheafe, and Creyghton; Quirke in attendance.

[ ] Larke was admitted a vicar choral for one year on probation, and was assigned the stall of [ ] and Mr Winscombe as *auscultator* [*sic*].

p351 The chapter was adjourned for convenience to Dr Selleck's house between 2 pm and 6 pm, and then by Sheafe and Creyghton to July 19.

July 19 Between 9 am and 12 noon [place not stated] Peirs and Sheafe adjourned the chapter to July 24.

July 24 In the chapter house between 9 am and 12 noon. Present: Bathurst, Peirs, Holt, Sheafe, and Creyghton; Quirke in attendance.

The stall of Wedmore I was assigned to Mr Webb.

The stall of Henstridge was assigned to Mr Larke.

No indenture granting any lands, rectories, or tenements whatsoever belonging to

[1] Thomas Brickenden, prebendary of Worminster, elected a residentiary on 2nd April 1689.

[2] The figure is indistinct, and could be either 10 or 12.

[3] In both entries *eiusdem diei* appears in error.

the dean and chapter would in future be sealed, except on the condition that whoever *p352* procures and receives from the dean and chapter such a charter or indenture should pay or cause to be paid to the dean and chapter, or for their use, the former and ancient rents which were wont and accustomed to be paid, after deducting the rates or taxes imposed or about to be imposed upon the said rents.

No indenture granting a rectory or property belonging to the dean and chapter would be sealed unless this condition had been inserted in the charter or indenture.

pp353–354 blank

p355 The chapter was adjourned to between 4 pm and 6 pm, when it was again adjourned and continued by Bathurst, Peirs, Holt, Selleck, Sheafe, and Creyghton to the next afternoon.

July 25 Between 4 pm and 6 pm [place not stated] Bathurst, Peirs, Holt, Selleck, and Sheafe adjourned the chapter to July 27.

July 27 Between 10 am and 12 noon [place not stated] Holt, Sheafe, and Creyghton adjourned the chapter to the afternoon.

Between 4 pm and 6 pm [place not stated]. Present: Bathurst, Peirs, Holt, Selleck, Sheafe, and Creyghton; Quirke in attendance.

An indenture was sealed granting the rectory of Mudford to Mr Francis Holt for his life and those of his wife Sarah and Avice her mother.

The chapter was adjourned to July 29.

p356 **July 29** Between 9 am and 12 noon [place not stated] Bathurst, Holt, Selleck, and Creyghton adjourned the chapter to Aug. 3.

Aug 3 Between 4 pm and 6 pm [place not stated]. Present: Bathurst, Selleck, Sheafe, and Creyghton.

Mr Robert Aulderly, executor of Mr Arthur Aulderly, lately subtreasurer of the cathedral church, attended and humbly handed over and restored to the chapter certain gold vessels given and consecrated for the use of the cathedral, viz. one flagon [*meropherum*] and two chalices with their covers.

The chapter was adjourned to the next afternoon.

Aug 4 Between 4 pm and 6 pm [place not stated] Bathurst, Holt, Selleck, Sheafe, and Creyghton adjourned the chapter to Aug. 30.

Aug 30 Between 9 am and 12 noon [place not stated] Sheafe adjourned the chapter to the next morning.

p357 **Aug 31** Between 9 am and 12 noon [place not stated] Holt and Sheafe adjourned and continued the chapter to Sept. 3.

Sept 3 Between 9 am and 12 noon [place not stated] Holt and Sheafe adjourned the chapter to the next morning.

Sept 4 Between 9 am and 12 noon [place not stated] Bathurst, Holt, and Peirs adjourned and continued the chapter to the next afternoon.

Sept 5 Between 4 pm and 6 pm [place not stated] they concluded the chapter.

p358 **Oct 1** In the chapter house between 9 am and 12 noon. Present: Bathurst, Holt, Selleck, and Sheafe; Quirke in attendance.

The following officers were elected: Baron of the exchequer, Dr Sheafe; Auditors, Dr Holt and Dr Selleck; Communar, Mr Creyghton; Master of the fabric, Mr Creyghton; Overseers of the houses, Dr Peirs and Dr Fane; Tabellar, Mr Shallett; Escheator, the vicars nominated Messrs Lasher and Winscombe and the chapter elected Mr Winscombe; Bailiff of the grange and *cursor ecclesiae*, James Gilbert.

p359 The chapter was adjourned to the next morning.

Oct 2 Between 9 am and 12 noon [place not stated]. Present: Bathurst, Holt, Selleck, and Sheafe; Quirke in attendance. [No further entry].

pp360–420 blank

1677-8

p421 **Jan 16** In Dr Selleck's house between 4 pm and 6 pm [or 9 pm]. Present: Holt, Selleck, Fane, and Creyghton; Quirke in attendance.

"It was then agreed betweene the Deane and Chapter . . . and Thomas Jordan and Thomas Callowhill of the City of Bristol that the said Thomas Callowhill and Thomas Jordan shall have and Convert to their owne proper use the tenth parte of all such Coles as was digged by Mary Greene, Denis Hollyster, the said Thomas Callowhill and Thomas Jordan, or their Agents, or any of them, in Westerly within the Manor of Pucklechurch belonging unto the said Deane and Chapter, unto the the Day of the Date hereof, haveing secured to pay one hundred pounds to the said Deane and Chapter in leiw and full satisfaction thereof."

pp422–490 blank[1]

1679

p491 **July 2** In the chapter house between 4 pm and 6 pm. Present: Peirs, Holt, Selleck, and Creighton; Quirke in attendance.

Edwyn Sandys, M.A., sought election and admission as a canon residentiary in accordance with the letters of king Charles II to the dean and chapter, and deposited his caution of 100 marks. He was elected and admitted, and took the usual oaths. His

[1] During this period when no entries were made, the chapter received a letter from the king dated 4th July 1678 recommending Henry Dutton for election to residence when other outstanding claims to election had been satisfied; see W.C.L., Documents, series III, box 4, 190.

caution was divided, 10 marks going to the fabric, 10 marks to the vicars choral, and the rest to the dean and six residentiary canons. He was to commence residence on *p492* Oct. 1, 1680, and was not to receive any emoluments as canon residentiary before that date; and if he should die before then, his caution money would be repaid to his executor.

July 4 "Balls cast the 4th of July 1679, as followeth". [The benefices are listed, but no names are inserted].[1]

pp493–494 blank

p495 **Aug 20** Between 9 am and 11 am [place not stated] Bathurst, Selleck, and Creighton, with Healy in attendance, adjourned the chapter to the next morning.

Aug 21 Between 10 am and 12 noon [place not stated] Holt and Selleck, with Healy in attendance, adjourned the chapter to the next afternoon.

Aug 22 Between 4 pm and 6 pm [place not stated] Bathurst, Holt, Creighton, and Sandys, with Healy in attendance, adjourned the chapter to the next afternoon at Dr Selleck's canonical house.

Aug 23 In Dr Selleck's house between 2 pm and 4 pm. Present: Bathurst, Peirs, Holt, Selleck, Creighton, and Sandys; Healy in attendance.

Dr Piers was deputed to hold the next court at North Curry for and in the name of the dean and chapter, which duty he accepted.

The chapter was concluded.

p496 **Sept 30** Between 10 am and 12 noon [place not stated]. Present: Bathurst, Peirs, Holt, Selleck, Creighton, and Sandys; Healy in attendance.

Officers for the ensuing year were elected as follows: Baron of the exchequer, Dr Creighton; Communar, Dr Busby; Master of the fabric, Dr Busby; Auditors, Dr Piers and Dr Selleck; Overseers of the houses, Dr Creighton and Mr Sandys.

Pursuant to a mandate from the bishop, Dr Busby was elected as proctor for the chapter in the Convocation to be held in London on Oct. 18.

p497 **Oct 1** Quarterly Chapter. In the chapter house between 10 am and 12 noon. Present: Bathurst, Piers, Holt, Selleck, Creighton, and Sandys; Healy in attendance.

The following vicars choral appeared: Shallet, Beaumont, Walkley, Greene, Jackson, Webb, Kelway, Martin, and Cooper; excused; Lasher, Winscomb, and Hobbs.

Henry Winscomb was elected tabellar.

The vicars nominated Messrs Webb and Jackson for the office of escheator, and the chapter elected Mr Webb.

The dean and Dr Selleck exchanged presentations: "Mr Deane to have the next Presentation to Bishop's Lydeard, and Dr Selleck to Allerton."

The chapter was adjourned to the next morning.

[1] For the allocation of chapter benefices to the residentiaries lots were drawn, apparently by means of balls—see further, p.xxii and n.4.

p498 **Oct 2** Between 9 am and 12 noon [place not stated] Bathurst, Piers, Holt, Selleck, Creighton, and Sandys, with Healy in attendance, continued the chapter to between 4 pm and 6 pm, when Bathurst, Holt, Selleck, Creighton, and Sandys, with Healy in attendance, adjourned it to the next morning.

Oct 3 Between 10 am and 12 noon [place not stated] Bathurst, Peirs, Holt, Selleck, and Creyghton, with Paine in attendance, adjourned the chapter to the next morning.

Oct 4 In the chapter house between 10 am and 12 noon Bathurst, Piers, Holt, Selleck, and Creyghton, with Healy in attendance, adjourned the chapter to Oct. 6.

Oct 6 Between 10 am and 12 noon [place not stated] Bathurst, Piers, Holt, Selleck, Creighton, and Sandys, with Healy in attendance, adjourned the chapter to the afternoon. Between 3 pm and 5 pm [place not stated].[1] Present: Bathurst, Piers, Holt, Selleck, and Creighton; Healy in attendance.

"... for the future, no Patent, Lease, Indenture, or any thing whatsoever of that nature, shall passe the Chapter Seale, before all the fees, due and payable upon the p499 Account, and for the setting of the said Seale, be payd to the Chapter, or to the Comminer, for the time being, by them in whose behalfe, and for whose good and behoofe the said Patent, Lease and Indenture is so sealed."

Letters patent were confirmed under the seal of the chapter, by which Dr Piers, archdeacon of Taunton, granted to John Bennett of Milverton and to John Southey his sister's son [*eius a Sorore nepoti*] the office of registrar of the archdeaconry of Taunton.

The dean charged Dr Holt (deputy communar and deputy master of the fabric) and Dr Selleck and Dr Creighton (deputies for the steward) to discharge their duties faithfully; and also enjoined Richard Healy on the Gospels faithfully to execute his office of deputy chapter clerk, and not to reveal the secrets of the chapter.

According to the statutes and the laudable customs or usage and practice of the cathedral, and the conditions [declared] prior to election, no canon only just elected [or, on the strength of election—*tantummodo electus*] ought to, or can as of right, claim or receive any daily distribution, any dividend, any stipend, emolument, or profit pertaining to a residentiary canonry before admission to full residence. So that this declaration on the matter might be valid and sufficiently guarded against all future disputes and doubts, the members present subscribed their names:[2]

"Rad. Bathurst Dec̄.
Will: Peirs — J: Selleck
Tho: Holt — Rob. Creyghton"

The chapter was adjourned to the next afternoon.

p500 **Oct 7** Between 3 pm and 5 pm [place not stated] Bathurst, Piers, Holt, Selleck, and Creighton, with Healy in attendance, adjourned the chapter to the next morning.

Oct 8 Between 10 am and 12 noon [place not stated] Bathurst, Holt, and Creighton, with Healy in attendance, adjourned the chapter to the next morning.

[1] The meeting was actually in the chapter house, see below on 15th October.

[2] Dr Creyghton revoked his subscription to this act on 1st July 1680, and Drs Peirs and Holt did likewise on 9th April 1681; see below on those dates.

Oct 9 In the chapter house between 10 am and 12 noon Piers, Holt, and Creighton, with Healy in attendance, adjourned the chapter to Oct. 11.

Oct 11 Between 10 am and 12 noon [place not stated] Bathurst, Holt, Creighton, and Sandys, with Healy in attendance, adjourned the chapter to between 3 pm and 5 pm, when Bathurst, Peirs, and Creighton, with Healy in attendance, again adjourned it to Oct. 15.

Oct 15 Between 10 am and 12 noon [place not stated]. Present: Bathurst, Peirs, and Sandys; Paine in attendance.

p501 Before the adjournment Mr Sandys presented a declaration, dated Oct. 12, which he asked to be recorded, protesting at the trouble caused to him on account of a certain chapter act made in the chapter house between 3 pm and 5 pm on Oct. 6 last in which, among other things, it was decreed that no canon only just elected ought to, or can as of right, claim or receive any daily distribution, etc. Specially he protested against the insertion of the words *Quotidianas Distributiones*, because it was not sufficiently clear to him that these distributions did not belong to him by right as a true residentiary; and on this point he appealed to the bishop, now engaged on his visitation.

p502 The chapter was adjourned to between 3 pm and 6 pm, when Peirs, with Paine in attendance, further adjourned it to the next afternoon.

Oct 16 Between 3 pm and 6 pm [place not stated] Piers, with Healy in attendance, adjourned the chapter to Oct. 18.

Oct 18 Between 10 am and 12 noon [place not stated] Piers and Sandys, with Healy in attendance, adjourned the chapter to Oct. 20.

Oct 20 Between 10 am and 12 noon [place not stated]. Present: Bathurst, Piers, Holt, and Creighton; Healy in attendance.

"... notwithstanding an Act of the Chapter, or any Custome whatsoever heretofore used to the contrary, the Tenants of the Deane and Chapter shall for the future have Copies of their grants made before the said Deane and Chapter, as usually they have had."

It was decreed that the care of the public library be committed to some one skilled in letters and a graduate of either university, whose office it would be to dispose the *p503* books in suitable places, to arrange the titles in alphabetical order, and to enter in a register the donations of benefactors.

If any books were lent (which should not be done, except for some pressing reason, and then only to the clergy or to benefactors, after permission had been sought from the dean or his deputy), the librarian must ensure that borrowers bind themselves, under their own signatures, to return borrowed books within the space of one month at most.

He must also take care that fines and other sums destined for the use of the library were recorded in a register and shown every quarter to the dean and chapter; and from these sums he himself would be assigned a yearly stipend of 40*s*., or whatever more might seem good to the chapter.

If any stranger were admitted to use the library (which should only be done if permission had first been sought from the dean or his deputy), the time of his admission must be entered in a register, and he must pay to the librarian the sum of 2*s*. 6*d*.

The chapter committed the care and custody of the public library to Richard Healy, M.A.

The chapter was adjourned to the next morning.

Oct 21 In the audit room between 9 am and 12 noon Bathurst, Piers, Holt, Selleck, and Creighton, with Healy in attendance, adjourned the chapter to between 3 pm and 6 pm, *p504* when the same members, with Paine in attendance, again adjourned it to the next morning.

Oct 22 In the audit room between 10 am and 12 noon Bathurst, Peirs, Holt, Selleck, and Creyghton, with Paine in attendance, adjourned the chapter to between 3 pm and 6 pm, and then to the next morning.

Oct 23 In the audit room between 10 am and 12 noon Bathurst, Piers, Holt, Selleck, and Creighton, with Healy in attendance, adjourned the chapter to between 3 pm and 6 pm, and then to the next morning.

p505 **Oct 24** In the audit room between 10 am and 12 noon Holt, Selleck, and Creighton, with Healy in attendance, adjourned the chapter to the next afternoon.

Oct 25 In the audit room between 3 pm and 6 pm Holt, Selleck, Peirs, and Creyghton, with Paine in attendance, adjourned the chapter to Nov. 3.

Nov 3 In the chapter house between 10 am and 12 noon Piers, Holt, and Creighton, with Healy in attendance, adjourned the chapter to the afternoon.

In the chapter house between 4 pm and 6 pm. Present: Piers, Holt, and Creighton; Healy in attendance.

An indenture was sealed and confirmed, by which the bishop granted to John Baylie Esq., of the city of Wells, the rectory of Weston in Somerset, with the profits from Middlezoy and Othery pertaining thereto.[1]

The chapter was immediately adjourned to Dr Selleck's house, from which the same members, with Dr Selleck, again adjourned it to the chapter house on Nov. 8.

p506 **Nov 8** In the chapter house between 10 am and 12 noon Peirs, Holt, Selleck, and Creyghton, with Paine in attendance, adjourned the chapter to the afternoon.

In the chapter house between 3 pm and 6 pm. Present: Peirs, Holt, Selleck, and Creyghton; Paine in attendance.

An indenture was sealed and confirmed, granting to Michael Hunt of the city of Bristol the rectory of Congresbury with its revenues.[2]

A caution or obligation was sealed, by which the dean and chapter bound themselves in a sum of 200*l*. to George Doddington Esq., on condition that they should submit themselves to the judgement or arbitration of George Long Esq. and George Musgrove gen. in a certain controversy between themselves and Mr Doddington concerning the chancel at Cheddar.

The chapter was adjourned to Dec. 4 in the exchequer.

[1] See W.C.L., Ledger G, 696. [2] See ibid. 698.

p507 **Nov 13** In the chapter house between 2 pm and 5 pm. Present: Peirs, Holt, Selleck, Creighton, and prebendaries Shallett, Winchcombe, and Nathaniel Selleck; Quirke in attendance.

Charles Symes, M.A., was installed by Messrs Shallett and Winchcombe in the prebend or canonry of Taunton, vacant by the death of [George] Brush.

p508 **Dec 4** In the audit room between 9 am and 12 noon Holt, Selleck, and Creighton, with Healy in attendance, adjourned the chapter to between 2 pm and 6 pm, when they again adjourned it to the next morning.

Dec 5 In the audit room between 10 am and 12 noon Holt, Selleck, and Creighton, with Healy in attendance, adjourned the chapter to the next morning.

Dec 6 In the audit room between 9 am and 12 noon. Present: Peirs, Holt, Selleck, and Creighton; Healy in attendance.

An indenture was sealed, granting the rectory of South Barrow to John Martin, Eleanor his wife, and John Hughes, clerk, for their three lives successively.[1]

An indenture was also sealed in the name of James Williams, for a term of forty years.[2]

The chapter was adjourned to Dec. 8.

Dec 8 In the audit room between 10 am and 12 noon Piers, Holt, and Creyghton, with Healy in attendance, adjourned the chapter to between 2 pm and 6 pm, when Piers, Holt, and Selleck, with Healy in attendance, again adjourned it to the next afternoon.

p509 **Dec 9** In the audit room between 2 pm and 6 pm Piers, Holt, and Creyghton, with Healy in attendance, adjourned the chapter to the next morning.

Dec 10 In the audit room between 9 am and 12 noon Piers, Holt, and Creighton, with Healy in attendance, concluded the chapter.

p510 blank

p511 **Dec 18** In the chapter house between 10 am and 12 noon. Present: Piers, Holt, and Creighton; Healy in attendance.

Mr Thomas Haddon appeared and presented a letter from king Charles under the royal privy seal in favour of the admission of the subdean, William Levinz, M.D., to a residentiary canonry. It was decreed that this letter be deposited in the archives.[3] The chapter was then concluded.

[1] See ibid. 704.

[2] See ibid. 701: properties in East Wells (St Thomas street) and Tor lane (Tor street).

[3] See, in this connexion, a letter from dean Bathurst to Dr Pierce (*sic*) or in his absence the senior canon, written at Oxford on 15th December 1679 in commendation of Dr Levinz: W.C.L., Documents, series III, box 4, 191. A further letter from the king on 8th January 1679–80 ordered that Mr Dutton (see below, 24th January 1679–80) should have precedence over Dr Levinz for election: ibid. 192.

1679-80

p512 **Jan 1** Quarterly chapter. In the chapter house between 10 am and 12 noon. Present: Peirs, Holt, and Creyghton; Paine in attendance. The chapter was adjourned to the next morning.

Jan 2 In the chapter house between 10 am and 12 noon. Present: Peirs and Holt; Paine in attendance.

[Roll-call of vicars choral]. Present: Beaumont, Lasher, Winscombe, Wakely, Greene, Webb, Kelway, Martin, Cooper. Absent: Shallett, Jackson, and Hobbs.

The chapter was adjourned to the next morning.

p513 **Jan 3** In the chapter house between 9 am and 12 noon Holt and Creyghton, with Paine in attendance, adjourned the chapter to Jan. 7.

Jan 7 In the chapter house between 9 am and 12 noon Holt and Creyghton, with Paine in attendance, continued the chapter to Jan. 9.

Jan 9 Between 9 am and 12 noon [place not stated] Peirs and Holt, with Healy in attendance, adjourned the chapter to Jan. 12.

Jan 12 Between 9 am and 12 noon [place not stated] Piers, with Healy in attendance, adjourned the chapter to the next morning.

Jan 13 Between 9 am and 12 noon [place not stated] Piers, Holt, and Creyghton, with Healy in attendance, adjourned the chapter to the next morning.

p514 **Jan 14** Between 9 am and 12 noon [place not stated] Piers, Holt, and Creyghton, with Healy in attendance, adjourned the chapter to the next morning.

Jan 15 Between 9 am and 12 noon [place not stated] Piers, Holt, and Creyghton, with Healy in attendance, adjourned the chapter to the afternoon.

Between 3 pm and 5 pm [place not stated] Peirs, Holt, and Creyghton, with Healy in attendance, adjourned the chapter to Dr Selleck's house between 4 pm and 6 pm, whence, with him, they adjourned the chapter again to the chapter house on the next morning.

Jan 16 In the chapter house between 8 am and 12 noon Peirs, Holt, and Creyghton, with Healy in attendance, adjourned the chapter to the next morning.

Jan 17 Between 9 am and 12 noon [place not stated] Peirs, Holt, and Creyghton, with Healy in attendance, adjourned the chapter to Jan. 19.

p515 **Jan 19** Between 9 am and 12 noon [place not stated] Holt, with Healy in attendance, adjourned the chapter to the afternoon.

Between 3 pm and 6 pm [place not stated]. Present: Piers, Holt, and Creyghton; Healy in attendance.

Dr Peirs declared that he had completed his residence for the current year.

The chapter was adjourned to Jan. 21.

Jan 21 Between 9 am and 12 noon [place not stated] Peirs and Holt, with Healy in attendance, adjourned the chapter to between 9 am and 12 noon on Jan. 23. [No entry appears for that day].

p516 **Jan 24** In the chapter house between 9 am and 12 noon. Present: Peirs, Holt, and Creyghton; Healy in attendance.

Henry Dutton, S.T.B., prebendary of Whitelackington, appeared and exhibited a letter from king Charles under the royal privy seal directed to the dean and chapter, which was received with respect and deposited in the archives.

The chapter was then concluded.

1680

p517 **April 1** In the chapter house between 9 am and 11 am. Present: Peirs, Holt, and Creyghton; Paine in attendance.

The following vicars choral appeared: Shallett, Beaumont, Lasher, Wakely, Greene, Jacksons, Webb, Kelway, Martin, Hobbs, and Cowper; Winscombe excused.

With Dr Selleck also present, the chapter was adjourned to the next morning.

April 2 In the chapter house between 9 am and 12 noon Peirs, Selleck, and Creyghton, with Paine in attendance, adjourned the chapter to the next morning.

April 3 In the chapter house between 9 am and 11 am Peirs, Selleck, and Creyghton, with Paine in attendance, adjourned the chapter to April 5.

p518 **April 5** Between 10 am and 12 noon [place not stated]. Present: Piers, Selleck, and Creyghton; Healy in attendance.

It was decreed that the communar should pay 20*s*. on behalf of the dean and chapter to a certain Mr [ ] Pittard,[1] clerk, whose house had lately been burnt down.

The chapter was adjourned to the next morning.

April 6 Between 9 am and 12 noon [place not stated] Peirs and Selleck, with Healy in attendance, adjourned the chapter to the next morning.

April 7 Between 9 am and 12 noon [place not stated] Peirs, Selleck, and Creighton, with Healy in attendance, adjourned the chapter to the next morning.

April 8 In the chapter house between 10 am and 12 noon Peirs, Selleck, and Creyghton, with Paine in attendance, adjourned the chapter to between 4 pm and 6 pm when, with Paine again in attendance, they further adjourned it to April 14.

p519 **April 14** Between 10 am and 12 noon [place not stated] Holt and Creyghton, with Healy in attendance, adjourned the chapter to the afternoon.

[1] Probably Robert Pittard, B.A., instituted to the prebendal benefice of Haselbury Plucknett on 12th May 1674 on the presentation of Daniel Mew, prebendary of Haselbury: see *Somerset Incumbents*, ed. F. W. Weaver, 98.

Between 4 pm and 6 pm [place not stated]. Present: Holt and Creyghton; Healy in attendance.

Guy Clynton, registrar of the bishop of Bath and Wells, surrendered to Dr Holt the letters patent under which, not long ago, the office of registrar of the dean and chapter had been granted to him.

The chapter was adjourned to the next morning.

April 15 Between 9 am and 12 noon [place not stated]. Present: Peirs, Holt, and Creyghton; Healy in attendance.

Letters patent were sealed, by which the office of registrar of the dean and chapter was granted to John Paine, notary public.[1]

It was ordered that the chapter's prison in the Canons' Barn in the Liberty of St Andrew should be repaired.

The chapter was concluded.

p520 blank

p521 **April 29** In the chapter house between 4 pm and 6 pm. Present: Peirs, Holt, and Creyghton; Healy in attendance.

Henry Dutton, S.T.B., prebendary of Whitelackington, sought election and admission as a canon residentiary in accordance with the royal letter addressed to the dean and chapter, and deposited his caution of 100 marks. He was admitted after taking the usual oaths, and his caution was divided—to the fabric, 10 marks; to the vicars choral, 10 marks; and the rest to the dean and canons. He was to commence residence on *p522* Oct. 1, 1681, and was not to receive any emoluments as canon residentiary before that date; and if he should die before then, his caution money would be repaid to his executor.

With the concurrence of Mr Dutton, Dr Creyghton was elected steward and official of the dean and chapter for the remainder of the year of office of Dr Sheafe, deceased, and his officialty was confirmed under seal.

The chapter was adjourned to the next morning.

April 30 Between 10 am and 12 noon [place not stated]. Present: Peirs, Holt, Creyghton, Dutton, and Sandys; Healy in attendance.

Henry Winchcombe, M.A., was elected and admitted on the nomination of the chancellor, Dr Holt, to the mastership of the grammar school, vacant by the cession of Mr Charles Thirlby.

p523 The chapter was adjourned to May 3.

At the time of his admission, Henry Winchcombe thus subscribed:

"I, Henry Winchcombe . . . now to be admitted to the Grammar Schoole within the Liberty of St Andrews in Wells . . . , do voluntarily and *ex animo* subscribe to the three Articles mentioned and contained in the 36th Canon of the Canons and Constitucions Ecclesiasticall of this Kingdome, and to all things therein contained.

Hen: Winchcombe."

p524–p526 **May 3** In the chapter house between 10 am and 12 noon. Present: Peirs, Holt, Creyghton, Sandys, Dutton, and prebendary Brickenden; Healy in attendance.

[1] See W.C.L., Ledger C, 707.

Charles Thirlby, M.A., was installed by Dr Creyghton and Mr Dutton in the archdeaconry of Wells with the prebend of Huish and Brent annexed, vacant by the death of Grindall Sheafe.

p527 **May 12** In the chapter house between 4 pm and 6 pm. Present: Peirs and Dutton; Healy in attendance.

Thomas Brickenden, S.T.B., prebendary of Worminster, appeared and exhibited a letter from king Charles dated May 3, 1680, and directed to the dean and chapter, which was received with respect and lodged in the archives.

p528 blank

p529–p530 **June 15** In the chapter house between 3 pm and 5 pm. Present: Selleck, Creyghton, archdeacon Thirlby, and prebendaries Shallett and Winchombe; Healy in attendance.

Edward Waple, S.T.B., by his proxy Morgan Jones, was installed by Messrs Shallett and Winchcombe in the prebend or canonry of Wiveliscombe, vacant by the cession of Charles Thirlby.

p531–p532 **June 16** In the chapter house between 9 am and 12 noon. Present: Selleck, Creyghton, and prebendary Shallett; Healy in attendance.

Samuel Mew,[1] S.T.B., by his proxy Joshua Lasher, was installed by Dr Creyghton and Mr Shallett in the prebend or canonry of Henstridge, vacant by the resignation of Edward Waple.

p533 **July 1** Quarterly chapter. In the chapter house between 10 am and 12 noon. Present: Peirs, Holt, Selleck, Creyghton, Sandys, and Dutton; Westley in attendance.

The following vicars choral appeared: Beaumont, Shallett, Lasher, Winchcombe, Walkley, Hobbs, Greene, Webb, Kelway, Martin, and Cooper; absent: Jackson.

Dr Creyghton asked that this declaration be inscribed in the acts of the chapter; namely, that although he had approved and subscribed the chapter act of Oct. 6 last, *p534* he had afterwards been moved by certain just and legitimate reasons to dissent entirely from it, and now, as far as in him lay, openly and publicly annulled and revoked it. He confirmed this declaration with his signature.

The chapter was adjourned to the next morning.

July 2 In the chapter house between 9 am and 12 noon. Present: Peirs, Holt, Selleck, Creyghton, Sandys, and Dutton; Healy in attendance.

Drs Peirs, Holt, and Creyghton, and Mr Sandys, unanimously confirmed that the election of Mr Dutton as canon residentiary on April 29 was good and valid in law as to its force, form, tenor, and effect; but Dr Selleck asserted that as the election did not take place during a quarterly chapter,[2] Mr Dutton should be re-elected.

Lots were cast for presentations to benefices:

p535 The dean—Stogumber and Mudford.

Dr Peirs—Cheddar and Shipham.

Dr Busby—St Cuthbert's, Wells, and North Curry.

Dr Holt—Dulverton and Burnham.

[1] Spelt Mews several times in the course of the entry.

[2] See chapter act of 18th January 1607–8, *Cal.* ii. 355.

Dr Selleck—Pucklechurch and East Lambrook.
Dr Creyghton—Bishop's Lydiard and Winscombe.
Mr Sandys—Buckland Abbas.
Mr Dutton—Allerton and Long Sutton.
Drs Peirs, Holt, and Creyghton, and Mr Dutton unanimously decreed that part of Mr Dutton's caution should be assigned and paid to Mr Sandys, because he ought to receive a portion with the rest of the canons. Dr Selleck protested against this. *p536*
The chapter was adjourned to the afternoon.

Between 4 pm and 6 pm [place not stated]. Present: Peirs, Holt, Creyghton, and Sandys; [Healy probably in attendance].

The validity of Mr Dutton's election in every legal particular was reaffirmed, notwithstanding the protestation by Dr Selleck in the morning; and this was confirmed with the following signatures:

"Guil: Peirs
P[raesidens]: C[apituli]:
Tho: Holt
Rob. Creyghton
Edwin: Sandys:"

The royal letter, exhibited at the meeting of the chapter on May 12 last, in favour of Mr Thomas Brickenden as the next canon for election after Dr Levinze, was reintroduced and accepted, and Mr Healy was instructed to deposit it again in the archives. *p537*

The chapter was adjourned to the next morning.

July 3 Between 10 am and 12 noon [place not stated]. Present: Peirs, Holt, Creyghton, and Dutton.

Guy Clynton brought the following letter from the bishop:

"To my Reverend Brethren the Canons of the Church of Wells at their Generall Chapter, These:

My Reverend Brethren,

I lately Complayned to som of you of a great Neglect in not signifying to the Dean if present, or the *Preses Capituli*, Who are to Preach for the Dignitaries or Praebendaries, especially if Strangers.

I likewise think fit at this your Generall Chapter to put you in mind of some other things formerly ordered for the better regulating the Affaires of the Church.

First, That all Books and Papers belonging to the Church be kept in the usuall place appointed for them.

Secondly, That all Dignitaries and Praebendaries bring in an Exact Terrier of the Lands and houses, Rents and Jurisdictions, belonging to them.

Thirdly, That they bring in Counterparts of the Leases of their Corps which they renew, to the Chapter, That so they may be Registred within one month after the sealing of the Leases. *p538*

These things do at present Occur to me as proper to put you in mind of, and I fear have hitherto bin neglected to the prejudice of the Church, The honour and interest of which ought to be our constant care and Study. I recomend them very earnestly to you, And you to God Almighties protection and am,

Your affectionate Brother,
P. Bath & Wells."

July 3rd 1680

This communication was received with respect and it was resolved that the chapter's humble thanks should be conveyed to the bishop for his paternal care of the Church and matters ecclesiastical; they assured him that the dean and chapter was ready and prepared to give due obedience to his injunctions, and to perform diligently the pre-eminently useful things stated in his letter.

A grant to Dr Peirs of the officialty of the dean and chapter within the Liberties of the cathedral was sealed, viz: to hear and determine only cases of urgency and of criminal proceedings within the Liberties.

The chapter was adjourned to July 5.

July 5 Between 10 am and 12 noon [place not stated]. Present: Peirs and Creyghton (proxy for Holt).

p539 Mr Francis Cox of Winchcombe[1] appeared and respectfully requested "That leave may be granted him to spitt[2] the Common call'd Woodborow's green within the parish and mannor of Winchcombe, to mend his Ploughed ground adjoyning to the said Common." Consideration of this petition was deferred until the dean and the greater part of the chapter were present.

The chapter was adjourned to between 4 pm and 6 pm, when the same members, with Healy in attendance, again adjourned it to the next morning.

July 6 Between 10 am and 12 noon [place not stated] Peirs and Creyghton (proxy for Holt), with Healy in attendance, adjourned the chapter to between 4 pm and 6 pm, when they again adjourned it to the next morning.

July 7 Between 10 am and 12 noon [place not stated] Peirs and Creyghton, with Healy in attendance, adjourned the chapter to the next morning.

p540 **July 8** Between 10 am and 12 noon [place not stated] Peirs and Creyghton, with Healy in attendance, adjourned the chapter to between 4 pm and 6 pm, when, with Westley in attendance, they again adjourned it to the next morning.

July 9 Between 10 am and 12 noon [place not stated] Peirs and Creyghton, with Westley in attendance, continued the chapter to the next morning.

July 10 Between 10 am and 12 noon [place not stated] Peirs and Creyghton, with Healy in attendance, adjourned the chapter to July 12.

July 12 Between 10 am and 12 noon [place not stated] Peirs and Creyghton, with Healy in attendance, adjourned the chapter to the next afternoon.

July 13 Between 4 pm and 6 pm [place not stated] Peirs, with Healy in attendance, adjourned the chapter to the next afternoon.

p541 **July 14** In the chapter house between 4 pm and 6 pm. Peirs and Creyghton (proxy for Holt), with Healy in attendance, adjourned the chapter to the next morning.

[1] Probably Winscombe. [2] I.e. to plough up.

July 15 Between 10 am and 12 noon [place not stated]. Present: Peirs and Creyghton (proxy for Holt); Healy in attendance.

Dr Sheafe had bequeathed in his will a sum of 20*l*.—10*l*. for the poor and needy in the Liberty, and 10*l*. for the poor of St Cuthbert's parish, to be distributed in the presence of the chapter. It was decreed that these sums should be distributed as directed.

The chapter was adjourned to July 28.

14th December 1681. I, William Peirs, communar of the dean and chapter, record and declare to all whom it may concern that the abovementioned twenty pounds has actually been distributed according to the tenor of the chapter act above written. Witness, James Williams, who distributed it at my order and the chapter's.

"James Williams Rob. Creyghton Will: Peirs."

p542 **July 21** Specially moved by certain considerations, and particularly the insufficiency of the proxy lately exhibited on his behalf by Mr Morgan Jones, it seemed good to Edward Waple, S.T.B., to ask the dean and chapter to institute and install him afresh in the prebend of Wiveliscombe. The dean and chapter agreed, and the whole business of installation was gone through again, as follows:

In the chapter house between 4 pm and 6 pm. Present: Peirs, Creyghton, and prebendary Nathaniel Selleck; Healy in attendance.

p543–p544 Edward Waple, S.T.B., by his proxy Morgan Jones, M.A., clerk, was installed by Dr Creyghton and Mr Selleck in the prebend or canonry of Wiveliscombe, vacant by the cession of Charles Thirlby.

p545 **Sept 30** In the chapter house between 10 am and 12 noon. Present: Bathurst, Holt, Selleck, Creyghton, and Dutton; Healy in attendance.

The following officers of the chapter were elected for the ensuing year: Baron of the exchequer, Dr Creyghton; Communar, Dr Peirs; Master of the fabric, Dr Peirs; Auditors, Dr Peirs and Dr Selleck; Overseers of the houses, Dr Selleck and Mr Sandys; Bailiff of the grange and *cursor ecclesiae*, James Williams. The vicars choral *p546* nominated Messrs Jackson and Hobbs as escheator, and the chapter deferred election to the next day, but there and then chose Mr Webb as tabellar.

p547 **Oct 1** Quarterly chapter. In the chapter house between 10 am and 12 noon. Present: Bathurst, Holt, Selleck, Creyghton, and Dutton; Healy in attendance.

Mr Hobbs was elected escheator.

The following vicars choral were present at the roll-call: Shallett, Beaumont, Winchcombe, Walkley, Jackson, Webb, Hobbs, Kelway, Martin, and Cowper; absent: Lasher (excused) and Green (sick).

p548 John Cowper, vicar choral, was perpetuated.

Charles Tudway was admitted a vicar choral for one year on probation, and was *p549* assigned Mr Beaumont as *auscultor*.

The chapter was adjourned to the afternoon.

Between 4 pm and 6 pm [place not stated]. Present: Bathurst, Holt, Selleck, Creyghton, and Dutton; Healy in attendance.

It was decreed "That for the future at St Martin's day there shall be no Martin's wheat received by any of the Officers of the Chapter from any Tenant, unlesse it be

paid in the old great measure, as it was before the act of Parliament[1] for setting the measures of the Kingdome".
Charles Tudway was assigned the stall of Worminster.
The chapter was adjourned to the next morning.

Oct 2 Between 10 am and 12 noon [place not stated] Bathurst, Holt, Selleck, Creyghton, and Dutton, with Healy in attendance, adjourned the chapter to the afternoon.

p550 Between 4 pm and 6 pm [place not stated]. Present: Bathurst, Holt, Selleck, and Creyghton; Healy in attendance.
An indenture was confirmed under the seal of the chapter, by which the bishop granted to John Baylie, LL.D., chancellor of the diocese of Bath and Wells, the rectory of Weston together with the revenues of the parishes of Middlezoy and Othery pertaining thereto.[2]
The chapter was adjourned to Oct. 4.

Oct 4 Between 4 pm and 6 pm [place not stated] Bathurst, Holt, Selleck, and Creyghton, with Healy in attendance, adjourned the chapter to the next afternoon.

Oct 5 Between 4 pm and 6 pm [place not stated] Bathurst, Holt, Selleck, Creyghton, and Dutton, with Healy in attendance, adjourned the chapter to the next morning.

Oct 6 Between 10 am and 12 noon [place not stated] Bathurst, Holt, Selleck, and Creyghton, with Healy in attendance, adjourned the chapter to the next morning.

p551 **Oct 7** Between 10 am and 12 noon [place not stated] Bathurst, Holt, Selleck, and Creyghton, with Healy in attendance, adjourned the chapter to the afternoon.
In the chapter house between 2 pm and 6 pm. Present: Bathurst, Holt, Selleck, and Creyghton, with Healy in attendance.
An indenture was sealed, confirming to William Evans, hosier, of the city of Wells the grant of a certain tenement in Chamberlain Street for 40 years.[3]
It was decreed "That every person, who liveth in any house bordering upon the Church-yard, and hath a doore opening into it, shall pay or cause to be paid to the Deane and Chapter, or to the Master of the Fabrick for the time being to the use of the Fabrick, two shillings yearly, or their doores into the Church-yard to be shut up; The payment of the said summe to commence from Michaelmas last. And that for the future there be a Covenant inserted in every lease to be let of any house which borders upon the Church yard for the payment of the said summe of 2*s*. yearly during the terme of the said lease. And then appeared Mrs Broderweek of the City of Wells, *p552* widdow, and humbly requested that leave might be granted her, to have a doore out of her backside into the Church yard: which request of hers the Chapter granted, under the conditions before-mentioned, vizt. upon the payment of 2*s*. per annum."
The chapter was adjourned to Oct. 11.

Oct 11 Between 10 am and 12 noon [place not stated]. Present: Bathurst, Selleck, and Creyghton; Healy in attendance.

[1] Proably 22 Car. II c.8 and 22 & 23 Car. II c.12. [2] See W.C.L., Ledger G, 708. [3] See ibid. 710.

The dean declared that he had completed his residence for the year ended Sept. 30, 1680, and Drs Selleck and Creyghton accepted his declaration.

The chapter was adjourned to Oct. 19.

Oct 19 In the audit room between 3 pm and 6 pm Bathurst and Selleck, with Healy in attendance, adjourned the chapter to the next afternoon.

Oct 20 In the audit room between 3 pm and 6 pm. Present: Bathurst, Holt, Selleck, and Creyghton; Healy in attendance.

It was decreed "That the widdow Browne shall be paid for the future but twelve *p553* pence a week by the Chapter, and that to continue but till Michaelmas next."

It was further decreed "That for the future at the installation of any Prebendary, the Prebendarie to be installed be desired to pay 20*s*. to the Library instead of the Collation usually made at the time of such installment."

The chapter was adjourned to the next afternoon.

Oct 21 In the audit room between 3 pm and 6 pm. Present: Bathurst, Holt, Selleck, Creyghton, and Dutton; Healy in attendance.

It was decreed "That There shall be a Seat in the Cathedrall appointed for the present Chancellor of the Diocesse, to be set up in such a place as the Deane and Chapter shall see requisite."

The chapter was adjourned to the next afternoon.

Oct 22 In the audit room between 3 pm and 4 pm. Present: Bathurst, Holt, Selleck, and Creyghton; Healy in attendance.

It was decreed "That there be speedy course taken for all mortuaries due to the Deane and Chapter within the mannors of East Curry and Winchcombe, and in other places whence they are payable, and the Steward and Commoner for the time being, by *p554* vertue of this Act, are required to take care for the effectuall prosecution of such persons as ought to pay the said mortuaries."

It was further decreed "That the Reeves and Bailiffes and Tenants of the severall mannors or farmes belonging to the Deane and Chapter be required to collect and pay the Rents for the severall farms and mannors according to their leases, and times and termes of Custome by the Copies for collecting and paying the same. And in case of neglect, the Steward and the Commoner and Master of the Fabrick for the time being are required to take all effectuall and legall wayes to prosecute all such of them as shall neglect their duty and offices herein. And that Mr Nicholas Dowthwaite, Clerke of their Courts, doth search the Records of the Church and the evidences thereof, and make as true a state as he can of what Lands, Tenements, Franchises, Privileges, Rents, or other hereditaments or encroachments whatsoever are witheld or withdrawne from the Deane and Chapter, and represent them to the Chapter; and that hee shall have Satisfaction for the paines which hee shall take in any of the premisses. And that the Reeve of East Curry for the time being be forthwith required to collect and gather up by St Martin's day next 14 Bushells of wheat and Arreares, and to pay it to the Reeve of West Hatch when it becomes due; otherwise that hee be speedily prosecuted by the Steward and Commoner *pro tempore*, as by law they shall be *p555* advised."

The chapter was adjourned to the next afternoon.

Oct 23 In the audit room between 3 pm and 6 pm. Present: Bathurst, Peirs, Holt, Selleck, and Creyghton.

An indenture was sealed, granting to Drs Peirs, Holt, Selleck, and Creyghton, and Mr Sandys, or any two of them the right to hold courts in the old almshouse.

Letters patent were confirmed under seal, by which the office of registrar of the archdeacon of Bath was granted to Tristram Evans, notary public, for his life and that of John Paine, notary public.[1]

It was decreed "That in pursuance of their act of Chapter of the 21st instant, the place in the Cathedrall Church where the present Chancellor of the Diocesse shall sit at prayer time shall be in the Seat behind the South doore of the Quire of the Church, in the Quire, where Mrs Keene and Mrs Westley have heretofore used to sit; and that leave is granted hereby to the present Chancellor of the Diocesse to sit there."

The chapter was adjourned to Dec. 4.

p556 **Dec 4** In the audit room between 10 am and 12 noon Peirs, Selleck, Holt, and Creyghton ,with Healy in attendance, adjourned the chapter to Dec. 6.

Dec 6 In the audit room between 10 am and 12 noon Peirs, Holt, Selleck, Creyghton, and Dutton, with Healy in attendance, adjourned the chapter to the afternoon.

In the audit room between 4 pm and 6 pm. Present: Peirs, Holt, and Creyghton; Healy in attendance.

It was decreed "that the Seat before that which is now erected for the present Chancellor of the Diocesse shall be and is assigned to Mrs Keene and Mrs Westley, and that leave is hereby granted to them to sit there during the pleasure of the Deane and Chapter".

The chapter was adjourned to the next morning.

Dec 7 In the audit room between 10 am and 12 noon. Present: Peirs, Holt, Selleck, and Creyghton; Healy in attendance.

It was decreed "That Dr Creyghton shall be desired to preach in the Cathedrall the 22nd of December next, being a day appointed by his Majestie for a Publick Fast *p557* throughout the Kingdome, and that the Chapter will pay for the supplying Dr Creyghton's next turne, which will be in the 2nd Sunday in January next."

Dr Creyghton agreed to this arrangement.

The chapter was adjourned to the next morning.

Dec 8 In the audit room between 9 am and 12 noon Peirs, Holt, Selleck, and Creyghton, with Healy in attendance, continued the chapter to 7 pm, and then adjourned it to the next morning.

Dec 9 In the audit room between 9 am and 12 noon Peirs, Holt, Selleck, and Creyghton, with Healy in attendance, adjourned the chapter to between 2 pm and 4 pm, and then to the next morning.

Dec 10 In the audit room between 10 am and 12 noon Peirs, Holt, Selleck, and Creyghton, with Healy in attendance, adjourned the chapter to between 3 pm and 6 pm,

[1] See ibid. 713.

and then to between 10 am and 12 noon on Dec. 13. [There is no record of a meeting then].

p558 blank

1680-1

p559 **Jan 3** Quarterly chapter. In the chapter house between 9 am and 12 noon. Present: Peirs, Holt, and Creyghton; Healy in attendance.

The following vicars choral appeared: Lasher, Walkley, Jackson, Webb, Hobbs, Cooper, and Tudway; absent: Shallet and Beaumont (excused), Winchcomb and Martin (sick), and Green.

The chapter was adjourned to the next morning.

p560 **Jan 4** Between 10 am and 12 noon Peirs and Holt adjourned the chapter from the chapter house to Dr Selleck's canonical house and continued it there, joined by Selleck and Creyghton; Healy in attendance.

It was decreed "that the present Commoner shall pay eight and twenty shillings and eight pence due to Mr Deane for books in the Library of the Deane and Chapter", and "that the Commoner shall pay ten pounds to Mr Harris for an hundred and two new Pipes put into the Chaire Organ of the Church".

The chapter was adjourned to between 3 pm and 6 pm in Dr Selleck's house, where Peirs, Holt, Selleck, and Creyghton adjourned it to the next morning, Healy in attendance.

p561 **Jan 5** In the chapter house between 10 am and 12 noon Peirs adjourned the chapter to Jan. 7.

Jan 7 In the chapter house between 9 am and 12 noon Peirs and Holt adjourned the chapter immediately to Dr Peirs's house[1] where, joined by Creyghton, with Healy in attendance, they adjourned it to the afternoon.

In Dr Peirs's house between 3 pm and 6 pm Peirs and Creyghton, with Westley in attendance, adjourned the chapter to the next morning.

Jan 8 In Dr Peirs's house between 10 am and 12 noon Peirs, Holt, and Creyghton, with Healy in attendance, adjourned the chapter to 5 pm, and then to Jan. 10.

p562 **Jan 10** In Dr Peirs's house between 9 am and 12 noon Peirs, with Healy in attendance, adjourned the chapter to the next morning.

[1] At this time Dr William Peirs, archdeacon of Taunton, was living in the eastern portion of the 'Archdeacon's house', until recently the Theological College library, opposite the north porch of the cathedral. His father, bishop Peirs, had obtained the house on a 60 years lease in the names of William and his brother John, intending that William should live there. But in his will the bishop altered this arrangement and instructed William to grant a 50 years lease of the western portion of the house to his step-mother Mary Peirs, retaining the rest of the building for his own residence. (See PCC 63 Penn).

Jan 11 In Dr Peirs's house between 10 am and 12 noon. Present: Peirs and Creyghton, with Healy in attendance, who, in the name of the whole chapter, decreed:

"That if Richard Healy their deputed Chapter Clarke be assign'd *Promotor Officii* in the Cause to be commenc'd *ex officio mero* in the Dean and Chapter's Consistory, against William Hawkins and William Robins of Chedder about the repaire of the Chancell of the parish Church of Chedder aforesaid, They do promise for the whole Deane and Chapter to save harmlesse and indemnifie the said Richard Healy, and to pay all Costs which the said Ri: Healy as *Promotor* aforesaid may be put to about the businesse aforesaid, either by a Sentence read against him in the said Businesse, Prohibition, or Appeale, or by any other meanes whatsoever."

The chapter was adjourned to Dr Peirs's house between 3 pm and 6 pm, when Peirs and Creyghton, with Healy in attendance, were joined by Holt, who assented to the act made in the morning; the chapter was then adjourned to the next morning.

p563 **Jan 12** In Dr Peirs's house between 9 am and 12 noon. Present: Peirs, Holt, and Creyghton; Healy in attendance.

An indenture was sealed, granting to Mr Nathaniel Selleck a parcel of land, meadow and pasture, in area more or less 24 acres, situate in the parish of Wick St Lawrence, and lately held by Anthony Shepheard.

It was decreed "that Mr Dowthwaite be hereby required and authorised to sue in their name in any of his Majesties temporall Courts for all arrearages of Rents due to them, and all other things owing to them, and recoverable in the said Courts as their Atturney"; and "that Richard Healy aforesaid be hereby requested and authorised for the Dean and Chapter to sue for all Pensions and Mortuaries which are due to them in arreares, and which are recoverable in his Majesties Ecclesiasticall Courts."

The chapter was adjourned to the next morning.

Jan 13 In Dr Peirs's house between 9 am and 12 noon. Present: Peirs, Holt, Creyghton, and Dutton; Healy in attendance.

It was decreed "That in obedience to the Injunctions of my Lord Bishop's Letter receiv'd in the Chapter-house the 3rd of July last, every private Canon be hereby required to deliver into the Chapter Clerk's hands all such Chapter books and other Records as are in each or any of their Custodies, and that James Williams their *p564* mandatary be commanded to wait upon the Canons for all such books, and that Mr Douthwaite do prepare a place to receive them there."

The chapter was adjourned to Dr Peirs's house between 3 pm and 4 pm, when Peirs and Holt, with Healy in attendance, adjourned the chapter to the next morning.

Jan 14 Between 10 am and 12 noon Peirs and Creyghton, with Healy in attendance, adjourned the chapter from Dr Peir's house to Dr Selleck's canonical house between 2 pm and 5 pm. [There is no record of a meeting at that time].

p565 & p568 **Feb 7** In the chapter house between 2 pm and 5 pm. Present: Peirs, Creyghton, and prebendaries Shallet and Lasher; Healy in attendance.

Wykes Huntley, B.A., LL.B., was installed by Messrs Shallet and Lasher in the prebend or canonry of Combe XI, vacant by the death of Thomas Willis.

pp566 and 567 blank and stuck together

p569 **Feb 23** In the chapter house between 2 pm and 4 pm. Present: Peirs, Selleck, Creyghton, and Dutton; Healy in attendance.

Mr Dutton stated that the vicarage of Long Sutton was vacant by the death of the last incumbent, Mr [Henry] Batten, and that he wished to present to the living Humphrey Smith, B.A. The nomination was accepted and the deed of presentation sealed.

p570 blank

p571 **March 5** In the chapter house between 9 am and 12 noon. Present: Peirs, Creyghton, and prebendaries Shallet, Huntley, and Jones; Healy in attendance.

Henry Allyne, M.A., of Magdalen college, Oxford, was installed by Messrs Shallet and Jones in the prebend or canonry of Combe XIII, vacant by the free resignation of Abraham Allyne.

p573 **March 10** In the chapter house between 10 am and 12 noon. Present: Peirs, Creyghton, and Dutton; Healy in attendance.

A mandate was received from the bishop for the election of a proctor for the chapter at the Convocation to be held in London on March 22; Dr Busby, treasurer, was elected, and his election was certified to the bishop.

p574 blank

1681

p575 **April 1** Quarterly chapter. In the chapter house between 9 am and 12 noon. Present: Peirs, Selleck, Creyghton, and Sandys; Healy in attendance. Being Good Friday, the chapter was adjourned to April 6.

April 6 Between 9 am and 12 noon [place not stated]. Present: Peirs, Holt, Selleck, Creyghton, Sandys, and Dutton; Healy in attendance.

The following vicars choral appeared: Lasher, Beaumont, Jackson, Hobbs, Green, Webb, Martin, and Tudway; absent: Walkley (sick), Shallet, Winchcomb, and Cooper.

p576 The chapter was adjourned to between 4 pm and 6 pm, when the same six canons again adjourned it to the next morning.

April 7 Between 10 am and 12 noon [place not stated]. Present: Peirs, Holt, Selleck, Creyghton, Sandys, and Dutton; Healy in attendance.

Dr Peirs the communar paid to Drs Holt, Selleck, and Creyghton, and Mr Sandys in full chapter their daily distributions due to April 1 last. Mr Dutton asked that he might have his daily distributions as if he were a canon residentiary, and Dr Selleck then immediately withdrew from the chapter. After this, Mr Dutton asked the president that the canons remaining in chapter should vote, as to whether or not it seemed [just] that he should receive his daily distributions. The president forthwith enjoined them to vote individually on this question; and Mr Sandys, Dr Creyghton, and Dr Holt, with the president himself, voted with one consent that Mr Dutton should have his arrears of the daily distributions, and that he should have the right to *p577* them in future. Then Dr Holt, Dr Creyghton, and Mr Sandys asked Dr Peirs as communar to pay to Mr Dutton his arrears—a sum of 5*l.*; and this he undertook to do. The chapter was adjourned to the afternoon.

Between 4 pm and 6 pm [place not stated]. Present: Peirs, Holt, Creyghton, Sandys, and Dutton; Healy in attendance.

James Williams was ordered to visit each canon residentiary, and in the name of the chapter require him to send, bring, or cause to be sent or brought into the chapter house all books whatsoever, and all other writings or records pertaining in any way to the cathedral church; and to report to the chapter at the same hour on the following day the response of each canon.

The chapter was adjourned to the next morning.

April 8 Between 10 am and 12 noon [place not stated]. Present: Peirs, Holt, Creyghton, Sandys, and Dutton; Healy in attendance.

James Williams appeared and assured the chapter that he had himself gone to the canons individually according to the order made yesterday in full chapter. From Dr Selleck he brought one large folio book beginning *Arreragia pendeñ in Compto* *p578* *Ministrorum* and ending "Before us Commissioners Geo. Walrond, Guydo Clynton, P. Roynon Commissioners";[1] also another book beginning *Die Jovis primo vizt. die mensis Aprilis A° 1591*, and ending "Benjamin Heyden Januar. 12. 1604";[2] and a third beginning *Die Sabbati 2° Januarii 1607*, and ending *Veñelis Viri Joannis Bowrne*;[3] and another beginning "To William and Alexander Towse gent.", and ending "Jo: Blake, Will: Doble, N. Marshall";[4] and a large folio book without any writing in it. Dr Holt brought in a book beginning "Lawrentius Rech, Agnes and Jana Rech", and ending "in Burnham Dr Wood sibi".[5] Mr Sandys brought in the book commonly called the Red Book.[6]

The chapter was adjourned to between 3 pm and 4 pm, when Peirs, Holt, Creyghton, and Dutton, with Healy in attendance, further adjourned it to the next morning.

April 9 Between 10 am and 12 noon [place not stated]. Present: Peirs, Holt, Creyghton, Sandys, and Dutton; Healy in attendance.

Dr Peirs and Dr Holt made the following statement in full chapter and asked that it be recorded in the chapter acts, viz: Notwithstanding that they had consented and had individually subscribed to the chapter act of Oct. 6, 1679, they now openly and publicly declared that on account of certain just and legitimate reasons which had specially moved them after the passing of that act, they wholly dissented jointly and *p579* severally from it, and as far as in them lay, annulled and revoked it. They immediately confirmed and endorsed this statement by their signatures:

"Guil: Peirs
Tho: Holt".

[1] W.C.L., Book of Arrears, 1590–1631.

[2] This book now forms part of W.C.L., Act Book 1591–1607. "Benjamin Heyden . . . 1604" occurs at the end of f.183d, but the book continues to f.215.

[3] W.C.L., Act Book 1607–22. [4] I cannot trace this book. [5] W.C.L., Steward's Book, 1629–30.

[6] W.C.L., *Liber Ruber*, described as Register II and calendared in *Cal.* i. and ii.

It was then decreed "that Mr Deane of Wells for the yeare begun the first of October last and now current shall be allowed his Residence in this Cathedrall Church, with all profits and commodities to the same belonging in as large and ample a manner as any other of the Canons resident do enjoy them for this yeare."
The chapter desired that a certain act made on Oct. 17, 1670, and attested by the signatures of Ralph Bathurst, William Peirs, Thomas Holt, and Grindall Sheafe, should be reaffirmed as valid in every respect at law, and to this end should be read and again inserted. The junior canons then confirmed the act by subscribing their names, so that all disputations and doubts in the future might be avoided; and it was desired that each succeeding canon should do likewise.

"Rob. Creyghton Precntor
Edwin Sandys.
Hen: Dutton."

The chapter was adjourned to April 12.

p580 **April 12** Between 3 pm and 6 pm [place not stated]. Present: Holt, Creyghton, Sandys, and Dutton; Healy in attendance.

An indenture was sealed, granting to Jane Keene, widow, for 40 years a certain tenement in Wells among the dwellings commonly called New-Works.[1]

Another indenture was sealed, granting a certain messuage in the parish of Shipham with its appurtenences to Jane Keene, widow, for her life and the lives of William Westley, gen., and his wife Sarah successively.[2]

Then Dr Peirs came in and took his place in chapter as president, and it was decreed "That the Commoner shall pay to Thomas Davis of this Liberty Shooe-maker, towards the reliefe of his necessities, fifty shillings."

The chapter was adjourned to the next morning.

April 13 Between 9 am and 12 noon [place not stated]. Present: Peirs, Holt, Creyghton, Sandys, and Dutton; Healy in attendance.

". . . Whereas there was a Contract made by Mr Nathaniell Selleck the 9th of December 1680 for an estate in Congresbury, for a fine of five shillings, And Whereas *p581* there is a Warrant issued out to the Clerke of their Courts upon the said Contract, to make out a Copy thereupon, The Chapter taking the same into Consideration againe, at the Request of Mr Sandys one of the Canons, and Mr Dutton another of the Canons resident aforesaid, do decree and order that the Steward and Clerke of their Courts do not grant any estate in Court, nor issue out any Copy upon the said Contract, before the matter be debated in full Chapter, whether the majority of the Chapter can conclude those that are absent."

The chapter was concluded.

p582 blank

p583 **July 1** Quarterly chapter. In the chapter house between 9 am and 12 noon. Present: Peirs, Holt, Creyghton, Sandys, and Dutton; Healy in attendance.

The following vicars choral appeared: Lasher, Winchcomb, Beaumont, Walkley,

[1] See W.C.L., Ledger G, 716: the 3rd house from the eastern end, with a garden in the 'New Works gardens'—on the north side of the present Recreation Ground.

[2] See W.C.L., Ledger G, 714.

Jackson, Hobbs, Green, Webb, Martin, Cooper, and Tudway; absent: Shallet, excused.

Dr Holt, to whom the nomination had fallen by lot, nominated John Bower, B.A., for presentation to the vacant vicarage of Burnham; this was approved, and the deed of presentation was sealed.

The chapter was adjourned to between 3 pm and 6 pm, when the same five canons, *p584* with Healy in attendance, adjourned it to the next morning.

July 2 Between 9 am and 12 noon [place not stated] the same five canons, with Healy in attendance, adjourned the chapter to July 4.

July 4 Between 9 am and 12 noon [place not stated] the same five canons, with Healy in attendance, adjourned the chapter to between 3 pm and 6 pm, and then to the next afternoon.

July 5 Between 3 pm and 6 pm [place not stated]. Present: Peirs, Holt, Creyghton, Sandys, and Dutton; Healy in attendance.

Mr Sandys declared publicly and openly in full chapter that he had completed his *p585* residence for the current year; this declaration was accepted by the other canons.

The chapter was adjourned to the next morning.

July 6 Between 9 am and 12 noon [place not stated] Holt, Peirs, Creyghton, and Dutton, with Paine in attendance, adjourned the chapter to between 4 pm and 6 pm, and then to the next morning. [There is no record of a meeting then].

p586 blank

p587–p588 **Aug 3** In the chapter house between 9 am and 12 noon. Present: Bathurst, Peirs, Holt, Creyghton, and prebendaries Waple, Brickenden, and Shallett; Healy in attendance.

Samuel Thomas, S.T.B., was installed by Messrs Waple and Shallett in the prebend or canonry of Compton Bishop, vacant by the death of Robert Collier.

p589 **Sept 30** In the chapter house between 9 am and 12 noon. Present: Bathurst, Peirs, Holt, Sandys, and Dutton; Healy in attendance.

The following officers of the chapter were elected for the ensuing year; Baron of the exchequer, Dr Holt; Communar, Dr Peirs; Master of the fabric, Dr Peirs; Steward, Dr Creyghton; Auditors, Dr Creyghton and Mr Sandys; Overseers of the houses, Dr Selleck and Mr Dutton; Bailiff of the grange and *cursor ecclesiae*, James Williams; *p590* Escheator, the vicars nominated Messrs Jackson and Martin and the chapter elected Mr Jackson; Tabellar, Mr Martin.

p591 **Oct 1** Quarterly chapter. In the chapter house between 9 am and 12 noon. Present: Bathurst, Peirs, Holt, Sandys, and Dutton, five residentiary canons; Healy in attendance.

The following vicars choral appeared: Shallet, Lasher, Winchcombe, Beaumont, Walkley, Jackson, Greene, Webb, Hobbs, Martin, Cooper, and Tudway.

Charles Tudway was perpetuated.

p592 The chapter was adjourned to Oct. 3.

Oct 3 Between 9 am and 12 noon [place not stated] the same five canons, with Healy in attendance, adjourned the chapter to the next afternoon.

Oct 4 Between 3 pm and 6 pm [place not stated] Bathurst, Holt, Creyghton, Sandys, and Dutton, with Healy in attendance, adjourned the chapter to the next morning.

Oct 5 Between 10 am and 12 noon [place not stated] Bathurst, Peirs, Holt, Creyghton, Sandys, and Dutton, with Paine in attendance, adjourned the chapter to between 3 pm and 6 pm, when, with Healy in attendance, they adjourned it to the next morning.

p593 **Oct 6** Between 9 am and 12 noon [place not stated]. Present: Bathurst, Peirs, Holt, Creyghton, Sandys, and Dutton; Healy in attendance.

Residences for the ensuing year were settled as follows:

Dr Peirs and Dr Selleck—October, November, December.

Mr Sandys and Mr Dutton—January, February, March.

Dr Holt and Dr Creyghton—April, May, June.

The dean and Dr Busby—July, August, September.

Lest this allocation should be detrimental to any one of the canons to whom a later turn of residence had fallen, it was decreed that all stipends, dividends, obventions, and all other kinds of commodity and emolument should be due and paid, not only to those who had completed their residences in the first quarter of the year, but also to those who were prepared to do so, even though their turns fell in the later months, so that they could not complete or even begin their actual residence. And if, after a period of three or four months at the beginning of the year, a canon should die *p594* before commencing his residence, it was unanimously decreed that his executors or administrators ought to receive, not only the dividend and stipends due to him for that year, but also the profits and stipends for the following year, as a dividend for the *annus post mortem*—and ought to receive them as of right.

It was resolved to give a charitable donation of 5*l*. to Mr John Ball, vicar of Mudford, and Dr Peirs the communar was asked to pay this immediately.

It was decreed "That a ninth part of the generall dividend be every yeare laid by for the Fabrick."

The chapter was adjourned to the next morning.

Oct 7 Between 9 am and 12 noon [place not stated]. Present: Bathurst, Peirs, Holt, Creyghton, Sandys, and Dutton; Healy in attendance.

An indenture was sealed, granting the rectory of St Cuthbert's to Edward Bisse, Esq. for his life and the lives of Jane his wife and Amy their daughter and the life of the longest liver of them.

p595 The chapter was adjourned to between 3 pm and 6 pm, when the same members, with Healy in attendance, again adjourned it to the next afternoon.

Oct 8 Between 3 pm and 6 pm [place not stated]. Present: Bathurst, Peirs, Holt, Creyghton, and Dutton; Healy in attendance.

Letters confirmatory were sealed of an indenture by which the bishop granted to John Baylie, LL.D. his chancellor the rectory of Weston together with the profits pertaining thereto in the parishes of Middlezoy and Othery.[1]

The chapter was adjourned to Oct. 10.

[1] See ibid. 718.

Oct 10 Between 9 am and 12 noon [place not stated] Peirs, Holt, Creyghton, and Dutton, with Healy in attendance, adjourned the chapter to the next afternoon.

Oct 11 Between 3 pm and 6 pm [place not stated] Bathurst, Peirs, Holt, Creyghton, and Dutton, with Healy in attendance, adjourned the chapter to the next morning.

p596 **Oct 12** Between 9 am and 12 noon [place not stated]. Present: Bathurst, Peirs, Holt, Creyghton, Sandys, and Dutton; Healy in attendance.

An indenture was sealed, granting the rectory of Cheddar to George Dodington, Esq., for his life and the lives of William Dodington his son and George Reding, son of John Redding deceased, and the life of the longest liver of them.

The chapter was adjourned to the next morning.

Oct 13 Between 9 am and 12 noon [place not stated] Bathurst, Peirs, Creyghton, Sandys, and Dutton, with Healy in attendance, adjourned the chapter to the next morning.

Oct 14 Between 9 am and 12 noon [place not stated]. Present: Bathurst, Creyghton, Sandys, and Dutton; Healy in attendance.

An indenture was sealed, granting a certain tenement in High Street, Wells, next to the inn commonly called 'The Catherine Wheel', to Charles Baron, gen., now *praetor* of the city of Wells, for 40 years.

p597 The chapter was adjourned to Oct. 21.

Oct 21 Between 10 am and 12 noon [place not stated] Peirs, Holt, Selleck, Creyghton, and Dutton, with Clynton in attendance, adjourned the chapter to the next morning.

Oct 22 Between 10 am and 12 noon [place not stated]. Present: Bathurst, Peirs, Holt, Selleck, Creyghton, and Dutton; Paine in attendance.

An indenture was sealed, granting the rectory of Stogumber with the chapel of Bicknoller thereto annexed to Mr John Sydenham for his life and the lives of his sons John and Philip, and the life of the longest liver of them.

Letters of attorney or deputation were sealed for the holding of courts at the old almshouse.

The chapter was adjourned to Oct. 25.

Oct 25 In the chapter house between 9 am and 12 noon Bathurst, with Healy in attendance, adjourned the chapter to the audit room, commonly called the exchequer, where, with Peirs, Holt, and Creyghton, the chapter was adjourned to *p598* the afternoon.

In the audit room between 3 pm and 6 pm. Present: Bathurst, Peirs, Holt, Creyghton, and Dutton, five residentiary canons; Healy in attendance.

It was decreed "That ten pounds shall be given by the Chapter towards the Redemption of the Captives in Algiers."

The chapter was adjourned to the next morning.

Oct 26 In the audit room between 10 am and 12 noon Bathurst, Peirs, Holt, Selleck, Creyghton, and Dutton, six residentiary canons, with Healy in attendance, adjourned the chapter to between 3 pm and 6 pm, when Holt and Dutton, with Healy in attendance, adjourned it to the next morning.

p599 **Oct 27** In the audit room between 9 am and 12 noon Bathurst, Peirs, Holt, Creyghton, and Dutton, five residentiary canons, with Healy in attendance, adjourned the chapter to between 3 pm and 6 pm, and then to the next morning.

Oct 28 In the audit room between 9 am and 12 noon Peirs, Holt, Creyghton, and Dutton, with Healy in attendance, adjourned the chapter to between 3 pm and 6 pm, when the same four canons, with Healy in attendance, adjourned it to the next morning.

p600 **Oct 29** In the audit room between 9 am and 12 noon Peirs, Holt, and Creyghton, with Healy in attendance, adjourned the chapter to between 3 pm and 6 pm, and then to Nov. 3.

Nov 3 In the audit room between 9 am and 12 noon Creyghton immediately adjourned the chapter to Dr Selleck's house. Present there: Peirs, Selleck, and Creyghton; Healy in attendance.

An indenture was sealed confirming the grant of a tenement and cottage with its appurtenences in the manor of Winscombe to Charles Francis of Wilton, Wilts., gen., for his life and the lives of his son and daughter, and the life of the longest liver of them.

The chapter was adjourned to the next morning.

p601 **Nov 4** In the audit room between 9 am and 12 noon Peirs, with Healy in attendance, adjourned the chapter to the morning of Dec. 5.

Dec 5 In the audit room between 9 am and 12 noon Peirs, Holt, Creyghton, Sandys, and Dutton, with Healy in attendance, adjourned the chapter to the next morning.

Dec 6 In the audit room between 9 am and 12 noon Peirs, Holt, Creyghton, Sandys, and Dutton, with Healy in attendance, adjourned the chapter to the next morning.

Dec 7 In the audit room between 9 am and 12 noon Peirs, Holt, Creyghton, Sandys, and Dutton, with Healy in attendance, adjourned the chapter to the next morning.

p602 **Dec 8** In the audit room between 9 am and 12 noon Peirs, Holt, Creyghton, Sandys, and Dutton, five residentiary canons, with Healy in attendance, adjourned the chapter to the next morning.

Dec 9 In the audit room between 9 am and 12 noon Peirs, Holt, Creyghton, Sandys, and Dutton, with Healy in attendance, adjourned the chapter to the next morning.

Dec 10 In the audit room between 9 am and 12 noon Peirs, Holt, Creyghton, Sandys, and Dutton, with Healy in attendance, adjourned the chapter to Dec. 12.

p603 **Dec 12** In the audit room between 9 am and 12 noon. Present: Peirs, Holt, Creyghton, Sandys, and Dutton, five residentiary canons; Healy in attendance.

Since several canons had brought before the chapter a complaint that they had at various times been inconvenienced by not receiving part of their dividends for several years now past (as appears at the foot of divers accounts now subscribed and inspected by the Baron and the auditors), any canon so inconvenienced would receive from the communar for 1681 (and from succeeding communars, until satisfaction had been made to the canon in question) the said sum or sums (provided they had not been received from another source). The communar or his successors, in the account for 1681 and, if necessary, in subsequent accounts, would deduct such sum or sums from the dividends of those canons whose emoluments had originally been incorrectly augmented, so that the accounts would be corrected and just compensation made to the brethren.

"Rob. Creyghton — Guil: Peirs
Edwin: Sandys: — *P:C:*
Hen: Dutton. — Tho: Holt."

p604 The chapter was adjourned to the next morning.

Dec 13 In the audit room between 9 am and 12 noon. Present: Peirs, Holt, Creyghton, Sandys, and Dutton, five residentiary canons; Healy in attendance.

The following letter had been received from the bishop:

"To my Reverend Brethren the Canons of Wells at their Chapter.

My Reverend Brethren,

I thought to have spoken with you in person, but some Publick Businesse commands mee abroad. This is therefore to remind you of a former Order[1] I made, That 10 pounds should be layd down at the Admission of a Canon in the Commoners hands towards the repaire of the ruinous Houses,[2] which, I doubt, *p605* hath not been constantly observ'd. I likewise think fit to put you in mind of the poore Captives, some of your Body having formerly told mee that it would be most proper to give a Summe out of the Common Stock. I commit you to God's protection and am,

Your Affectionate Brother
P. Bath & Wells."

Wells Decr.12th
1681.

It was decreed that the bishop should be told that the chapter gratefully accepted his paternal care for them and that, approving his desire, they had already by public decree set aside 10*l.* for the redemption of the captives. As to his other injunction, they had received from Dr Creyghton and Mr Sandys the sum of 10*l.* mentioned,[3] and had it in mind to receive the same sum from each succeeding canon.

The chapter was adjourned to the next morning.

Dec 14 In the audit room between 9 am and 12 noon Peirs, Holt, Creyghton, Sandys, and Dutton, with Healy in attendance, adjourned the chapter to the afternoon.

[1] There is no other record of this order by bishop Mews.

[2] These were "two canonicall houses, lying on the east of the cathedral church . . . utterly ruined in the time of the late civill warres" (*Cal.* ii. 465). They were in the bishop's gift, and stood between the house until recently the Theological College principal's house and Tor street.

[3] There is no trace of the receipt of these sums, but the communar's accounts for 1689–90 show that contributions of 10*l.* each were in hand from Dr Creyghton, Mr Sandys, Mr Dutton, and Dr Levinz; similar sums were received from two new residentiaries, Mr Brickenden (accounts for 1691–2, *Cal.* ii. 471) and Mr Cheney (accounts for 1693–4, *Cal.* ii. 473). There is no evidence that this money was applied for the rehabilitation of the ruinous houses.

p606 In the audit room between 3 pm and 6 pm. Present: the same five canons, with Healy in attendance.

Mr Nicholas Painter appeared and handed to the president of the chapter certain letters patent granted by Philip and Mary in the 2nd and 3rd years of their reign, on May 10, concerning the archdeaconry of Wells; and another parchment containing four schedules beginning *Gilbertus permissione divina Bathoñ. et Wellen. Epũs* and ending *Año Dñi millesimo quingentesimo quinquagesimo sexto*; and thirdly a paper document effecting a composition between the bishop and the archdeacon of Wells.[1] He left these three documents with the chapter and asked that they should be deposited in the archives.

The chapter was adjourned to the next morning.

Dec 15 In the audit room between 9 am and 12 noon Peirs, Holt, Creyghton, and Dutton, with Healy in attendance, adjourned the chapter to the next morning.

Dec 16 In the audit room between 9 am and 12 noon. Present: Peirs, Holt, Creyghton, Sandys, and Dutton; Healy in attendance.

p607 At the petition of Humphrey Smith, vicar of Long Sutton, a dispensation was sealed, relieving him from rebuilding "An Hall having a Porch and little Buttery adjoyning and a Chamber over it" at the vicarage house, which had become dilapidated and almost demolished during the time of Henry Batten the last vicar, so that neither he nor his executors or administrators should be legally obliged to restore the ruin.

The chapter was adjourned to the next morning.

Dec 17 In the audit room between 9 am and 12 noon Peirs, Creyghton, and Sandys, with Healy in attendance, adjourned the chapter to Dec. 19.

p608 **Dec 19** In the audit room between 9 am and 12 noon Peirs, Holt, Creyghton and Sandys, with Healy in attendance, adjourned the chapter to the next morning.

Dec 20 In the audit room between 9 am and 12 noon. Present: Peirs, Holt, Creyghton, and Sandys; Healy in attendance.

It was decreed "that Mr Lasher shall be paid for preaching the course of the Prebend of Wedmore 2nd last Sunday morning 20*s*. out of the Salary of the said Prebend". *Et deinde Domini praedicti decre-* [Here the record breaks off].

1681-2

p609 **Jan 2** Quarterly chapter. In the chapter house [time not stated]. Present: Creyghton, with Healy in attendance.

The following vicars choral appeared: Shallet, Lasher, Winchcomb, Beaumont, Hobbs, Walkley, Jackson, Greene, Webb, Martin, Cooper, and Tudway.

The chapter was adjourned to the next morning.

[1] The particulars of these papers given here are insufficient to enable them to be traced.

Jan 3 In the chapter house between 9 am and 12 noon Holt, Creyghton, and Sandys, with Paine in attendance, adjourned the chapter to Dr Peirs's house in the Liberty between 4 pm and 6 pm, where Peirs, Holt, Creyghton, Sandys, and Dutton, with *p610* Paine in attendance, adjourned it to the next morning in the chapter house.

Jan 4 In the chapter house between 10 am and 12 noon Holt, Creyghton, Sandys, and Dutton, with Paine in attendance, adjourned the chapter to Dr Peirs's house, where the five canons adjourned it to the next morning.

Jan 5 In the chapter house between 10 am and 12 noon Sandys and Dutton adjourned the chapter immediately to Dr Peirs's house, where Peirs, Holt, Creyghton, Sandys, and Dutton, with Healy in attendance, adjourned it to Dr Peirs's house between 3 pm and *p611* 6 pm, when they again adjourned it to the next afternoon.

Jan 6 In Dr Peirs's house between 3 pm and 6 pm Peirs, Holt, Creyghton, Sandys, and Dutton, with Healy in attendance, adjourned the chapter to Jan. 24.

Jan 24 In the chapter house between 9 am and 12 noon Holt, Creyghton, Sandys, and Dutton adjourned the chapter to Dr Peirs's house on the north side of the cathedral where, with Healy in attendance, the five canons adjourned it to the same place between 3 pm and 6 pm, and then to the next afternoon.

p612 **Jan 25** In Dr Peirs's house between 3 pm and 6 pm Peirs, Holt, Creyghton, Sandys, and Dutton, with Healy in attendance . . . [the entry is not completed].

p613–p614 **Feb 20** In the chapter house between 3 pm and 6 pm. Present: Creyghton, and prebendaries Shallett, Nathaniel Selleck, and Winchcombe; Healy in attendance.

Thomas Davis, M.A., was installed by Messrs Shallett and Winchcombe in the prebend or canonry of Wedmore II, vacant by the death of Walter Hungerford.

1682

p615 **April 1** Quarterly chapter. In the chapter house between 9 am and 12 noon. Present: Holt, Creyghton, and Dutton; Healy in attendance.

The following vicars choral appeared; Shallet, Lasher, Winchcomb, Hobbs, Walkley, Greene, Jackson, Webb, Martin, Cooper, and Tudway.

The stall of Sutton, vacant by the death of Mr Beaumont, was assigned to Mr Lasher.

The chapter was adjourned to April 3.

April 3 In the chapter house between 9 am and 12 noon Holt, Creyghton, and Dutton, with Healy in attendance, adjourned the chapter to Dr Peirs's house.

p616 An indenture was sealed, granting to Mr Dowthwaite for forty years a parcel of land commonly called the Camery on the south side of the cathedral.[1]

Then the canons declared that they would meet in chapter at the same house at 8 pm.

[1] The lease was granted to Mr Dowthwaite "only in trust to and for the use and behoof of... William Peirs..."; W.C.L., Documents, Series V, 25.

In Dr Peirs's house at 8 pm. Present: Peirs, Holt, Creyghton, and Dutton.

An indenture was sealed, granting to John Palmer Esq. of Wells for his life and the lives of William and Thomas Peirs, gen., sons of Dr Peirs, the rectory of Bishop's Lydiard, in hand by the death of Charles, late Earl of Rochester. Mr Palmer gave an undertaking to pay at Michaelmas next, as part of the fine, the sum of 266*l.* 13*s.* 4*d.*, from which 8*l.* would be paid to Mr Dowthwaite and Richard Healy for their diligence in looking after the chapter's business. After the sealing of this indenture it was decreed "That if within two yeares Mr Palmer aforesaid shall desire to change any of the Lives now mentioned in his Lease, provided the said Lives be in being, hee shall change the lifes for five shillings and the fees. And they then gave him a Release under the chapter seale of the 2400*l.* fine."

The chapter was adjourned to the chapter house on the next afternoon.

p617 **April 4** In the chapter house between 3 pm and 6 pm Holt and Dutton, with Healy in attendance, adjourned the chapter to the next morning.

April 5 In the chapter house between 9 am and 12 noon *coram tribus canonicis praedictis*, with Healy in attendance, the chapter was adjourned to the next morning.

April 6 In the chapter house between 9 am and 12 noon Holt and Creyghton adjourned the chapter to the next morning.

April 7 In the chapter house between 9 am and 12 noon Holt, Creyghton, and Dutton adjourned the chapter to the afternoon.

In the chapter house between 3 pm and 6 pm. Present: Holt, Creyghton, and Dutton; Healy in attendance.

The "Leas-fees" in the manor of North Curry were granted to Arthur Weaver for one year for the sum of 30*s.*

It was decreed "That in conformity to an Act of Chapter made the 6th day of October last past and pursuant to the same, Mr Dean of Wells for the yeare begun the *p618* first of October last and now current shall be allowed his Residence in this Cathedrall Church with all profitts and commodities to the same belonging, in as large and ample a manner as any of the Canons Resident do enjoy them for this yeare."

10*s.* would be given to John Hobbs, one of the vicars choral, as an act of charity.

The chapter was adjourned to the next morning.

April 8 In the chapter house between 9 am and 12 noon the same three canons, with Healy in attendance, adjourned the chapter to April 10.

April 10 In the chapter house between 9 am and 12 noon the same three canons, with Healy in attendance, adjourned the chapter to the next morning.

April 11 In the chapter house between 9 am and 12 noon the same three canons, with Healy in attendance, adjourned the chapter to April 20.

p619 **April 20** In the chapter house between 9 am and 12 noon. Present: Holt, Creyghton, and Dutton; Healy in attendance.

William Levinze, M.D., president of St John's college, Oxford, and subdean of the cathedral sought admission as a canon residentiary in accordance with the royal letter deposited in the archives by the capitular decree of Dec. 18, 1679. He brought his caution money of 100 marks, which the chapter accepted and decreed to be divided and distributed in the customary manner, and took the usual oaths. He was *p620* admitted, and was not to commence residence before Oct. 1, 1683, or to receive any emoluments as canon residentiary before that date; and if he should die before then, his caution money would be repaid to his executor.

Lots were cast for benefices, as follows:

The dean—Stogumber and Mudford.

Dr Holt—Dulverton and Burnham.

Dr Busby—Cheddar and Shipham.

Dr Selleck—Bishop's Lydiard and Winscombe.

Dr Creyghton—Pucklechurch and East Lambrook.

Mr Sandys—St Cuthbert's and North Curry.

Mr Dutton—Allerton and Long Sutton.

Dr Levinze—Buckland Abbas.

With the concurrence of Dr Levinze, Mr Dutton was elected communar and master of the fabric for the rest of the current year, on the death of Dr Peirs. Orders were given to Mr Dowthwaite to inspect and complete the accounts of Dr Peirs or his *p621* executors, and to pass them to the auditors for revision and approval.

The chapter was adjourned to the afternoon.

Between 3 pm and 6 pm [place not stated]. Present: Holt, Creyghton, and Dutton; Healy in attendance.

The stall of Henstridge was assigned to Mr Hobbs and the stall of Timberscombe to Mr Tudway.

The chapter was then concluded.

p622 blank

p623–p624 **April 22** In the chapter house between 3 pm and 6 pm. Present: Selleck, Creyghton, Levinze, and prebendary Shallett; Healy in attendance.

Edward Waple, S.T.B., was installed by Dr Creyghton and Dr Levinze in the archdeaconry of Taunton with the prebend of Milverton I annexed, vacant by the death of William Peirs.

p625–p626 **April 29** In the chapter house between 9 am and 12 noon. Present: Selleck, Creyghton, and Levinze; Healy in attendance.

James Aston, M.A., was installed by Dr Creyghton and Dr Levinze in the prebend or canonry of Wiveliscombe, vacant by the cession of Edward Waple.

p627–p628 **May 1** In the chapter house between 3 pm and 6 pm. Present: Selleck, Creyghton, and Levinze; Healy in attendance.

John Yeadle, M.A., was installed by Dr Creyghton and Dr Levinze in the prebend or canonry of Buckland Dinham, vacant by the cession of James Aston.

p629 **July 1** Quarterly chapter. In the chapter house between 9 am and 12 noon. Present: Holt, Selleck, Creyghton, and Sandys; Healy in attendance.

Dr Selleck exhibited the following letter in favour of the election of Edward Waple as a canon residentiary after Mr Brickenden; it was received with due respect and deposited in the archives until the time and opportunity should arise for it to be produced:

"Charles R

Trusty and well-beloved, Wee greet you well. Having received good Information that Edward Waple . . . is a person very deserving of our Royall favour and encouragement, and for his Learning and piety duly qualifyed for the Dignity of a Canon Residentiary in our Cathedrall Church of Wells, Wee have thought fitt, and do hereby in a particular manner recommend the said Edward Waple unto you to be chosen into the next Canon Residentiaries place that shall become voyd in our said Church, next after such as have already obtain'd our Letters for the like Dignity, To hold and enjoy the same with all rights privileges profits and advantages thereunto belonging in as ample manner as other the Canon Residentiaries there do

p630 hold and enjoy their said places. And also that you bestow upon him . . . after hee shall be so elected the next Canon Residentiaries house that shall become vacant.[1] And our pleasure is that you cause these our Letters to be entered in your Register, to the end they may be produced when Occasion requires. And so wee bid you Farewell. Given at our Court at Windsor the 23 day of May 1682 in the 34th yeare of our Reigne.

By his Majesties Command

Examinat per Nos L. Jenkins

Ri: Healy

Nic: Dowthwaite

To our Trusty and well beloved the Deane and Chapter of our Cathedrall Church of Wells."

The following vicars choral appeared: Shallet, Winchcombe, Hobbs, Walkley, Jackson, Webb, Martin, Cooper, and Tudway; absent: Lasher, and Greene (sick).

It was decreed "That Mr Edward Waple, Archdeacon of Taunton, shall have the next Canonicall house in the gift of the Deane and Chapter, if Mr Brickenden be before that provided for.

And afterwards appeared Mr Guydo Clynton of Wells, at whose petition the said Canons Residentiary gave him leave to levell the Camery granted by Lease to Dr Peirs deceased,[2] lying on the south side of the Quire of the said Cathedrall Church."

p631 The chapter was adjourned to July 3.

July 3 Between 9 am and 12 noon [place not stated] Holt, Creyghton, Sandys, and Dutton, with Healy in attendance, adjourned the chapter to the afternoon.

In the chapter house between 3 pm and 6 pm. Present: Holt, Creyghton, Sandys, and Dutton; Healy in attendance.

Mr Dutton declared that he had completed his residence for the current year, and his declaration was accepted.

The chapter was adjourned to the next morning.

July 4 In the chapter house between 9 am and 12 noon Holt, Creyghton, Sandys, and Dutton, with Westley in attendance, adjourned the chapter to between 3 pm and 6 pm when, with Healy in attendance, they adjourned it to the next morning.

[1] Possession of a canonical house was properly a precondition of co-option and admission to residence—hence the decree made at this meeting and entered after the roll-call of vicars choral.

[2] See the entry for 3rd April 1682, p.94 and n.1.

July 5 Between 9 am and 12 noon [place not stated]. Present: Holt, Creyghton, Sandys, and Dutton; Healy in attendance.

p632 Letters patent from archdeacon Waple of Taunton were sealed, granting the registrarship of the archdeaconry of Taunton to John Bennett and Thomas Newman, notaries public, for their lives and the life of the longest liver of them.

An indenture was sealed, granting a certain house or cottage with garden in Chamberlain Street, [Wells], to Archibald Harper for 40 years.

The chapter was adjourned to the afternoon.

Between 3 pm and 6 pm [place not stated]. Present: Holt, Creyghton, Sandys, and Dutton; Healy in attendance.

The election and admission of Dr Levinze as canon residentiary on April 20 was confirmed and pronounced to be fully valid in law, and was attested by the signatures of those present:

"Tho: Holt. *P.C*:
Rob. Creyghton
Edwin Sandys:
Hen: Dutton."

"Mem[oran]d[um] 20*s*. for the Library from Saffin."

The chapter was adjourned to July 7.

p633 **July 7** In the chapter house between 9 am and 12 noon Holt, Creyghton, Sandys, and Dutton, with Healy in attendance, adjourned the chapter to the afternoon.

Between 3 pm and 6 pm [place not stated]. Present: Holt, Creyghton, and Sandys; Healy in attendance. Later, Mr Dutton appeared and took his place in chapter.

Mr Sandys was elected steward for the period of two years beginning on Oct. 1 next.

The chapter was adjourned to Aug. 9 between 9 am and 12 noon.

Aug 9 In the chapter house between 12 noon and 2 pm Holt, Selleck, Creyghton, Dutton, and Sandys, with Neblett in attendance, adjourned the chapter to the next morning.

Aug 10 In the chapter house between 9 am and 12 noon. Present: Holt, Selleck, Creyghton, Sandys, and Dutton; Healy in attendance.

An indenture was sealed, granting a parcel of land, meadow and pasture, in East Curry to Richard Sam of East Curry for the lives of William Buncombe, Katherine Buncombe, and Robert Rowswell.

p634 John Yeadle, M.A., prebendary of Buckland Dinham and chaplain to Maurice, Lord Fitzharding, appeared and brought a letter from the king recommending him for a *p635* residentiary canonry. Dated at Whitehall, July 4, 1682.[1] This letter was obediently received and the chapter ordered that it should be deposited in the archives.

p636 blank.

p637 **Sept 30** In the chapter house between 9 am and 12 noon. Present: Bathurst, Holt, Sandys, and Dutton; Healy in attendance.

Officers for the ensuing year were elected as follows: Baron of the exchequer, Dr Creyghton; Communar, Mr Dutton; Master of the fabric, Mr Dutton;

[1] For the letter, see W.C.L., Documents, series III, box 4, 195. Yeadle was again recommended for election to residence by a royal letter dated 30th June 1685 (ibid. 199), but was passed over by the chapter.

Auditors, Dr Holt and Mr Sandys; Overseers of the houses, Dr Selleck and
p638 Mr Dutton; Bailiff of the grange, James Williams; *cursor ecclesiae*, Allen Lawe; Escheator, the vicars nominated Messrs Martin and Cooper and the chapter elected Mr Martin; Tabellar, Mr Cooper.

p639 **Oct 1** In the chapter house [time not stated]. Present: Holt, Creyghton, and Sandys; Paine in attendance. The chapter was adjourned to the next morning.

Oct 2 In the chapter house between 10 am and 12 noon. Present: Bathurst, Holt, Creyghton, Sandis, and Dutton; Paine in attendance.

The following vicars choral appeared: Lasher, Winscombe, Hobbs, Walkley, Greene, Jackson, Webb, Cooper, and Tudway; absent: Shallett and Martin.

p640 The chapter was adjourned to the afternoon.

Between 3 pm and 6 pm [place not stated]. Present: the same five canons; Healy in attendance.

Resolved "That the Seat in the grates on the south side of the Quire of the Cathedrall Church, called Beckington's Monument, within which grates the effigies of the said Bishop Beckington's body lies, which Seat the Lady Wroth, lately deceased, by the permission of the Dean and Chapter, did in her life time sit in, shall be and is hereby granted to the present Wife of the Reverend Dr Ralph Bathurst the Dean of Wells, to sit there in the time of divine Service, and that a lock be put upon the said Seat set apart for her use, as aforesaid."

An indenture was confirmed, by which the bishop granted to Marshall Bridges and William Fiennes for twenty one years the rectory of Weston Zoyland.

It was decreed "That forty shillings shall be given towards the making a new bell at St Cuthbert's Church by the Dean and Chapter, which said 40*s*. the Commoner is hereby authorized to pay."

p641 The chapter was adjourned to the next morning.

Oct 3 In the chapter house between 9 am and 12 noon. Present: Bathurst and the four canons aforesaid [Holt, Creyghton, Sandys, and Dutton]; Healy in attendance.

Mr Sandys was appointed official of the dean and chapter for the ensuing two years in respect of its external jurisdiction, and the appointment was sealed.

The chapter was adjourned to between 3 pm and 6 pm, when the same five canons, with Healy in attendance, adjourned it to the next morning.

Oct 4 Between 9 am and 12 noon [place not stated]. Present: the same five canons; Healy in attendance.

It was decreed "That, whereas Mr John Palmer gave Bond to the Dean and Chapter for the payment of two hundred and sixty six pounds thirteen shillings and four pence,
p642 which said money upon the Bond aforesaid (*prout per actum Capituli 3° Aprilis ult. plenius liquet*) was due and payable at Michaelmas last, The Chapter, in consideration of the ruines and decayes in the house, barns, Pigeon-house, and other out-houses, and in the Chancell of the Church of Bishops Lidyeard, parcell of the Rectory of Bishops Lidyeard aforesaid, and for other good considerations them thereunto moving, have thought to remit, and by these presents do remit to the said John Palmer his executors and administrators the Summe of seventy four pounds thirteen shillings and four pence, part of the money due upon the said Bond, towards the Reparation of the said houses and premises; and therefore the Chapter do decree that

only the summe of one hundred ninety two pounds shall be payable from the said Mr Palmer to the said Dean and Chapter upon the said Bond; and upon payment of the said one hundred ninety two pounds, the Commoner is hereby ordered to deliver up to the said Mr Palmer the said Bond."

The chapter was adjourned to between 3 pm and 6 pm, when the dean and four canons present in the morning, with Paine in attendance, adjourned the chapter to the next morning.

p643 **Oct 5** In the chapter house between 9 am and 12 noon. Present: the same members of the chapter as on the previous day; Healy in attendance.

Residences for the ensuing year were fixed:

Dr Selleck and Mr Sandys—October, November, December.

Dr Creyghton and Mr Dutton—January, February, March.

Dr Holt and Dr Levinze—April, May, June.

The dean and Dr Busby—July, August, September.

The usual declaration about the emoluments of residence was made.

The chapter was adjourned to the afternoon.

p644 Between 3 pm and 6 pm [place not stated]. Present: Bathurst, Holt, Creyghton, Sandys, and Dutton; Healy in attendance.

Dr Holt, to whom the patronage had fallen by lot, nominated Hugh Lloyd, B.A., for presentation to the vacant vicarage of Dulverton; the deed of presentation was sealed.

The chapter was adjourned to the next morning.

Oct 6 In the chapter house between 9 am and 12 noon the dean and the same four canons, with Paine in attendance, adjourned the chapter to the afternoon.

p645 Between 3 pm and 6 pm [place not stated]. Present: the same five canons; Paine in attendance.

An indenture was sealed, granting to Edward Slade for forty years a tenement in Chamberlain Street, [Wells], next to the former 'Antelope', now called 'The King's Arms', and one acre of land in East Wells Fields or East Walls Fields.

The chapter was adjourned to the next morning.

Oct 7 Between 9 am and 12 noon Bathurst, Holt, Dutton, and Sandys, with Paine in attendance, adjourned the chapter to Oct. 24.

Oct 24 In the chapter house between 9 am and 12 noon. Present: Bathurst, Holt, Creyghton, Sandys, and Dutton, five canons residentiary; Healy in attendance. The chapter was adjourned to the audit room.

Certain requisitorial letters were sealed, directed to Mr Robert Wyseman, the official principal of the Canterbury Court of Arches in London, for the hearing of a case of dilapidations between Mr Sandys and William and Thomas Peirs, gen.[1]

p646 The chapter was adjourned to between 3 pm and 6 pm in the audit room, when Holt, Creyghton, and Dutton adjourned it to the next morning.

Oct 25 In the audit room between 9 am and 12 noon. Present: Bathurst, Holt, Creyghton, Sandys, and Dutton; Healy in attendance.

[1] See p.xxx.

It was decreed "That the Commoner shall pay Thomas Lane 10*s.* towards his losses in paying the Lords Rent and Chimney money due before hee came into the possession of his house."
The chapter was adjourned to between 3 pm and 7 pm, when the same canons adjourned it to the next morning.

Oct 26 In the audit room between 9 am and 12 noon. Present: as on the previous day; Healy in attendance.
It was decreed "That leave be granted to Mr William Westley to set up railes in the Church-yard against his house, and they are to stand but 6 foot from the wall of the house in the cleare."
The chapter was adjourned to between 3 pm and 6 pm, and then to the next morning.

p647

Oct 27 In the audit room between 9 am and 12 noon. Present: Bathurst, Holt, Creyghton, Sandys, and Dutton; Healy in attendance.
It was decreed "That the Commoner shall pay Mr Jackson the Organist 40*s.* for his pains in procuring Services for the Quire, and pricking Services and Anthems in the books."
The chapter was adjourned to between 3 pm and 7 pm, and then to the next afternoon.

Oct 28 Between 3 pm and 6 pm [place not stated]. Present: Bathurst, Holt, Creyghton, Sandys, and Dutton; Healy in attendance.
It was decreed "That Eight pounds shall be given by the Chapter and paid by the Commoner towards the Reliefe of the French Protestants"; also that orders be given to James Williams, the bailiff of the grange, "That hee doth forthwith collect all such amerciaments as shall be estreated to him within the Mannor of Canons Grange".
The dean, having already contributed 50*l.* for the use of the chapter, openly and publicly declared that this sum was given to the chapter with the intention that at the beginning of the year it should be consigned to the communar commencing office, to lighten and discharge the expenses necessarily incurred by successive communars at the beginning of the year—like the money formerly given by Dr Powell;[1] and thus it should be passed on from year to year for ever.
The chapter was adjourned to the audit room on Dec. 4.

pp648–649 blank
p650

Dec 4 In the audit room between 9 am and 12 noon Holt, Creyghton, Sandys, and Dutton, with Healy in attendance, adjourned the chapter to the next morning.

Dec 5 In the audit room between 9 am and 12 noon the same canons adjourned the chapter to the next morning; Healy in attendance.

Dec 6 In the audit room between 9 am and 12 noon the same canons adjourned the chapter to the next morning.

[1] Dr William Powell was elected to residence on 2nd October 1581 and was installed as archdeacon of Bath on 7th April 1584. He died in March 1612 and left a sum of 10*l.* to be used for the assistance of tradesmen within the Liberty (see W.C.L., Act Book 1608–22, f.95d and ibid. Act Book 1635–45, p.95—*Cal.* ii. 426); but there is no record of his leaving money for the use of the communar.

Dec 7 In the audit room between 9 am and 12 noon. Present: Holt, Creyghton, Sandys, and Dutton; Healy in attendance.

p651 A certain public register, commonly called a Legier book, belonging to the dean and chapter, beginning *Indentura Praebendae de Tyngherst* and ending "The day and yeare first above-written", and containing 241 pages,[1] had now been returned by John Gutch, gen., in whose possession it had lately been, to be deposited in the archives for the future. It was decreed that he should receive without any fee any copies whatever of the indentures, letters patent, and other records contained in the book, when and as often as he pleased. Then at his request the chapter decreed that copies of all letters patent issued by the bishop's registry and contained in the book, and also of indentures pertaining to the archdeaconry of Wells, should be supplied to him whenever he should request them.

The chapter was adjourned to the next morning.

Dec 8 Between 9 am and 12 noon [place not stated] the same canons adjourned the chapter to the next morning.

Dec 9 In the audit room between 9 am and 12 noon Holt, Creyghton, Sandys, and Dutton, with Healy in attendance, adjourned the chapter to Dec. 11.

p652 **Dec 11** In the audit room between 9 am and 12 noon Holt, Creyghton, and Dutton adjourned the chapter to the next morning.

Dec 12 Between 9 am and 12 noon [place not stated] Creyghton continued the chapter to between 2 pm and 4 pm, and then adjourned it to the next morning.

Dec 13 Between 9 am and 12 noon [place not stated], Creyghton, Sandys, and Dutton, with Healy in attendance, adjourned the chapter to the next morning.

Dec 14 In the audit room between 9 am and 12 noon. Present: Holt, Creyghton, Sandys, and Dutton; Healy in attendance.

It was decreed "That, whereas an Act of Chapter was made the twelfth day of January in the yeare 1664, That the Stewards for the time being should receive to their own use all the herriots accruing and belonging to the Deane and Chapter for the yeares of their Stewardships respectively, The Reverend Dr Creyghton, late Steward *p653* of the Deane and Chapter, shall have and receive to his own use all the herriots belonging to the Deane and Chapter from the first day of October 1681 to the same day of October 1682".

It was further decreed "That the Stewards of the Deane and Chapter for the time being for futurity shall receive to his own use or their own use respectively all such herriots as shall fall, in the time of their respective Stewardships, and become due to the said Deane and Chapter."[2]

The chapter was adjourned to between 9 am and 12 noon on the next day. [There is no record of a meeting then].

p654 blank

[1] W.C.L., Ledger F.

[2] Against this entry there is a marginal note: "Revoc^{r} Oct 23° 1683".

1682-3

p655[1] **Jan 2** Quarterly chapter. In the chapter house between 9 am and 12 noon. Present: Selleck, Creyghton, and Sandys; Healy in attendance.

The following vicars choral appeared: Shallett, Lasher, Winchcombe, Hobbs, Walkley, Jackson, Greene, Webb, Martin, Cooper, and Tudway.

The chapter was adjourned to between 3 pm and 6 pm in the chapter house, when the same canons, with Healy in attendance, adjourned it again to the next morning.

p656 **Jan 3** In the chapter house between 9 am and 12 noon Holt, Creyghton, Sandys, and Dutton, with Healy in attendance, adjourned the chapter to between 3 pm and 6 pm and then, with Healy in attendance, to the next morning.

Jan 4 Between 9 am and 12 noon [place not stated]. Present: Holt, Creyghton, Sandys, and Dutton; Healy in attendance. Later Selleck appeared and took his place.

The five canons present were authorized to hold a court in the old almshouse.

The chapter was adjourned to the afternoon.

Between 3 pm and 6 pm [place not stated]. Present: Holt, Creyghton, Sandys, and Dutton; Healy in attendance.

Letters patent were sealed, conferring upon Richard Healy the office of exercising ecclesiastical jurisdiction within the peculiar jurisdictions of the deanery of Wells.

p657 The chapter was adjourned to the next morning.

Jan 5 Between 9 am and 12 noon [place not stated]. Present: Holt, Selleck, Creyghton, Sandys, and Dutton; Healy in attendance.

It was decreed "That the Steward and the Commoner and Dr Creyghton, or any two of them, do take care to prosecute the businesse now depending in the Exchecquer against Mr Edward Strode of Downside, in the name of them the said Deane and Chapter."

The chapter was adjourned to Jan. 8.

Jan 8 Between 9 am and 12 noon [place not stated] Selleck, Creyghton, and Dutton (later joined by Holt), with Healy in attendance, adjourned the chapter to Jan. 18.

Jan 18 Between 2 pm and 6 pm [place not stated]. Present: Holt, Creyghton, Sandys, and Dutton.

It was decreed "That the Master of the fabric do forthwith take care to lay out monies [for] the necessary repaire of the Fabrick, as [he] shall [judge] convenient."

pp658–663 blank

p664 [upside down] "July 30th 1679. I, Thomas Davis, now to be collated to the Rectory or parish Church of Allerton alias Alverton in the Diocess of Bath and Wells doe voluntarily and *ex animo* subscribe to the 3 articles menconed and Contained in the 36th Canon of the Canons and Constitucions Ecclesticall of this Realme and to all things therein contained.

Tho: Davies"

[1] Pp. 655–8 consist of a double loose leaf inserted into the book.

pp665–667 blank

p668 "Mr Deane
Dr Busby 8° Julii 1670

N.B.

There is an addicional clause to be put to the Act of rescinding a former Act that deprives the Residentiaries from all Claime of Quotidians and Divident whatever causes they had, were they never so necessary and Legall, and such as could not but be approved off and admitted by the Chapter, which seeme to them an unreasonable decree for want of explanacion of their true intencions in the making of it."

So nevertheless that the statute concerning the abrogation or diminution of quotidians and dividends in the case of absence shall have the force which it fully possesses in the charter of the cathedral, unless that absence has been approved by the chapter as necessary.

Wm. Crofts, B.A., to be presented to the vicarage of Winscombe.

1670, Dec 14 Between 1 pm and 4 pm [place not stated]. Present: Peirs (proxy for Smith), Holt, Sheafe, and Fane.

"Mr Deanes proxie exhibited by Dr Holt and Dr Fane and was accepted *nemine contradicente*."

["All unanimously agreed that there should be an appeale to my Lord Bishopp by reason there is an obstruction in the Accompts, for that the late Commoner Dr Selleck refuseth the Charges given him by the Steward."][1]

"Whereas the late Commoner Dr Selleck hath and doth still refuse to receive the Charges renderd him by the Steward and other officers, and thereby obstructs the passing and perfecting of his Accompts for the yeare immediately passed, to the great detriment of the Church and Chapter, the aforesaid worshipfulls agreed to make their Legall and humble appeale to the Lord Bishopp their Visitor, which they accordingly doe, hopeing that thereby there wilbe an amicable composure of the differences betweene the said Dr Selleck and themselves."

p669 "*28 Octobris 1682 Ds Decanus Dr Bathurst dono dedit Capitulo 50l. 00s. 00d.*"

p670 blank

[1] The entry within brackets has been deleted.

Index

Each reference covers all the entries (sometimes numerous) on the page or pages in question.

Abbott, Edward, precentor, x, xiv
Alderley (Alderly, Aulderly),
Arthur, vicar choral, 1, 3, 5–8, 10–14, 16–18, 20, 21, 25, 28, 29, 30, 33, 38, 39, 58, 61
Robert, 66
Alderson, William, 37
Algiers,
donation for redemption of captives in, 90, 92
mission of John Selleck to, xiii
Allen (Allyne),
Abraham, prebendary, 45, 85
Henry, prebendary, 85
Allerton, xxii n.1, 22, 38, 40, 41, 54, 68, 77, 96, 103
Bradenhurst in, 56 n.4
Andrews, William, 16
Annus post mortem, xxi, 55
Antiquaries, Society of, 28 n.1
Aprice, Thomas, xxx
Archer, Edmund, archdeacon of Wells, viii, xxvii n.4
Arches, Court of, xxviii, 100
Ashbrittle, xvi
Ashbury, Berks,
fields, xxx
Parson's Wood in, xxx, 36
rectory, lease of, xxx–xxxii, 14, 33, 35–37
Wick (Wycke), chapel of, in, xxx, 36
Aston, James, prebendary, 11, 96
Atkins, Francis, prebendary, 1, 20, 39
Atwell, John, 40 n.4

Baildon, W. P., i
Baily (see also Baylie), Dr ——, 36
Ball,
John, 38, 89
Philip, 51 n.1
Balls cast for benefices, see Wells cathedral, Dean and Chapter
Bampfield, George, 43
Bampton, Oxon, 35
Bargrave, John, canon of Canterbury, xiii
Barker,
G. F. R., xii n.1
Joseph, prebendary, 21, 57, 65
Barlow, William, bishop of Bath and Wells, v
Baron, Charles, 90
Batcombe, xii
Bate, R. S., i
Bath,
archdeacon of, iv (see also Peirs, William; Powell, William; and Selleck, John)
archdeaconry of, registrar, 82
prior of, see Holleway, William
Bath and Wells,
bishop of,
apparitor general of, 3
auditor general of, 10
deputy registrar of, see registrar
election of, 21, 45
mandate for, 21, 45
enthronement of, xxii, 23, 47
leases granted by, 71, 80, 89, 99
registrar of, xxxi, 33, 75
deputy, xli, 35
registry of, 102
vicar general of, 9
See also Barlow, William; Bekynton, Thomas; Clerk, John; Hooper, George; Ken, Thomas; Kidder, Richard; Mews, Peter; Peirs, William; Ralph of Shrewsbury; Robert of Lewes; Savaric [Bath and Glastonbury]; Stafford, John
diocese of, chancellor of, 81, 82 (see also Baylie, John; Pope, Henry)
Bathurst,
Mary, 99
Ralph, dean, xii, xv, xvii, xviii, xxi, xxvi, xxvii, xxix, xxxiii n.8, xxxvii, 21–34 *passim*, 37, 39–44 *passim*, 45 n.3, 47, 49, 55, 58, 61, 65–71 *passim*, 76, 79–83 *passim*, 95, 96, 98–101 *passim*, 104
Batten, Henry, 37, 85, 93

Baylie, John, chancellor of Bath and Wells, xxix, 71, 89
Beaton, Mrs ——, xlv
Beauchamp, John, vicar choral, xxxiii
Beaumont, Thomas, vicar choral, 1, 3, 5–8, 10–14, 16–18, 20, 21, 25, 28–31, 33, 34, 38, 39, 42, 61, 68, 73, 74, 76, 79, 83, 85, 87, 88, 93, 94
Bec, abbey, 33
Bekynton, Thomas, bishop of Bath and Wells, 9 n.3, 16 n.2
Bellfounder, see Purdy, Thomas; Bilbie, Edward
Bells, see Wells cathedral, general, and Wells, St Cuthbert's
Benford, Augustine, vicar choral, 1, 3, 5–8, 10–17, 40 n.4
Bennett,
J. A.,
John, 69, 98
Berrier, Stephen, prebendary, 1, 5
Bicknoller, 90
tenement in, called Wayfish, 65
Bilbie, Edward, 28 n.1
Binegar, 51 n.1
Bishop's Lydeard, xxii n.1, 22, 41, 54, 68, 77, 95, 96, 99
Bisse,
Amy, 89
Edward, 30, 89
George, 3, 4, 15, 30
Jane, 30, 89
Philip, archdeacon of Taunton, vi
Blackwell, 35
Blake, John, 86
Blount, T, xiii n.3
Boniface IX, pope, xx n.5
Bower,
Anne, 30
John, 88
Thomas, 7, 30
William, 30
Bradenhurst, see Allerton
Brailsford, Matthew, dean, viii, 28 n.1
Braily, Thomas, 31
Brawdripp, Christopher, 10
Breathers, John, 3
Brickenden (Brigandine), Thomas, prebendary, 65, 75–77, 88, 92 n.3, 96, 97
Bridge, Mr ——, xxxix, 9
Bridges, see Brydges
Bristol, 67
see of, xv
Britten, William, 3
Broderweek, Mary, 80
Browne,
John, vicar choral, 1, 3, 5–8, 10–14, 16–18, 20, 21, 25, 28, 29, 30, 33, 38, 39, 49
widow, 81
Brush, George, prebendary, 37, 72
Brydges, (Bridges),
Frances, xvii
Marshall, chancellor, viii, xvii, 99
Buckland Abbas, Dorset,
benefice, xxii n.1, 22, 53, 77, 96
rectory, xxvi, xxxv, 19, 20
Buckland St Mary, xi
Buncombe,
Katherine, 98
Thomas, 34
William, 98
Burges, Cornelius, xxvii
Burgh, Edward, prebendary, 27
Burnham, xvii, xxii n.1, 22, 54, 76, 86, 88, 96
Busby, Richard, treasurer, xii, xv, xvii, xxiv, xxv, xxvi, xxvii, xxviii, xxxvi, xxxvii, 6, 20, 22–24 *passim*, 27, 28, 30, 31, 33, 39, 46, 47, 54, 68, 76, 85, 89, 96, 100, 104
Butts, Mrs ——, 5
Byam, Henry, prebendary, 1, 15
Byrne, W., 40 n.4
Bytall (Birstall, Bristall), William, prebendary, 1

Callowhill, Thomas, 67
Calvin, John, x
Cambridge,
King's college, xiv
professorship of Greek at, ix, xvi, 8
Queens' college, xv
Trinity college, xvi
university, xii
Cannington, Mr ——, 50
Canon Grange, Wells,
manor of, ix, 101
bailiff of, 12, 17, 25, 31, 42, 45, 49, 56, 58, 61, 67, 79, 88, 99, 101
Parliamentary survey of (1649), ix

Canons and Constitutions Ecclesiastical (1604), No 36, 50, 75
No 44, 26
Canterbury,
archbishop of, xxxii, xxxiii, 18
cathedral, xiii
Carhele, John, prebendary, 9
Carter, John, 28 n.1, 40 n.4
Cartwright, Thomas, prebendary, 17
Castle Cornet, Guernsey, xiv
Castor (Caistor), Lincs, ix
Cathedrals Commission (1835), vii
Cathedrals Measure (1963), xxi n.4
Charles II, king, xiii, 8, 27, 33, 36, 56, 67, 72, 74, 76, 82, 97, 98
Cheddar, x, xxii n.1, 22, 41, 54, 76, 96
parish church, chancel in, 71, 84
rectory, 33, 43, 90
Cheney, Thomas, canon residentiary, 92 n.3
Cheshire, William, xxxi, xxxii, 35, 36
Chester, bishop of (Brian Walton), xxxvii
Chew Magna, 18, 38
Christian Malford, Wilts., xi
Church, C. M., subdean, xxxv
Churchels, 51 n.1
Chyles (Chiles), Nathaniel, xviii, 56
Clarke,
Anne, 24 n.3
John, 24 n.3
Samuel jun., 24 n.3
Samuel sen., 24
Thomas, vicar choral, 1, 3, 5–8, 10–14, 16–18, 20, 21, 25, 28–31, 33, 38, 39
Cleeve, abbey, 33 n.2
Clerk, John, bishop of Bath and Wells, **xxxi**
Clifton Campville, Staffs, xiii
Clifton Maybank, Dorset, xviii
Clinton (Clynton),
Anne, 12, 33
Guy (Guydo), jun., 43, 49, 51, 53
Guy (Guydo), sen., xxii, xxix, xxxi, xli, xliii, 10, 12, 35, 39, 41, 42, 50, 53, 75, 77, 86, 90, 97
Coals, dug in the Manor of Pucklechurch, 67
Collier (Collyer), Robert, prebendary, 11, 39, 88
Coltishall, Norfolk, xiv
Combe St Nicholas, xvii, 41
prebend, v
Comer,
Mary, 48
Thomas, 48
Commons,
House of, x, xi
Speaker of, 57 n.1
Commonwealth, i n.3, xii, xxxv, xxxvii
Compton Dando, x
Congresbury, 87
sale of chapter's property in, 13
rectory of, 71
Convocation, 23, 68, 85
Cooke, Mr ——, 33
Cooper (Cowper), John, vicar choral, 68, 73, 74, 76, 79, 83, 85, 88, 93, 94, 97, 99, 103
Coventry,
Elizabeth, Lady, xiii
John, xiii
Thomas, 1st Lord, xiii
Coward,
Christopher, prebendary, 21
Mary, xi
Cowper, see Cooper
Cox, Francis, 78
Crane, George, 32
Creyghton (Creyghtone, Creighton),
Frances, wife of Robert Creyghton I, ix, x
Frances, daughter of Robert Creyghton II, xvii
Frideswide, xvi
George, x
Katherine, daughter of Robert Creyghton I, x
Katherine, daughter of Robert Creyghton II, xvii
Margaret, xvii
Robert I, dean, and bishop of Bath and Wells, ix, x, xiv, xv, xxi, xxiv–xxix, xxxi, xxxii, xxxvii, 1–4 *passim*, 7–9 *passim*, 11–21 *passim*, 23, 33, 35, 104
Robert II, precentor, viii, xv–xvii, xxix, xxxvii, 2, 5, 6, 8, 9, 15, 17, 27, 33, 37, 39, 45, 47, 49, 53–103 *passim*
Robert III, prebendary, xvii
Robert IV, prebendary, xvii
Thomas, x
Creyghtonian seventh, xvi n.3
Crofts, William, 24, 104
Cromwell, Thomas, dean, v, xxxi

Cross (Crosse), Robert, 18, 31, 38
Cudworth, Mr ——, xlv
Curry Mallet, xviii

Dakyn, Thomas, chancellor, v
Dane, John, viii
Davis,
Daniel, vicar choral, 1, 3, 5–8, 10–14, 16–18, 20, 21, 25, 28, 29
John, 51
Thomas, prebendary, 94, 103
Thomas, shoemaker, 87
widow, 55
Deane, Henry, 9, 38
Dight, Reginald, 19, 26
Ditcheat, xi
Doble, William, 86
Dodington (Doddington),
Christopher, 43
George, 71, 90
William, 90
Douch, James, prebendary, 9, 21
Downside, 103
Dowthwaite (Dowthwaight, Dowthwayte, Douthwaite, Douthwayt), Nicholas, xxxii, xxxv, xxxvi, xliii, xlv, 1, 5, 18, 22–24, 26, 44, 50–52, 81, 84, 94–97
Dugdale,
James, subdean, xiii, xviii
William, 28 n.1
Dulverton, xxii n.1, 22, 54, 76, 96, 100
Duncombe, John, prebendary, 1, 11
Dutch, naval attacks by, x
Dutton, Henry, canon residentiary, xviii, xxi, xxix, 1, 11, 65, 67, 72 n.3, 74–77 *passim*, 79–82 *passim*, 84–102 *passim*
Duvall (Duvoll), Henry, vicar choral, 28–30, 33, 34, 38–40, 42, 44, 49, 56
Dyke, Alexander, 38

East Brent, xi
East Curry, 13, 81, 98
East Horrington, 51 n.1
East Lambrook, xxii n.1, 22, 54, 77, 96
Easton, 51 n.1
Ecclesiastical Commission, (1560), The, v
Edmonds, John, vicar choral, 1, 3, 5–8, 10–14, 16–18, 20, 21, 25, 28–30, 33, 38, 39, 52, 61
Edward VI, king, v
Edwards, Kathleen, iii, xxi n.2, xxii n.6
Elizabeth I, queen, v, xxxv, 35
Elworthy, xiii
Evans,
Tristram, xxix, 82
William, 80
Evelyn, John, ix n.2, x, xii n.1, xv, xvi
Evercreech, xviii
Exon, Henry, 31

Fane, Hon. William, canon residentiary, xiv, xv, xxiv, xxv, xxvii, xxviii, xxxii, xxxvi, xliii, 1–16 *passim*, 18–34 *passim*, 37–51 *passim*, 53–55 *passim*, 57, 59–63 *passim*, 67, 104
Fea, Allan, xiii n.3
Ferrar (or Turner),
Mary, 8
Thomas, 8
Fiennes, William, 99
Fingest, see Thinghurst
Fitzharding, Maurice, Lord, 98
FitzWilliam, William, v
Florence, council of (1438), x
Foster, J., x n.3, xi n.2, xii n.4, xiii n.2, xv n.2, xviii n.3 & 5
Francis, Charles, 91
Freeman, E. A., vii, viii, 9 n.3
French Protestants, relief of, 101
Frycker, Mr ——, 40

Gale, Robert, prebendary, 15, 37
Gilbert, James, bailiff and *cursor ecclesiae*, 45, 49, 56, 58, 67
Goodman, John, dean, v
Gordge, Digory, 1
Gray, John, bailiff and *cursor ecclesiae*, 3, 17, 25, 31, 42
Green (Greene),
Gabriel, vicar choral, 40, 42, 44, 49, 58, 61, 63, 68, 73, 74, 76, 83, 85, 88, 93, 94, 97, 99, 103
Mary, 67
Greenwich, ix
Griffin, William, prebendary, 65
Gutch, John, 102
Gybes, William, see Holleway

Hacker, William, 62
Haddon, Thomas, 72

Haggat, Bartholomew, viii
Hague, The, ix
Halliday, J. O., 7 n.4
Hambledon, Bucks, x
Hamilton, Sir Richard, xx
Ham Mills, see North Curry
Hanson,
Thomas, 54, 55
William, 1
Hardy, T. D., ix
Harper, Archibald, 98
Harris,
David, 32
Renatus, 83
Harrison, Alexander, deputy chapter clerk, xxii, 1–12 *passim*, 14–32 *passim*
Haselbury Plucknett, 74
Hawkins, William, 84
Hawley, Francis, Lord, 46
Head, John, prebendary, 1, 53
Healy, Richard, deputy chapter clerk and librarian, i, viii, xxii, xxiii, xxxvi, 68–103 *passim*
Hearne,
T., 40 n.4
widow, 10
Heath, Thomas, xxii, 50, 51
Hele, xiii
Hembry, P. M., xi n.2
Henborrow, widow, 31
Henchman, Humphrey, xiii
Henry VIII, king, v, 36
Herbert, John, dean, vi
Heyden, Benjamin, dean, 86
Hitchman, Edward, prebendary, 13, 21, 45
Hobbs, John, vicar choral, 1, 3, 5–8, 10–14, 16–18, 20, 21, 25, 28–30, 33, 34, 38, 39, 61, 63, 68, 73, 74, 76, 79, 83, 85, 88, 93–97, 99, 103
Hole, Emanuel, 4
Hollar, Wenceslaus, 28 n.1
Holleway (or Gybes), William, prior of Bath, xxxi
Hollyster, Denis, 67
Holmes, T. S., chancellor, iii n.1
Holt,
Francis, 66
Francis, son of Thomas, xlv
Sarah, 66
Holt continued
Thomas, chancellor, xii, xiv, xvi, xxiv, xxv, xxvii, xxix, xxxvi, xxxvii, xliii, xlv, 1–16 *passim*, 18–34 *passim*, 37–104 *passim*
Hooper, Abigail, xvii, xx n.4
Horrington, see East and West Horrington
Horsey, Peter, vicar choral, 10, 11
Horstead, Norfolk, xiv
Horton, prebend of, see Salisbury cathedral
Huggate, Yorks, ix
Hughes, John, 72
Huish, Alexander, prebendary, 11
Hungerford, Walter, prebendary, 5, 6, 94
Hunt,
Michael, 71
William, xvii
Huntley, Wykes, prebendary, 84, 85
Hurdacre, Grisella, 2
Hyde, Mary, xiii

Ilchester, xi
Ile Brewers, x
Ilminster, xi

Jackson (Jacksons), John, organist and vicar choral, 55, 58, 61, 68, 73, 74, 76, 79, 83, 85, 88, 93, 94, 97, 99, 101, 103
James I, king, xxvii
Jenkins, L., 97
Jenkyns, Richard, dean, xxi
Jewers, A. J., 14 n.2
Jones, Morgan, prebendary, 76, 79, 85
Jordan, Thomas, 67

Keene,
Francis, 53
Jane, 82, 87
Kelway, Mr ——, vicar choral, 68, 73, 74, 76, 79
Ken, Thomas, bishop of Bath and Wells, xviii
Kidder, Richard, bishop of Bath and Wells, xvii n.1 & 2, xviii, xxx n.4 & 5
King, Daniel, 28 n.1
Kingsbury Episcopi, xi
Kingsbury, Richard, 3
Kirkby Laythorpe, Lincs, xviii
Knapp, see North Curry

Knappfee, see North Curry
Knowles, John, prebendary, 53

Lambeth, xiii
Lamyat, xii
Lane, Thomas, 101
Lanfire, Samuel, prebendary, 1, 13, 37
Larke, Mr ——, vicar choral, 65
Lasher, Joshua, prebendary and vicar choral, 48, 49, 53, 61, 63, 67, 68, 73, 74, 76, 79, 83–85, 87, 88, 93, 94, 97, 99, 103
Lawe, Allan, *cursor ecclesiae*, 99
Laws, Matthew, 41
Layng,
 Henry, subdean and archdeacon of Wells, xvii
 Katherine, xvii
Leas-fees, see North Curry
Le-Neve, John, ix n.2, x n.3, xi n.2, xii n.1 & 4, xiii n.2, xiv n.1, xvii n.2, xviii n.2 & 3, 1 n.3
Levinze, William, canon residentiary, xvii, xviii, 72, 77, 92, 95–96, 98, 100
Ley, Roger, prebendary, 8
Lincoln, cathedral, ix
Litton, 51 n.1
Lloyd, Hugh, 100
London, fire of, 42
Long, George, 71
Long Sutton, xxii n.1, 22, 37, 41, 54, 77, 85, 93, 96
Lonsdale, John, prebendary, 17, 53
Lovington, 4, 41

Macy, Mr ——, vicar choral, 58, 61, 63
Marsh, Humphrey, 40
Marshall, N., 86
Martin,
 Eleanor, 72
 John, 72
 John, vicar choral, 68, 73, 74, 76, 79, 83, 85, 88, 93, 94, 97, 99, 103
Martin's wheat, see Wells cathedral, estates
Marwood,
 Mary, xxxiv n.1
 Robert, vicar choral, xxxiv
Mary I, queen, v, 93
Mary II, queen, xviii
Matthews, A. G., ix n.2, x n.3, xi n.2, xii n.4, xiii n.3, xiv n.1, xviii n.3 & 5
Mattock,
 Arthur jun., 10, 19
 Arthur sen., prebendary, 39, 47, 53
 George, 19
 Thomas, 19
Meare Court, see North Curry
Mells, xviii
Merry, Richard, prebendary, 15
Mew (Mews),
 Daniel, vicar choral and prebendary, 31, 33, 38, 39, 41, 42, 53, 55, 74
 Samuel, prebendary, 76
Mews (Mew),
 Peter, bishop of Bath and Wells, xvii, xviii, xxix, xxx, 45, 47, 52, 77, 78, 84, 85, 92
  visitation of
   (1673), xxxix, xliii, 49
   (1679), xxix
Middlezoy, 71, 80, 89
Milverton, 69
Monmouth, duke of, xii, xvi
Morgan, Mrs ——, 42
Morris, Claver, 19 n.3
Moss (Mosse), John, vicar choral, 1, 3, 5–8, 10–14, 16–18, 20, 21, 25, 28–30, 33, 34, 38, 39, 42, 61
Mudford, xxii n.1, xlv, 22, 38, 50, 54, 66, 76, 89, 96
Mundy, Francis, subdean, xiv, xv, xxxi, xxxii, xlv, 5, 33
Musgrove, George, 71

Neblett,
 Margaret, 12, 33
 Nicholas, xiii, xxii, 12, 33, 53, 98
Newman, Thomas, 98
Newton, Sir Isaac, xii
Nicholls, Roger, prebendary, 5
Nixon, Thomas, 11
Northampton, fire damage at, 61
North Curry, x, xxii n.1, 22, 30, 41, 54, 68, 76, 95, 96
 Greenewayes Close in, 7
 Ham Mills in, 46
 hundred of, 46
 Knapp in, 31

North Curry continued
Knappfee in, 34
Leas-fees in, 95
March Close in, 4
Meare Court in, 19 n.1
Sheepfields Close in, 7

Obits, iv, viii, xxxiv
Odcombe, xvii
Osbaston,
Henry, prebendary, 17
Lambert, prebendary, 1
Osborne, Sir P., xiv
Osmund, St, iii
Othery, 71, 80, 89
Oxford, xxxix
bishop of, see Skinner, Robert
Christ Church cathedral, x
university, ix, xii, xix
Christ Church college, xii
Corpus Christi college, xviii
Magdalen college, xii
hall, xvii
professorship of Greek in, xviii
Trinity college, xv
vicechancellor of, 45

Packer,
Margaret, 15 n.1
Thomas, 15 n.1
Pain (Paine), John, chapter clerk, xxii, 69–71, 73–75, 82, 88–90, 94, 99–100
Painter, Nicholas, 10, 93
Palmer,
John, 95, 99, 100
Jonathan, prebendary, 14
T. F., iii
Parker, J. H., 9 n.3
Parliament, Acts of:
1 Ed. VI, c.14, xxxiv, 18
3 & 4 Ed. VI, c.10, xxxv
13 Eliz. I, c.10 ('Against Frauds'), xxxii
14 Chas. II, c.4, xviii, xxix
22 Chas. II, c.8, 80 n.1
22 & 23 Chas. II, c.12, 80 n.1
3 & 4 Vict. c.113, xxi
Parliamentary Survey of Canon Grange manor (1649), ix
Parson's Wood, see Ashbury

Peirs (Piers, Pierce),
Anne, 1st wife of bishop William, xi
Frideswide, xvi
John, prebendary, 8, 27
John, son of bishop William, 83 n.1
John, son of archdeacon William, 95, 100
Mary, 2nd wife of bishop William, xxviii, 83 n.1
Mary, wife of archdeacon William, xi
Thomas, xxix, xxx
William, archdeacon of Taunton and canon residentiary, xi, xii, xiv, xv, xvii–xix, xxiv–xxix, xxxvii, xliii, xlv, 2, 3, 5–16 *passim*, 21–34 *passim*, 37–58 *passim*, 61, 62, 64–79 *passim*, 82–97 *passim*, 104
William, bishop of Bath and Wells, x, xi, xxvi–xxviii, xxxi, 14 n.1, 83 n.1
William, son of archdeacon William, 95, 100
Pepys, Samuel, ix, x, xix
Peterborough,
bishop of (John Towers), xv
cathedral, x
Philip (II of Spain), king, 93
Phipps, Mr ——, vicar choral, 61
Pine, Mr ——, 61; and see Pyne
Pitchford, Elizabeth, xiii
Pittard, Robert, 74
Plumtre, E. H., xv n.2
Podimore, xvii
Pope,
Henry, chancellor of Bath and Wells, xvii
Margaret, xvii
Robert, 56
Potman, Thomas, prebendary, 27
Potterne, prebend of, see Salisbury cathedral
Pottinger (Potinger, Potenger), John, prebendary, xliii, 11, 14, 15, 17, 21, 27, 37, 45, 47, 49, 50, 53
Poulett (Paulet),
Catherine, 19
Francis, x, 19, 20, 41
John, 1st baron, x, xxvi, xxxv, 19, 20
Katherine, x
Letitia, 19
Powell, William, archdeacon of Bath and canon residentiary, vi, 101
Prebends, see Wells cathedral, prebends founded in

Presbyterians, x
Prickman, John, 50
Privy Council, xxxiii
Protestants, French, 101
Prowse, Anthony, prebendary, 39
Pucklechurch, Glos, xxii n.1, 20, 22, 41, 54, 67, 77, 96
Puddimore Milton, see Podimore
Purdy (Purde), Thomas, 19 n.2, 23, 28 n.1, 30, 40
Pyne, John, 4; and see Pine

Quirk (Quirke), Robert, deputy chapter clerk, xxii, 34, 37–61 *passim*, 63–67, 72

Raleigh, Walter, dean, xi
Ralph of Shrewsbury, bishop of Bath and Wells, 18 n.1
Randall, John, prebendary, 8
Rech,
Agnes, 86
Jane, 86
Lawrence, 86
Reding,
George, 90
John, 90
Reformation, v
Reynolds, H. E., vi n.3
Rivet, Timothy, 48
Robert of Lewes, bishop of Bath and Wells, iii
Robins, William, 84
Robinson, A. E., xvii n.1
Rochester
cathedral, 45
Charles, earl of, 95
Elizabeth, countess of, 41
John, earl of, 41
Rokes, Robert, xxxi
Romman, Thomas, 11
Rowswell, Robert, 98
Royal Society, The, xv
Roynon, P., 86
Rush, Thomas, 49

Sadbery, Christopher, prebendary, 6, 9
Saffin—, 20*s* for library received from, 98
St Buryan, Cornwall, ix
Salisbury,
bishops of, xxii n.5
cathedral, close, xiii
institution charter, iii
prebends founded in,
Horton, xxii n.5
Potterne, xxii n.5
Sam, Richard, 98
Sandys (Sandis),
Edwin, archbishop of York, xvii
Edwyn, archdeacon of Wells and canon residentiary, xvii–xix, xxi, xxix, xxx, xxxvi, xxxvii, xlv, 37, 45, 47, 53, 56, 57 n.1, 58, 67–70 *passim*, 75–77 *passim*, 79, 82, 85–94 *passim*, 96–102 *passim*
Francis, xvii
Saunders,
Elizabeth, 34
John, 34
Savaric, bishop of Bath and Glastonbury, 33
Sealy, William, 19
Selleck,
Joan, 2
John, canon residentiary, xii–xiv, xvii, xix, xxiv–xxvii, xxix, xxxii, xxxiii n.8, xxxv–xxxvii, xxxix, xlv, 1–23 *passim*, 25, 27, 30, 31, 34, 37–49 *passim*, 51–53 *passim*, 55–69 *passim*, 71–74 *passim*, 76, 77, 79–88 *passim*, 90, 91, 96, 99, 100, 103, 104
Nathaniel, 14, 72, 79, 84, 87, 94
Sguropulus, Sylvester, x
Shallett (Shallet), Joseph, prebendary and vicar choral, 42, 43, 49, 53, 58, 61, 67, 68, 72–74, 76, 79, 83–85, 88, 93, 94, 96, 97, 99, 103
Sheafe, Grindall, archdeacon of Wells and canon residentiary, xiv, xviii, xxiv, xxv, xxviii, xxxvi, xliii, 1–34 *passim*, 37–59 *passim*, 61–67 *passim*, 75, 76, 79, 87, 104
Shepheard, Anthony, 84
Shepton [Mallet], xlv
Shipham, xxii n.1, 22, 54–56, 76, 87, 96
Simes, William, 28 n.1, 40 n.4
Skinner, Robert, bishop of Oxford, xv
Slade, Edward, 100
Smith (Smyth, Smythe),
Edward, x
Humphrey, 85, 93
Sebastian, precentor and canon residentiary, viii–xii, xiv, xv, xxiv–xxviii,

Smith (Smyth, Smythe) continued
xxxix, 6, 16, 20, 22–24, 27, 29–34, 37, 47, 52, 54, 55, 104
Thomas, 47
Snead, an army trumpeter, xii
Somerset, Edward, duke of, v
South Barrow, 41, 56, 72
Southey, John, 69
Stacy, Mr ——, 48
Stafford, John, bishop of Bath and Wells, 20 n.2
Standish,
Francis, 37
Francis, prebendary and vicar choral, 1, 3, 5–8, 10–14, 16–18, 20, 21, 25, 28–31, 33
Mary, 24 n.3
Thomas, vicar choral, 1, 3, 5–8
Stanniford, Thomas, prebendary, 13
Stawell (Stowell), Ralph, 30, 39
Stephens, Thomas, 7
Sterky, John, xxx
Stogumber, xxii n.1, 22, 54, 76, 90, 96
Stoke St Gregory, 41
Storey, Samuel, xvi
Stowe, archdeaconry of, ix
Strangwayes, Mr ——, 1
Strode, Edward, 103
Stuckey, William, 25
Sugar, Hugh, treasurer, iv n.2
Sweeting,
John, 60
Mr ——, xxxix
Swetting,
George, 65
Giles, 65
William, 65
Sydenham,
John jun., 90
John sen., 90
Philip, 90
Symes, Charles, prebendary, 72

Tarleton,
Charles, xi
John, xi
Taunton (Tanton), xi
archdeacon of, iv, 96 (see also Archer, Edmund; Bisse, Philip; Peirs, William; Waple, Edward)
archdeaconry of, registrar of, 69, 98
Robert, 49
Thinghurst (Fingest), 8
prebend of, see Wells cathedral, prebends founded in, s.v. Dultingcote
Thirlby, Charles, prebendary and archdeacon of Wells, xliii, 6, 8–11, 13–15, 17, 20, 21, 23, 24, 27, 30, 32, 33, 37–39, 41, 45, 47, 50, 53, 75, 76, 79
Thistlethwaite, Gabriel, prebendary, 27
Thomas,
Nicholas, 3
Robert, 3, 38
Samuel, prebendary, 88
Tilly, Samuel, 22
Tiverton, Devon, 35
Towers, John, see Peterborough, bishop of
Towse,
Alexander, 86
Tristram, 7
William, 86
Trent, Dorset, xiii
Tudway, Charles, vicar choral, 79, 80, 83, 85, 88, 93, 94, 96, 97, 99, 103
Tulchils (? Tulse Hill), Surrey, xliii
Turner,
Thomas, see Ferrar
William, dean, v
Twerton, 1

Ulacq, Adrian, x n.1
Underdown, D., xxvii n.3
Uniformity, Act of, see Acts of Parliament
Uplowman, Devon, x, xvi

Vannam, John, prebendary, 21
Vannes, Peter, xxx–xxxii
Venn, J. & J. A., ix n.2, xii n.4, xiv n.1, xv n.1
Vergil, Polydore, archdeacon of Wells, v
Verney, Sir Ralph, ix

Walkley (Walkly, Wakely), Anthony, vicar choral, 25, 28–31, 33, 34, 38, 39, 49, 56, 59, 61, 68, 73, 74, 76, 79, 83, 85, 87, 88, 93, 94, 97, 99, 103

Walker,
J., xi n.2, xii n.4, xviii
Roger, xxxix, 9, 20 n.3
Thomas, canon residentary, xiv, xv, xxxix n.2, 2, 9, 20, 24, 32
Walrond,
Amos, 14
Frances, x
George, 86
William, x
Walton,
Brian, bishop of Chester, xxxvii
Waple, Edward, archdeacon of Taunton, 76, 79, 88, 96–98
Warburton, George, dean, xxvii
Ward, Hamnet, prebendary, 9
Watkin, Dom Aelred, iii
Watts, William, xi
Weaver,
Arthur, 10, 95
F. W., 74
Webb, Thomas, vicar choral, 63, 65, 68, 73, 74, 76, 79, 83, 85, 88, 93, 94, 97, 99, 103
Wells,
archdeacon of, iv, 76 (see also Archer, Edmund; Layng, Henry; Sandys, Edwyn; Sheafe, Grindall; Thirlby, Charles; Vergil, Polydore)
archdeaconry of, v, 76, 93, 102
registrar of, 3, 53
canonical houses, see under Wells cathedral; also below, Wells, houses and buildings in, nos 3, 11, 17, 21, 25 The Liberty, Tower House, 3 St Andrew st, and canonical houses in Market Place and in East Wells
deanery of, v, xxi
registrar of, 14, 50
houses and buildings in:
'Antelope', the, 100
archdeacon's house, xii, xix n.4, xxviii, 83, 84
Bubwith's (old) almshouses, 37, 46, 48, 51, 82, 90, 103
Canons' barn, 75
6 Cathedral Green (site of), v n.1
houses bordering on, 80
choristers' house, 9, 29
corner house in The Liberty, 3 n.4
east end of cathedral, house at, see 3 St Andrew st
East Wells, canonical house in, xv, xvii, xix
'Globe', the, 7
High Cross (in Market Place), house near, 38
'Katherine Wheel', the, 11, 90
'King's Arms', the, 100
3, The Liberty, ix n.4, xii
11, The Liberty (house on site of), xii
17, The Liberty, v n.1
19, The Liberty (house on site of), 19 n.3, 41
21, The Liberty, xiii, 13 n.1, 53, 63, 65, 67, 68, 71, 73, 83, 84, 91
25, The Liberty, xv, 43 n.1
Market Place, old canonical house in, xi, xvii, xxix
new canonical house in, xvii, xviii, xxvii, xxviii
New Works,
1st house from east, 16
3rd house from east, 87 n.1
5th house from east, 60
north side of cathedral, house on, see archdeacon's house
precentor's house, see Tower House
prison of dean and chapter, 75
ruinous houses, v, 92
3, St Andrew st, xvi, xvii, xviii, 92 n.3
'Three Horse Loaves', the, 7
Tower House, xvi, xvii, xxviii
undercroft, house on north-east of, 40 n.4
provost of, v
streets and localities in:
Camery, 94, 97
Cathedral Green, iv, v n.1, 9 n.3, 80, 101
Chamberlain st, 15, 80, 98, 100
Churchyard, see Cathedral Green
Close Hall, see Vicars' Close
College lane, 41
East Wells (East Walls) = St Thomas st, xvii, xix, 24, 30, 72
East Wells fields, 100
High Cross, The, 38
High st, 11, 90

Wells continued
Liberty, The, v n.1, ix n.4, xii, xiii, xv, 3, 8, 19, 41, 44, 45, 75, 78, 79, 87
Lymekill close, 7
Market Place, xi, xvii, xviii, xxvii, xxix, xxx, 16 n.2
Mill lane, 32
Mountroy lane=The Liberty, 3, 41, 43
New st, 7
New Works, 16 n.2, 37, 38, 87
Physic garden of vicars choral, 48
St Andrew st, 3
St Thomas st, 72
Tor lane = Tor st, 72, 92 n.3
Vicars' Close, xxxiv n.1

Wells cathedral,
canonical houses, xvii, 87
inspection of, iv, xxviii
lease of, xxviii
repair of, 92
residence in, xxviii
ruinous, 92
canons non-residentiary, iiif., vi, 77
collation provided by new, xx, 81
contribution to library on installation, xx, 81
estates of, vi, 77
installation of, xx, xxiii, 5, 8, 9, 11, 13–15, 17, 27, 33, 37, 39, 45, 53, 65, 72, 81, 84, 94, 96
canons residentiary, iiif., vi, ix–xix
admission of, xx, xxi, 22, 56, 67, 75, 92, 96
caution money deposited by, xx, xxi, 22, 25, 53, 67, 75, 77, 96
co-option or election of, vi, xiv, xv, xix, 22, 53, 54, 67, 69, 75, 76, 96, 98
emoluments of, xxi, xxiiiff., 18, 23, 27, 55, 69, 70, 75, 85–87, 89, 92, 95, 96, 100, 104
precedence of, ix, xxv
residence of, vi, xxiii–xxx, 26, 47, 52, 54, 55, 68, 73, 75, 77, 87, 88, 95, 97, 104
residence,
allocation of, 27, 31, 41
duties during, xxvii, 27
royal letters recommending as, xi, xiii–xv, xvii, xviii, 8, 53, 56, 57, 58, 67, 72, 74, 76, 77, 96, 98
See also Abbott, Edward; Archer, Edmund; Bathurst, Ralph; Bisse, Philip; Brailsford, Matthew; Brydges, Marshall; Busby, Richard; Creyghton, Robert I; Creyghton, Robert II; Church, C. M.; Dakyn, Thomas; Dugdale, James; Dutton, Henry; Fane, William; FitzWilliam, William; Goodman, John; Herbert, John; Holmes, T. S.,; Holt, Thomas; Hunt, William; Layng, Henry; Levinze, William; Peirs, William; Powell, William; Raleigh, Walter; Sandys, Edwyn; Selleck, John; Sheafe, Grindall; Smith, Sebastian; Sugar, Hugh; Turner, William; Vergil, Polydore; Walker, Thomas; Warburton, George; Wood, Roger; Young, John
chancellor, iv, viii (see also Brydges, Marshall; Dakyn, Thomas; Holmes, T. S.; Holt, Thomas; Young, John)
chapter, xix–xxiii
acts, rescinding of, 23
act books, i, xxii, xxiii
chairman, see president
clerk, xxii, xxiii, 44, 52, 84 (see also Paine, John; Westley, William)
deputy, xxii, 39, 69, 84 (see also Harrison, Alexander; Healy, Richard; Quirke, Robert)
acting, see Clinton, Guy[do]; Heath, Thomas; Neblett, Nicholas; Paine, John
duration of, xix
ledger books or registers, xxiii
mediaeval, constitution of, iiif
place of meeting, xx
audit room, xx, 3, 4, 13, 14, 34, 37, 51, 62, 63, 71, 72, 81, 82, 90–93, 100–102
cathedral, 23, 47
chapter house, xx, 1–103 *passim*
dean's house, xxv, 16–19
Dr Peirs's house, xix n.4, 83, 84, 94, 95
Francis Poulett's house, xx, 19

Wells cathedral continued
Dr Selleck's house, 13 n.1, 53, 63, 65, 67, 68, 71, 73, 83, 84, 91
president, xix
proxies, xxvi, 19, 23, 24, 29, 34
quarterly, xix
quorum, xix, 39 n.1
times of meeting, xix
charter, vi, vii, xix, xxiv, xxvii, 18
choristers, xxxiii, 1, 12, 18, 20 n.2, 24, 27, 32, 44, 49
clerks, negligent in duties, 6
cursor ecclesiae, see Wells cathedral, dean and chapter, officers; also Gilbert, James; Gray, John; Williams, James
dean of, iv, xix, xxi (see also Bathurst, Ralph; Brailsford, Matthew; Creyghton, Robert I; Cromwell, Thomas; FitzWilliam, William; Goodman, John; Herbert, John; Jenkyns, Richard; Raleigh, Walter; Turner, William; Warburton, George)
dean and chapter, xix
benefices, balls cast for, xxii, 68
presentation to, 22, 25, 37, 38, 41, 54, 55, 56, 68, 76, 85, 88, 100, 104
See also Allerton, Bishop's Lydeard, Buckland Abbas, Burnham, Cheddar, Dulverton, East Lambrook, Long Sutton, Mudford, North Curry, Pucklechurch, Shipham, Stogumber, Wells St Cuthbert's, Winscombe
books and records of, 84
consistory court of, 84
officers of:
auditors, iv, 8, 12, 17, 24, 31, 42, 43, 49, 56, 58, 61, 67, 68, 79, 88, 99
baron of the exchequer, iv, 8, 12, 17, 24, 31, 42, 49, 56, 58, 61, 67, 68, 79, 88, 98
chapter clerk, see under chapter
communar, iv, viii, 1, 8, 12, 17, 19, 23, 24, 31, 42, 43, 46, 47, 49, 56, 58, 61, 67, 68, 69, 79, 81, 83, 88, 92, 96, 98, 99, 100, 101, 103
cursor ecclesiae, 12, 17, 25, 31, 42, 45, 49, 56, 61, 67, 79, 88, 99
election of, iv, xix, 8, 12, 15, 16, 17, 24, 31, 42, 49, 56, 58, 61, 67, 68, 79, 88, 98, 99
escheator, iv, viii, 7, 12, 17, 18, 25, 31, 42, 49, 56, 58, 61, 67, 68, 79, 88, 99
master of the fabric, iv, viii, 1, 2, 8, 9, 12, 17, 19, 24, 28, 31, 42, 47, 49, 56, 58, 61, 67, 68, 79, 80, 88, 96, 98, 103
official, 8, 19, 56, 75, 78, 99, 103
overseers of houses, iv, 8, 9, 12, 17, 25, 29, 31, 42, 49, 56, 58, 61, 67, 68, 79, 88, 99
provost of Combe, v
registrar, 38, 75
for peculiar jurisdictions, 41
sacrist, 16
steward, v, viii, xxiv, xxv, xxvii, 8, 15, 16, 23, 26, 30, 33, 39, 40, 42, 44, 60, 75, 81, 98, 102, 103, 104
tabellar, 7, 12, 17, 25, 31, 42, 49, 56, 58, 61, 63, 67, 68, 79, 88, 99
patronage, distribution of, xxi, xxii, 22, 40, 53, 68, 76, 96 (see also benefices)
prison of, 75
proctor in Convocation for, xxvi, 23, 68, 85
seal of, 24
fees for, 69
visitation, right of, 24
Whitsun visitation by, vi, viii, xxxiv, 2, 15
dignitaries, iii, iv, vi–ix, 77 (see also Wells: dean of, precentor of, archdeacon of, chancellor of, treasurer of)
emoluments of, xxiii
estates of, 77
installation of, xx, 21, 53
lesser, iv, vi (see also Bath, archdeacon of; Taunton, archdeacon of; Wells cathedral: subdean, succentor)
residence of, vi
estates, viii, 3
bailiffs, 81
court rolls, copies of, 1, 13, 44
courts, 20, 37, 42, 46, 48, 68, 82, 90, 103
clerk of, 81, 87
escheatory lands, xxxiii–xxxv, 40
heriots, 13, 26, 102

Wells cathedral continued
leases, 25, 34, 66, 69
confirmation of, xli, 71
copies of, 70
counterparts to be produced, xli
granted, 4, 7, 8, 14, 16, 19, 24, 30, 32, 34, 37, 38, 41, 42, 43, 46, 47, 48, 49, 50, 56, 60, 61, 65, 66, 71, 72, 80, 87, 89–91, 98, 100
manors, 23, 25, 81 (see also Canon Grange, East Curry, Lovington, North Curry, West Hatch)
rentals of, 23
Martin's wheat, 51, 79, 81
mortuaries, 81, 84
nomination of lives, xliii, 25, 26, 34, 42
rents, 66, 81, 84
collection of arrears of, 22, 50
reeves, 43, 44, 81
tenants, 81
terriers, xli
fabric, repairs to, 103
finance, 19
audit, xlv, 23, 43
caution money (see also under canons residentiary)
amount of, xx
distribution of, xxi, xxiv, xxix, 25, 53, 68, 75, 77
daily distribution, see quotidians
dividends, xxiii–xxvi, xxix, xliii, 18, 20, 23, 26, 27, 69, 92, 104
donations, 50*l*. by dean for use of chapter, 101, 104
to the city of London, 42
to the town of Northampton, 61
for relief of French Protestants, 101
for redemption of Algerian captives, 90, 92
to John Edmonds, 52
escheatory revenues, viii, xxiii, xxiv, xxxiii, xxxix, 18, 40
fabric fund, iv, 26, 32, 53, 89
fines, xxvi, xxxiii, xxxiv, 20
pensions, 18, 20, 21, 32, 38, 50, 84
quotidians, xxiii–xxvi, xxix, 8, 18, 23, 27, 69, 70, 85, 86, 104
steward's accounts, xxvii
stipends, 27, 69
general:
altar, high, 3
rails before, xliii
in Lady chapel, 59
audit room, xx, xxvii n.4, 3, 4, 13, 14, 22, 34, 37, 51, 62, 63, 71, 72, 81, 82, 90–93, 100, 101, 102
bells, casting of, 28, 40
clock, 28
'Harewell', 19 n.2, 28 n.1
in small steeple, 28
in central tower, 28 n.1
Bekynton's chantry, 99
best pulpit cloth and cushion, use of, 31
books and papers, 77, 84, 86
chapter house, xx, 1–103 *passim*
cloister,
south, 19
west, xx n.1, 9 n.3
doors, to be closed, 16
exchequer, see audit room
Lady chapel, 40 n.4, 59
holy table in, 59
morning prayer in, 16, 23
library, see Wells cathedral, s.v.
organ, 49, 83
quire,
seats in, 12, 33, 44, 81, 82, 99
stalls in, iv, 2, 44
St John Baptist chapel, 14 n.2
central tower, 28 n.1
south-west tower, 28 n.1
vessels, 66
grammar school, xliii, 50, 75
master's stipend, xxxiii
see also Pottinger, John; Thirlby, Charles; Williams, ——; Winscombe, Henry
library, i, xxxv–xxxvii, xli, xliii
arrangement of, xxxvi, 22, 70
books and papers to be kept in, 77
to be returned to usual places, 84, 86
custodian, xxxvi, 22, 71
donations to, xxxvi, xxxvii, 81
gifts to, xii, xviii, xxxvi, xxxvii, 83
loans of books or MSS from, xxxvi, 22, 70
missing books returned to, xxxvi, 102

Wells cathedral continued
Red Book (*Liber Ruber*), xxxvi, 86
repair of, xxxv, xxxvi, 19, 22, 46, 47
music: anthems and services,
appointing of, xliii
by Robert Creyghton II, xvi
procuring and pricking of, 101
organist, see Jackson, John
preachers, xli, xliii, 32, 77
prebendaries, see canons non-residentiary
prebends founded in:
Barton St David, 65
Buckland Dinham, 11, 96, 98
Combe St Nicholas, 15 prebends of, 32
Combe I, 9
Combe II, xii
Combe VII, 17, 53
Combe VIII, x, 8
Combe XI, 84
Combe XII, v
Combe XIII, 13, 45, 85
Compton Bishop, 20, 39, 88
Compton Dundon, 15
Cudworth, xi, xii
Curry, v
Dinder, xv, xvii, 13, 37
Dultingcote, 8, 27
East Harptree, xviii, 11, 39
Easton in Gordano, 1
Haselbury, 53, 74
Henstridge, 76
Holcombe, xviii
Huish and Brent, xiv, 76
Litton, xii
Milverton I, 96
North Curry, see Curry
St Decumans, xiii
Shalford (Scanford), 17
Taunton, ix, xv, 37, 72
Timberscombe, xvi, xvii, 2, 6, 8
Wanstrow, xvii, 53
Warminster or Luxville, 15
Wedmore, 4 prebends of, 32
Wedmore I, v
Wedmore II, 5, 93, 94
Wedmore III, 33
Wedmore IV, xvii, 14, 15, 37, 53
Wedmore V, 27
Whitchurch, xi
Whitelackington, xviii, 11, 74, 75
Wiveliscombe, v, 30, 39, 76, 79, 96
Worminster, x, 65 n.1
Yatton, xvi, 5
precentor, iv, viii (see also Abbott, Edward; Creyghton, Robert II; Smith, Sebastian)
services, 44
morning prayer, 16, 23
Statuta Antiqua, vii
statutes, iv, vii
subdean, iv (see also Church, C. M.; Dugdale, James; Mundy, Francis)
subtreasurer, iv, 66
succentor, iv
estates of, v
treasurer, iv, ix (see also Busby, Richard; Creyghton, Robert I; Sugar, Hugh)
vicars choral, xviii, xliii, 27, 53, 55 (see also Alderley, Arthur; Benford, Augustine; Beauchamp, John; Beaumont, Thomas; Browne, John; Clarke, Thomas; Cooper, John; Davis, Daniel; Edmonds, John; Greene, Gabriel; Hobbs, John; Horsey, Peter; Jackson, John; Kelway, ——; Larke, ——; Lasher, Joshua; Macy, ——; Martin, John; Mew, Daniel; Moss, John; Standish, Francis; Standish, Thomas; Tudway, Charles; Walkley, Anthony; Willis, Thomas; Willmott, James; Winscombe, Henry; Woodson, Samuel)
admission of, xx, xxiii, 10, 25, 28, 31, 39, 40, 42, 48, 55, 58, 63, 65, 79
auscultor, xx, 10, 25, 28, 31, 33, 39, 40, 42, 48, 55, 58, 63, 65, 79
charter of (1592), xxxv
communar elected from, iv, viii
controversy with chapter, xxxiiff., 18, 40
emoluments, xx, xxxii–xxxv
escheator elected from, iv, viii, 7, 12, 17, 25, 31, 42, 49, 56, 58, 61, 67, 68, 79, 88, 99
master of the fabric elected from, iv, viii
pension from Chew Magna due to, 18 n.1

Wells cathedral continued
perpetuation of, xx, 13, 31, 34, 42, 48, 49, 79, 88
physic garden of, 48
priest vicars, 23
roll-call of, xix, 1, 3, 5, 6, 8, 10, 11, 12, 13, 14, 16, 17, 18, 20, 21, 25, 28, 29, 30, 33, 38, 39, 42, 61, 68, 73, 74, 76, 79, 83, 85, 87, 93, 94, 97, 99, 103
vicarial stalls, xx, xxxiv
Combe I, 10
Combe II, 10, 12
Combe III, 10, 12
Combe VIII, 12
Combe IX, 25, 30
Combe XIII, 30
Compton Bishop, 1, 43
Henstridge, 65, 96
Litton, 12
Old Cleeve, 33, 59
St Decumans, 1, 44
Sutton, 94
Timberscombe, 96
Warminster or Luxville, 48, 49
Wedmore I, 12, 65
Wiveliscombe, 28, 63
Worminster, 12, 80
Yatton, 31, 43

Wells, St Cuthbert's, xxii n.1, 20, 22, 48, 50, 54, 76, 79, 96
new bell for, 99
pension due from, 20, 21, 32, 50
rectory of, 3, 4, 15, 30, 89

Westerham, Kent, xiv
Westerly (Westerleigh), Glos, 67
West Hatch, 10, 41, 47, 81
Nythewood in, 7
Woodbreach in, 7

West Horrington, 51 n.1
West Huntspill, xv
Westley,
Sarah, xxxvii, 82, 87
William, chapter clerk, xxii, xxx, xxxvi, xxxvii, 3, 10, 12, 13, 14, 15, 22, 23, 33, 39, 51, 52, 53, 76, 78, 83, 87, 97, 101

Westminster,
abbey, xii
St Margaret's, x
school, xii, xvi, xxvi, 23

Westmorland, Francis, earl of, xv
Weston Zoyland, xii, 71, 80, 89, 99
Wharton, T, xv n.2
White, Thomas, 7
Whitehall chapel, x
Wick (Wycke), see Ashbury
Wick St Lawrence, 14, 84
Willan, Samuel, prebendary, 53
William III, king, xviii
Williams,
——, schoolmaster, 10
James, sacrist, *cursor ecclesiae*, and bailiff of the grange, xxxvi, 2, 24 n.3, 30, 40, 72, 79, 84, 86, 88, 99, 101
T. W., xxxv

Willis, Thomas,
prebendary, 84
vicar choral, 10–14, 16–18, 20, 21, 25, 28, 29, 30

Willmott (Willmot, Wilmott),
Charles, Lord, 41
James, vicar choral, 10–14, 16–18, 20, 21, 25, 28–31, 33, 34, 38, 39

Winchester cathedral, xxvii
Windsor, xvi, 97
Winscombe (Winscomb, Winchcombe), xxii n.1, 22, 25, 37, 54, 77, 81, 91, 96, 104
felling trees in, 48
Woodborow's Green in, 78
Henry, vicar choral, 61, 65, 67, 68, 72–76, 79, 83, 85, 87, 88, 93, 94, 97, 99, 103

Winsham, 41
Wood,
Anthony, ix n.2, x, xi n.2, xiv, xviii
Gerard, 86
John, prebendary, 15
Roger, canon residentiary, xi

Woodson (Wootson), Samuel, vicar choral, 39, 43, 48, 49
Wootton, xxiii, 35
Worminster, 51 n.1
Wraxall, xii
Wroth, Lady, 99
Wyndham, colonel Francis, xiii, 19
Wyseman, Robert, 100

Yanworth, Glos, xviii
Yatton, xvii
Yeadle, John, prebendary, 96, 98

Yeovil, xiii
Yeovilton, xvii, xviii
Yerwoth, Samuel, 2
Young, John, chancellor, xxvii

Printed in England for
Her Majesty's Stationery Office
by Hobbs the Printers Ltd, Southampton

469 Dd503607 K6 6/73